That's Living

Based on the Award Winning Radio Talk Show

Henry Janzen, Ph.D.
John Paterson, Ed.D.
Carl Blashko, M.D.

ISBN 0-88864-867-7
Copyright@1989 Three Pears Publishing

Printed in Canada

Published by
Three Pears Publishing

Printed and bound by
University of Alberta
Printing Services.

Cover graphics – Trina Irons
Line drawings – Sylvia Blashko
                Barbara Paterson

Enquiries and orders write to:
Three Pears Publishing
922 Burley Drive
Edmonton, Alberta
Canada   T6R 1X3

CONTENTS

ACKNOWLEDGEMENTS

Writing a book is no easy task, as we have discovered. Since we chose not to involve a publishing company on this edition, the task was left to us to organize. Fortunately we had excellent cooperation and assistance from friends and staff. Special thanks and gratitude go to Susan Whalen-Janzen, who coordinated the manuscript typing and worked closely with Barbara Paterson and Sylvia Blashko on selection of the line drawings. We acknowledge the expert and competent assistance of our secretarial staff, Roberta McLaughlin, Deb LaFranchise, Sonia Rywak and Deb Black. Without their dedication this book would not have been finished. There is also deep appreciation to Ken Machon and our departmental chairman; Dr. Gene Romaniuk, for providing the help when we needed it. And finally, we thank the many staff at the University Printing Services who offered careful and competent advice on the final draft of the book on publishing matters. Needless to say, we are indebted to 930 CJCA, Bob Lang in particular, for allowing us the opportunity to serve, on radio, for allowing us to use the title of the radio-show for our book title, for encouraging us to complete the task. To these wonderful people, and to all listeners to "That's Living" who indulged our creativity, we give thanks.

Dr. H.L. Janzen
Dr. C. Blashko
Dr. J.G. Paterson

FOREWORD

The contents of this book are the ideas of the authors, for which we take full responsibility. Nevertheless, it was the listeners to our radio program and the thousands of people who took time to write us that shaped our programs and our views. This book began with compilation of sixty well-received, requested programs. Eventually, we narrowed them down to fourteen chapters, some topics remaining, others deleted. Many of the program-notes had already been mailed to those requesting them.

The idea for the book was spawned two years ago. Instead of mailing cryptic versions of our radio notes, why not provide a more detailed discussion on all programs for which there was a massive response? This demanded further research and writing. In May, 1988, the writing began. All chapters, in rough draft, were completed in four months, months during which we had no teaching duties at the University. Revisions, and there were many, became a necessary task. Although most chapters were edited three or four times, we are still unhappy with some of our work. An expert editor would have been welcome. We ask the readers to bear with us. It is true for us, however, that the ideas are more important, but we know that readers do prefer proper grammar. We tried!

There is a semblance of logic, for the order of the chapters. We begin on the lighter side, move to increasingly more serious and complex issues. Within each chapter are wide-ranging topics pertinent to the main chapter theme. We have deliberately chosen not to identify specific authors for each chapter. We chose to write on issues where we felt prepared.

As you read the book you will be met with personal views as well as studied ideas. Keep in mind that scholarly books as well as popular books have been written on each topic. This book represents our interpretation of the scientific literature and our clinical experience. Each topic is written for easy reading, yet designed to be sophisticated enough to allow the complexity to be revealed. It is not a self-help book as such. It was designed to bring understanding, plus our insights, to the many people who will choose to read this book.

Dr. H.L. Janzen
Dr. C.A. Blashko
Dr. J.G. Paterson

INTRODUCTION

Over the many years that we worked as private practitioners in our office, consulted to a variety of agencies and institutions, and on our radio program "That's Living", we were always asked questions such as "Where can I read about depression? Where could I get more information about Alzheimer's Disease? What is a learning disorder?" We have a very highly educated population that hungers for information. Very often this information is available in large libraries and written in a very academic and scientific manner. It is very difficult for an individual not trained in this area to understand these books and articles. With this in mind, we undertook to give you information on medical, psychiatric and psychological topics in a readable form. Where possible, we will use simple language in order that you may understand what is being said. However, it is sometimes impossible to use plain language and a specific psychological term such as "empathy" or "catatonia" will be used. We will define these terms in the clearest manner possible. Also, because our readers may want to read further on specific topics, we have chosen to introduce you to a variety of terms so that you can use them for library searches. Many articles written in popular magazines use relatively complex medical terms such as "Tricyclic antidepressants" and "Dyslexia". Some sections may be very easily read and understood such as the one on alcoholism. Other chapters may have to be read several times or may only be important to you if it involves you or your family.

As we wrote, we tried to visualize who we would be reaching. As we thought about our audience, we realized that we would have a wide variety of readers. We believe that parents will gain a great deal of information from this book and make it available to their children. Since topics are covered that will refer to all stages of life from infancy to the aged, it did not seem possible to focus this book to only one reader. As you can imagine, it would be so much easier to write a book only directed to adolescents or to the aged. We will therefore compromise and hope that, no matter what your age, your education, or your experience, you will gain from this book.

CHAPTER 1

Humor on Radio

HUMOR ON RADIO

Introduction

In the first instance, the authors of this book should start out by apologizing. In this chapter we plan to share with you many of the vignettes our listeners have shared with us over the years. Of course we will attempt to give credit where we have been able to trace the source. Many of the poems, sayings, and truisms presented to us are either anonymous, or written by one of our listeners. Where we are infringing on copyright, it is by accident.

The three authors of this book are quite different; different backgrounds, different ages, and even representing two different professions. We came together to do a radio show. It stands to reason that people changing careers all of a sudden, thrust into unfamiliar situations, would make mistakes and have fun doing it. That is exactly the case.

The following chapter simply details some of the humor we've found in radio as well as presenting some of the many listener suggestions brought to us to share.

The Cast of Characters
Dr. Paterson

Dr. Paterson has been continuously with "That's Living" so undoubtedly had time to get into the most trouble. He did. Actually, his debut in radio was rather inauspicious. The earliest days of "That's Living" involved a psychiatrist, Dr. Robbie Campbell. When Dr. Campbell was ill one day he asked his friend, John Paterson, to substitute. John, because he was a friend, feigned knowledge of the program. About 20 seconds before air time he was asked by CJCA's

Gord Whitehead what his topic would be. The idea of a topic had never occurred to this neophyte broadcaster. The next hour and a half was probably one of the worst radio shows in history. It would have been *the* worst if it was not for the skill and talents of the above mentioned professional announcer, Gord Whitehead.

Things didn't get very much better when Drs. Blashko and Paterson came to radio professionally. On his very first show, John Paterson was faced with a caller who indicated he believed he was a moose. After some realistic suggestions about seeking psychiatric help, the gentleman indicated the advice seemed okay but was still concerned about how he would get through doors because his horns kept getting in the way. It wasn't a terrific start.

Another female listener talked about low self-esteem to Dr. Paterson, and so he presented the following example. "What would happen if you were walking in front of a group of important people and you tripped and fell and didn't hurt yourself". She replied "That's just like me Dr. Paterson - that's exactly what I would do. I'd fall and make a terrific fool of myself". "No", he replied, "If you laughed at yourself, other people would laugh with you, not at you". The point seemed well made and our host was rather proud of himself. Several weeks later, John tripped on the way downstairs early in the morning, as his son had left books on the stairs. As the air became blue with bad language, the aforementioned son was heard to say "You must find this pretty funny Dad". Children, I suspect, find it difficult to separate advice to others from the family situation!

An elderly caller made Dr. Paterson's entire day when she advised that she was over 90, blind, and in a nursing home. She wanted to know what he looked like. "What do you think I look like?" he asked. "Dr. Paterson, I see you as a tall athletic looking man with wavy blond hair. You are probably in your early to mid-thirties". Dr. Paterson replied, "You've got it". Since then he has always advised people to take the word of senior citizens, rather than a piece of glass.

Perhaps Dr. Paterson's most interesting battle with his listeners and with the radio station is his love for dogs, particularly Dandie Dinmont Terriers. When questioned by Program Director Bob Lang about why he was always talking about dogs, Dr. Paterson indicated the importance that listeners place on advice he was giving about raising and caring for pets. Mr. Lang suggested that when one thousand letters had been received by the station asking for a show on dogs it would be time to proceed. Three months later George Payne and John Paterson counted the letters. There were 13. "Close enough," exclaimed Dr. Paterson and that was the start of approximately six to eight shows on dogs. One approximately every six months. If not totally impressed, listeners seem amused and show up in large numbers when Dr. Paterson's dogs are exhibited in dog shows throughout the province.

Dr. Janzen

Dr. Janzen is seen to be the most serious of the three authors of this book, but what appears on the surface is not always or necessarily true. There is probably no mental health professional better at handling a very serious topic or exposing his own personality on sensitive and touching issues. Yet Dr. Janzen is, and always has been, very willing to laugh at himself and take blame for his own and others mistakes. Dr. Janzen was told by his fellow co-hosts that his career in radio would be both challenging and fun. After a couple of years he was heard to remark "Challenging it has been!" It is not known by the other co-hosts how this happens, but Dr. Janzen's mailbox is always the fullest. He receives the most mail, he tends to also receive more gifts and goodies from listeners than the other co-hosts. He is very good-natured about this popularity and has advised the station that in order to save trouble in sorting mail, all positive mail and gifts could be delivered directly to him, leaving the job of answering disgruntled listeners to anyone else who might be interested. Only once has Dr. Janzen been known to lose his temper in the radio station. This occurred when a young announcer from the neighboring rock station left a note on the windshield of Dr. Janzen's car. The note evidently included some four letter words and Henry took exception. The situation was so serious with Hank Janzen prowling up and down the halls of the radio station, that our Program Director, notoriously tight-fisted Bob Lang, was heard to be offering to buy drinks for all to settle the situation. Dr. Janzen enjoyed the attention so much, that he is thinking of repeating the incident on a staged basis at least once a year. As Dr. Janzen is an expert on stress, a stress story might be appropriate. Whether or not this story is true or apocryphal is a moot question.

A recently elected executive director of the Canadian Chamber of Commerce was giving a maiden speech in Regina. Being an Executive Director was a new experience for this business person from Vancouver. It was the first time he had ever had speeches written for him. It became obvious that this particular speech, delivered in Regina, had been written by someone from eastern Canada. The man read for awhile and then realized that if he continued to talk about the need for subsidizing Eastern industrialists and supporting the "Crow freight rates" he might not be allowed to even finish his speech. He faked something and then had words with the speech writer.

Several months later this same executive director was presenting an important formal speech to a joint meeting of the Men's and Women's Canadian Club of Canada. It was indeed an important affair, with all Ambassadors, Members of Parliament, Senators, etc., in attendance. As he was reading his speech he said something like this; "Ladies and Gentlemen, I recognize that Canada is in tough shape. Central Canadians seem to hate the West and the feeling is reciprocated. The French and English don't like each other. Unemployment is at an all time high and our dollar doesn't seem to be worth anything. Our economy is in shambles, and people have lost confidence in all phases of Government. Our taxes are at the highest rate in history.

But, Ladies and Gentlemen, if the average Canadian family would only do five simple things, this problem could be solved. In fact this problem could be solved without costing anybody one cent and within two weeks we would be back on a positive course".

The man then turned to page six of his notes which was empty except for the following hand-written note "You're on your own, you bastard".

So much for Dr. Janzen's serious side.

Dr. Blashko

From the first day he was on radio, Dr. Blashko has had listeners talk to him about his infectious laughter. Many people believe that this psychiatrist cures people simply by enjoying them, and no one enjoys a good joke better than Carl. For that reason, many are played on him. In the very early days of "That's Living" our program director invited Drs. Blashko and Paterson to supper which was held at a first class Edmonton hotel. The three people then proceeded to work, and eat and drink, as they planned one of the first extravaganzas where the hosts of "That's Living" worked with other professionals on a community problem. By midnight, the bill had climbed to a point where it was a good idea to remember that CJCA was hosting the dinner. You guessed it, Dr. Blashko forgot. When the check came, Dr. Blashko immediately reached for it saying, "Let me take that", and Bob Lang with a straight face commented, "OK". Carl has been recovering ever since.

The entire story cannot be told, but it was. Dr. Blashko once made an off-air comment to a guest who was a personal friend. Unfortunately, the comment was "on-air". If he ever doubted it, the host of "That's Living" found indeed that we do have many listeners, as they all phoned the station to let us know they had heard the aside. Surprisingly and thankfully there were no complaints, just listeners with a good sense of humor who recognize that when we make a mistake, we too should be able to laugh at ourselves.

It was in the era of Blashko and Paterson when they were hosting the show in 1985 when "That's Living" won the award for the best Public Affairs Program in Canada. This gold ribbon statue was presented by the Canadian Association of Broadcasters. At any rate, Carl and John were indeed in Ottawa ready to receive the award. In fact, the major point of discussion throughout the meal was which of the two would accept on behalf of "That's Living". After a small argument, Dr. Blashko suggested that he would take the microphone, say a few words and pass it to Dr. Paterson to formally accept. When "That's Living" was announced as the winning program, both hosts went to the front to find the station manager, Terry Strain, had beaten them to the microphone. Terry took this opportunity to give a ten to fifteen minute talk on many of his favorite subjects. Drs. Blashko and Paterson said nothing, which is probably a first for both of them.

Unlike the other two authors of this book, Dr. Blashko comes from Northern Alberta and his family is very prominent in the surrounding community. Carl's mother invited all of the hosts for Thanksgiving one year and she was overheard telling Dr. Janzen that if he continued to improve he would be "almost" as effective as Carl. The Blashkos are quick learners though, and Carl's parents now are the proud owners of a Dandie Dinmont Terrier, courtesy of, guess who?

Carl Blashko was the first host, at least in this radio station, to encourage people to write in, to share jokes with the hosts, and to laugh with us. It's difficult on radio, but his infectious good nature has made it possible and believable. Carl has had many highlights on "That's Living". He announced the hiring of Jackie Parker, popular Edmonton Eskimo football coach. Another highlight would be a picture taken with him and Dr. Paterson and the Stanley Cup. If anyone wondered how mental health professionals would incorporate within a framework of a radio station, they would only need to follow the example of Carl Blashko. He belonged to the group because he wanted to belong. Carl has been off the radio as a regular participant for over two years but he remains friendly with CJCA broadcasters and staff, often trading insults with people as he always has. We have here a caring dedicated professional, totally out of control.

The Radio Game

When one changes from a hospital or university setting to private radio, the transition is, to say the least, confusing. It seemed to the authors of this book that radio people spend most if not all of their time joking with each other and trading insults, there are always tricks being played on someone. The analogy of the station to a family is not totally out of line. In the radio station milieu one will find father figures, mother figures, scapegoats, troublemakers, etc. There is, though, lots of love and caring in that environment, which is why this program has continued for so long, and with as few problems as have been encountered.

CHAPTER 2

Self-Concept

SELF-CONCEPT

Picture Yourself Positive:

People act and feel according to the pictures they carry around in their minds as to who they are. *Self-concept* refers to the internal experience and interpretation of that experience; it is formed and influenced by the evaluation of significant others and it is shaped by the self-statements, self-attributions of one's own behaviors. As a construct or dimension of the person, self-concept is thought to be the single greatest factor influencing our drive, motivation, persistence, influence, and even our intelligence. When the self-concept is negative, life and experiences are negative, few risks are taken. The drive to try any task becomes difficult. Read the actual problems shared by letter to the co-hosts on 930 CJCA "That's Living" program on the issue of self-concept:

> "...My problem is Me. I feel like I am running out of time to FIND MYSELF. I quit school after passing Grade IX. Now I regret very much, but I am terrified of trying...The worst enemy for me was taking criticism. Anytime that happened, I quit. It has been frustrating for my family as well as for me. I have left home to "find myself", stayed away for awhile then came back where I am now and I still haven't found any answers...The thing that tugs at the back of my mind is my husband's ex-wife. She went back to school and got her degree...and is now making excellent money on her way to a self-sufficient career while I am a high school dropout with NO guts and only able to get part time minimum wage jobs. I want to feel important and

proud of myself. I want other people to look up to me, but everytime I really want to do something, something inside of me says "It won't work" or "You'll fail". I have no friends (my fault) and I feel like I need someone to hold my hand and push me along until I can get started and move through life on my own..."

"...I am too shy and nervous. I am an adult child of an alcoholic and believe I have low self-esteem...I am not afraid to meet strangers, but I am very self conscious with my husband's family and with casual acquaintances. I am far too sensitive. I enjoy friends that relate to me on a "feelings" level but get annoyed with superficial people. I enjoy people one on one, but if there are more than four people present, I most often won't say anything. Crowds make me uneasy. Does some of this relate to my dad's alcoholism? I know I felt a tremendous amount of shame over that while growing up. Now it's like I don't want anyone to see *me* as I really am because I think they won't like what they see...I have to get out and involved. But my heart beats so hard when I have to speak out at a meeting, that I avoid speaking...Yes, I want to change and succeed in overcoming this. What can I do?"

"...I am a single mother of a 4 year old boy. Since my divorce I did have a boyfriend, someone whom I cared for very much. It took me a while to find out that he was at the same time seeing another woman. When I found out, I tried to kill myself because I couldn't take the hurt. I'm much better now but am having a big problem making friends - I have no close friends...now I find myself completely alone and very rarely go anywhere but my biggest problem is how to make close friends...My physician has said for the last year or so that my problem is lack of self worth or self esteem...Why is (my father) so inconsiderate and what makes him think he can control every minute of my working and free time and generally walk all over me? When I don't agree with his plans for me I'm screamed at...my mother gets the same kind of treatment and simply says "that's the way he is"...I hope very much that counselling will help me get inner peace and stop hating this man so much..."

In psychological terms, self-concept is usually referred to as low or high, positive or negative, poor or good. Sometimes the word "self-esteem" is used. We won't quibble about exact scientific definitions. People generally use the terms "self-concept" and "self-esteem" interchangeably, although self-esteem refers more to the subjective/emotional assessment of one's notion of self-worth, and self-concept refers to the private and public image we present.

The letters excerpted above show very clearly how powerful a force a negative self-concept can be. People want to feel important, proud, respected and liked, yet negative and unhealthy experiences produce negative evaluations of oneself. In the above examples, experiences of quitting school (self-evaluation of a dropout, quitter, unknowledgeable), lacking friends (self-evaluation of not being worthy to be liked), living in an alcoholic family situation (self-evaluation of unworthiness, shame and guilt), single-parent through divorce (self-evaluation of not being worthy of love and commitment), produce the psychological states of the self. These psychological states (I as learner, I as lover, I as friend, I as worker, I as spouse, I as good/bad looking, etc) are developed slowly over time, beginning in infancy and are shaped by experiences and evaluations by self and others of that experience. When the self-concept is low or negative it is hard to change, yet this self-concept will shape and color absolutely every behavior, every feeling, every task to be done. The self-concept is both descriptive (I am a psychologist) and evaluative (I am a good psychologist). Not only do people often not like the description of themselves, they have to learn to accept the evaluation of these descriptions. The descriptive part of the self-concept may be easier to change than the self-evaluations, other evaluations of that same description. It is difficult to argue a feeling about oneself. You might disagree with my evaluation of you, but it is difficult to argue over your own evaluation. This is why the low self-concept is so hard to change quickly. It took time and plenty of experiences, often negative experiences to shape the self-concept in the first place.

The self-concept is linked to every facet of our experiences and being. An example of the complexity of the self-concept, its interrelationship to personality, social development, sexuality, family life, conscience and responsibility, is clearly seen in the following letter:

> "...My problem is basically that I am painfully shy. I have done everything I can possibly think of to overcome this thing but haven't been able to. I have sometimes gotten so bad that I draw the drapes and don't answer the door until

> I get a little better. I now have children...and I find now that I can't hide anymore. The kids need me to be like other mothers...when I was a kid and growing up, I was very open and never had these problems in any way. I was not a terrific teenager and was very rebellious but also very popular. When I was 15 years old I was into almost everything that I shouldn't have been. One night hitch-hiking, I was picked up by a man who raped me. My entire life changed from that night on...that night being raped was not the worst of it all, the more tragic thing happened was that I got pregnant...I carried the child for nine months and placed her up for adoption...I simply can't face people. The problem now is that it's not just affecting me but my husband and children. My husband is very supportive about this problem, but doesn't know what I can do either..."

This woman sees herself as shy (a personality trait or state). Was she always shy? Oh no, she saw herself as very "open" and "popular", often "rebellious". Her traumatic experience at age 15, she felt, may have been precipitated by her rebelliousness (conscience, lack of self-responsibility). That experience changed her life, her social status, her evaluation of herself, her marriage and her relationship to her husband. Being raped and feeling degraded was compounded by the decision to give up the child for adoption. So one draws the drapes and closes the doors, hiding not just from others but also from oneself.

The self-concept is formed out of both positive and negative experiences and evaluations of one's behaviour in those experiences. Its effect is cyclical in nature. With low self-esteem come poorer coping skills; poorer coping skills produce less success in life and decision-making; with fewer success experiences come feelings of not being in control of one's life; less control begets anxiety, worry and frustration; these feelings give rise to defense mechanisms that often are ineffective; that ineffectiveness again confirms the low self-esteem. It is a vicious cycle! When the self-concept is negative, criticism is difficult to accept, change and risk become very difficult. People with negative self-concepts don't feel worthy of being loved. They see others as they see themselves. They often blame others for their problems. This produces further acrimony and negative evaluation from others. So they are singled out, "scapegoated", made fun of, and avoided. In the end, they become isolated and alone, afraid to reach out, afraid to look inside. Yes, self-concept is, indeed, a powerful force in our life. Developing a positive self-esteem in self and others is the most important thing we can do. How we start, and why it is so important, is discussed next in greater detail.

▍ The Value of a Positive Self-Esteem

Why is it so important to honor, respect and value the self? Is it mere selfishness or egotistical pride? No, I don't think so. To value the self is to value ourselves and our humanness above any other thing. There is for us nothing more precious than the life we've been given. This thought has become more important to me in the recent months and especially in the past year since my wife's illness and subsequent death. When serious life threatening illness struck my wife, we were made to realize that nothing in this world is more precious than the people we love. Nothing can replace the person you are. Time may dim the memories and heal the hurts and pains, but the value of one human life is more precious than all the wealth in all the world. But even when we are not threatened by death, we can lose sight of the value of people, persons with whom we share work, home or community. Honoring oneself and nurturing the self-esteem brings with it the strength to live and hope for the future, as well as a desire to succeed in our daily trials of life.

Self-esteem is a valued concept in psychology because it relates very strongly to our success in our work, our achievement in school, our relationship to people and the self-confidence that we hold to do all these things. Therefore, self-esteem is closely connected to all issues of life including making friends, accepting failures, fighting disease, coping with stress, achieving in school, holding a marriage together, coping with anxiety and serious mental and emotional illnesses, holding down a job, risking change and tackling new assignments. If the self-esteem is positive, you hold the view "I can" instead of "I can't" or "I give up".

The value of a positive self-esteem is in the fact that we can live actively, doing things that we enjoy, loving and living life and not sitting by passively and letting others tell us what life is all about. The value of the positive self-esteem is in understanding things in real terms and not fooling ourselves. It is not to give in to momentary feelings of defeat or helplessness. As Dr. Nathaniel Branden wrote, to honor the self is to hang on and try to understand. To value the self is to believe in our convictions and believe we can change things for the better. To value the self is not to rely too much on others or in other people's opinions. To value the self is willingness to follow one's dreams and to think independently, being honest with oneself. To value the self is to believe in one's convictions, attitudes and beliefs; it is fighting against evil and prejudices and living up to high standards based on consensus and input from others, but also based on one's own beliefs. To value the self is to desire to improve oneself, being aware of one's feelings and emotions and owning those feelings at each moment. Thus, to value the self is to provide a basic structure of honesty about oneself.

People have often doubted their value because in many areas of their life they simply were not as successful or felt as successful as others. It is very important to realize that any healthy person is not going to be competent in all things. For example, I do not have the talents and skills of others in fixing things around the house, repairing furniture or cars. I am not as competent as others in operating a business or in taking care of financial matters. But this is not necessarily a sign of a low self-esteem and it certainly isn't in my case. A healthy person doesn't have to feel adequate in all aspects of life. Living up to your own standards is a key to a healthy self-esteem. It is, in fact, an essential condition. This means that you and I realistically appraise who we are, what we can do, what we can expect of ourselves and live up to those standards and beliefs. This does not mean that you set artificially low standards and then feel good if you meet them. You cannot fool yourself that easily and certainly not for very long!

Parents Play a Key Role

People have often asked just where this self-esteem comes from. There are many factors that impact on the development of the self-esteem including one's upbringing, one's relationship to friends and family, one's experiences in life, one's acceptance by peers and so on. Probably the most important impact on the self-esteem does come from the home. All parents send messages to their children and this has an effect - for good or bad. A child needs to make sense of his world and when that need is frustrated, a tragic sense of self may result. If you send messages that the child is not good enough and does not have the potential, or that his/her behavior is unacceptable then that child will be coping with life in a different fashion than a child who gets sent more positive messages. How often do we concentrate on clothes and hair or on standing straighter or not being so emotional or excited? Many times as parents we forget that every interaction has an effect even though it will take years for a self-esteem to be brought down. As children get the impression that they're not good enough for you, their self-esteem suffers and they go through life exhausting themselves in order to try to be somebody or to try to please you. Even as adults we find this attitude in people who have developed a low self-esteem for whatever reason. We often hear adults say "if I only had a successful marriage" or "if I could only get that job" or "if I could only make a few more dollars so we could have a comfortable living" or "if I could only have that one more promotion, then I would be happy". These things in and of themselves are important but they speak more to the issue of how high or low that self-esteem is and what kind of confidence they have in themselves. Remember, a person's self-esteem is related to family living. Issues of how much money one makes, or what level of education one has, or what area of town we live in and what social class we are in and what mother and father do for a living are not the key factors related to one's self-esteem. Even in the conditions of dire poverty an individual can develop a positive self-esteem if the interaction is positive. Thus, it is in the nature of that interaction that we need to be most concerned. Children need to experience acceptance of thoughts, feelings and values as a person. Children need to operate in clearly defined limits that are fair but negotiable.

To develop a positive self-esteem it is important that we are rational, predictable and not contradictory in our behavior towards each other. We need to encourage others to think independently and not expect obedience just for obedience's sake. We can develop a positive self-esteem if we allow expressions of views, feelings and are treated with respect. It is important that we see others as psychologically visible, where we make them feel that we are interested in them. These interactions will cause others to believe in themselves and in their potential. It will help others accept mistakes as normal and make them feel that their humanness is valued and respected. We all need to be given explanations for what we do and how we react. The feedback we receive is very important and can have a tremendous impact on our lives and especially our self-esteem. Self-esteem is born out of how we see ourselves and how others see us. Self-esteem is not born out of our fantasies or out of fooling ourselves and others about who we really are and what we really think and feel. Self-esteem is born out of our own mental operations and out of interactions with other people.

How many of you have seen the sign on little children's T-shirts that read "I'm Good, Cause God Doesn't Make Junk"? School counsellors sometimes have children carry a tag on their shirt for the day reading "I.L.A.C.", meaning "I am loveable and capable". The counselor has engaged the children in a discussion of all the things they see as positive in themselves, making lists for each child. At the end of the discussion, the tag I.L.A.C. is made and pinned on the child's shirt. As the children routinely go through the exercises of a school day wearing that sign, positive things begin to happen. The tag invites questions, "What does ILAC stand for?" Many times a day the children experience the thrill of recognition, the acceptance of others, the chance to recognize their worthiness. They begin to see the inner worthiness of the person, regardless of circumstance or ability. ILAC encourages the children to look inside and see that "God Doesn't Make Junk". Try this exercise yourself for a day. Look inside and recognize your own worthiness. Dare to be you, because you are lovable and capable!

Dare To Be You

Do you secretly wish that you could be better looking, more intel-

ligent and more confident? Do you tend to put on an act in front of people making them think you are someone really important? Do you sometimes make up stories, brag or even lie about what you do, where you live, what you own so as to impress others? Do your stories about yourself sometimes get you into more difficulty by having to tell more stories to cover up? Do you secretly wish that you were someone else? If you answered "yes" to most or all of these questions, I feel that you have a problem in not daring to be you. You have difficulty in accepting who you are.

There is no doubt that all of us from time to time use and need the fences to protect ourselves because this world is not easy to live in. We rationalize away our shortcomings; we project our faults onto others; we play the "helpless me" game or we play the "I'm better than you" game, or we play the "there's nothing wrong with me" game - a basic defense of denial. We all do this, but when we do it too often and at inappropriate times and places it backfires on us and we fall deeper into disrespect with others. Our dislike for ourselves makes us lose the confidence we once had. Eventually this gives rise to the myriad of personal problems culminating for some people into psychological illnesses such as depression, anxiety states, phobias, insomnia, long term personality disorders and, for a few, schizophrenia. This is too high a price to pay for not daring to be you.

There Is No Person Like You

I ask you, no, I challenge you to try to be yourself. This means accepting yourself with faults, but also with strengths. You may not be highly educated, you may not be good looking, you may not have special talents, you may not have a glamorous or high profile job, you may not have as big a house or as many nice things as others - but you are still a person, a person who cannot be replaced by anyone else. There is no other like you. You're a person who can feel and cry and laugh with others. You are a person who can love and give as well as nurture and care. You are a person who has worth because you are capable of giving. You are a person who has needs, but who can also fulfil the needs of others. You are a person who is a friend, can be a friend to others, and one who needs friends. You are a person who has sensitivity, warmth and inner beauty. To dare to be you involves risks, and there will be setbacks! When you choose to manipulate, when you try to convince rather than appreciate, when you evaluate rather than listen, you involve yourself in risks. Daring to be you is difficult. It begins with liking yourself. If you can do this - you will also be yourself, the natural you, the more relaxed you, thus you will be able to like others because they will like you in return.

Daring to be you means that you are becoming less dependent on others. You are other-directed in the sense that you become sensitive to people's affection. You are also inner-directed; you trust your deepest feelings and you make your own decisions.

Daring to be you means that you have a meaning in life, a goal, and a future ahead of you. You don't live in the past or blame others for where you are in the present. To like oneself is to be self-trusting and self-justifying. It is feeling good and alive for the moment and for the day. It is feeling the joy in just running, walking, or being free. It is experiencing the joy of a good sleep or feeling that you've done enough for today.

Developing the Self-Concept

Daring to be you also means living in the present. Living fully in the moment is a difficult task because we tend to think about what needs to be done or what we have done in the past. It may be that you need to cry for this moment, or it may be that you also need to love or be loved, at this moment. It may mean saying to yourself "I am adequate now". For you, life is an exciting process of trusting yourself in the here and now. Be aware of your strengths and weaknesses so you won't need to project your blame on others or be critical. You are aware of how you feel and sensitive to how others may feel.

I have a word to the religious-minded as well. To the religious, daring to be you means stressing that the kingdom of God is within and that trusting oneself is the highest form of trusting God's handiwork. Religion becomes less and less a judgemental process and more and more a sharing and growing together.

Oscar Toscanini on his eightieth birthday was asked by his son what he thought was his greatest achievement. As you know, Toscanini was a great conductor and violinist. He replied that for him there was no such thing as the most important achievement. For him, whatever he happened to be doing at the moment was the biggest thing in his life, whether conducting a symphony or peeling an orange. This is the perspective in life that we need to "live in the present moment". It isn't in the high goals, the grand achievements, but whatever you are doing at the moment that you enjoy. Living in the present involves daring to be you. Much of the continual pressure that we feel or the demands we make of ourselves and others come about because we're always striving for goals and standards which are a little bit higher than our actual accomplishments. This is described by psychologists as the need for self-actualization, to move one step beyond where we are at the moment. Whereas I believe that the need for self-actualization is a strong one and ought to be followed, I think that we often over-emphasize it to our own detriment and hence we tend to be much too hard on ourselves. We see this in our daily living when we get angry at our children if they misbehave, or we want our babies to be toilet trained well before they think they're ready, or we get angry when our spouse doesn't do the things that we think she/he ought to do. We push ourselves to keep up to what we think are our own standards, whether it is wanting more money or improving our job. So we tend to work day and night to get the things we want. We borrow too much and we buy too big a house or own too many cars. All of these problems, and many others, come about because we just dare not be ourselves. We tend to place ourselves in a competitive situation that destroys others in the process of destroying ourselves.

The Challenge

So what can we do? I'm suggesting that we learn to be ourselves, to be average people not attempting to outdo anyone but to live in perfect peace and harmony with ourselves. How do we do this?

First, I think we need to assess our situation. Because it is our own situation, we have to do it ourselves. Don't look over the fence to another person's situation. Look at your own and decide what it is you want and then determine the limits of those wants in relation to being yourself.

Secondly, it is important that we set goals that are within our reach and learn to be happy with them. It is not necessary to go for the extra dollar or that bigger house or that second car or the extra clothes or the nicer furniture. This means that we dare to be average, dare to live within our means.

Thirdly, know your own limitations. If life is smooth and relaxing and not stressful now, then why reach for goals that will cause the extra stress? It is important to know when we are doing what comes naturally and easily, enjoy it and continue in it. Again, we should not look over the fence to what someone else is doing.

I recently received a new book that challenged the old principle that competitiveness is indeed a quality worth enhancing in ourselves and others. My understanding of it is that we ought to work more cooperatively rather than competitively. This on its own will take the pressures off us and we will dare to be ourselves within a setting of cooperation. Once we turn to competitive striving we cannot dare to be ourselves because we are continually forced to work up to someone else's standard. Being cooperative instead of competitive helps others bring happiness to our lives as well as we to theirs. If we all helped others there would be no competition and we would all win. To see someone else happy causes great joy in us. It satisfies our inner being, it makes us feel good, and this is the one true antidote to our own feelings of stress and a negative self-image.

Naturally, we should continue to expect that life is going to have its conflicts, deaths, sorrows, arguments and problems. If we tend to see these as a normal part of living and not as a sign that we are socially, mentally or emotionally failing, then we are already learning to accept ourselves. It is in the whole process of meeting and solving problems that makes life normal, not unusual. It is in solving daily problems in fact that life has its meaning. Problems are the cutting edge that distinguish between success and failure. It is not in how much we have, how high a job we've attained, how well our children do, how fast we can run or how much we've accomplished that gives meaning to life. Benjamin Franklin once said that "things that hurt, instruct". This is because life brings us problems. This is the norm. This should be expected. And if we expect them, we will not be overwhelmed or disappointed or hurt or frustrated when problems do come our way.

Even problems in mental health can be seen as signs that we are growing. Through mental health problems we change. We are given a sign that we are not slowing ourselves down enough, that we expect too much of ourselves. If we see our own emotional illness as a sign of growth we will have a new joy even in that. If we see the pain as a temporary step in changing the focus of our life to a more simple, enjoyable, relaxing experience we will grow as people, even through mental illness.

There is a distinct challenge in daring to be who we are. It begins with an understanding and acceptance of our worthiness. If you believe this, you are well on the road to developing a positive self-concept. But there is another challenge ahead. Learning to accept oneself, and one's worthiness, requires realistic self-appreciation and a basic honesty with oneself and others. Being honest sounds easy enough and simple, but it isn't. Being honest is a key to the development of a healthy self-concept.

Read this next section slowly and carefully. Coming to grips with honesty is the next step.

Being Honest: Beginning a Realistic Self

Honesty is a trait highly valued by people. We want to teach it to our children, we expect it of our friends, we like to count on it from salesmen, teachers, and professionals of all kinds including business people, government officials and politicians. But do we really believe in direct and forthright honesty? Do we really expect honesty? Further, how do we understand honesty? Is it being brutally frank? Is it careful phrasing? How many times have we heard people say "You've done a find job"? or "You're a good boy"? These general comments certainly are honest in and of themselves but I think they need further explanation. We could say, "The reason I think you've done a good job is ..." or "This is why I think you're a good boy ...". When we speak in very general phrases we are certainly being honest. But the message is never very clear and there is a hidden message under it all. In the areas of business and business contracts, the law in the courts, or a doctor's diagnoses, we expect truly upfront words - honesty in what is said. What we want to hear are things that are said in a way so we can understand the exact meaning - nothing left to interpretation. When my wife asked the oncologist at the Cross Cancer Clinic "How long do I have to live?", the doctor said "A few weeks". Truly she had seven weeks from that day on. The doctor was right. A few weeks certainly covered the time frame that she had left. It was a shock but it had to be said and we both wanted to know. But when it comes to relationships, to family or marriage, to friends and children, honesty becomes more complicated. Direct meaning is often left to the other person to interpret and we ourselves do not always know or understand the exact meaning of a message. So we hide behind words and explanations, we are not totally frank and honest. We hide behind hidden messages, causing splits between husband and wife, parent and child, friend to friend.

It has been found that negative feelings usually are less difficult to express honestly than positive feelings. Most people have less trouble being very direct and forthright in letting others know if we are angry, frustrated, feel rejected, depressed or disappointed. Our language is more direct, our emotions are consistent with words, our face and body express the negative feelings. But when it comes to positive emotions or feelings of caring and love, praise and pride or accomplishment, we become less direct. Why is this so? One reason may be that we feel people might get swelled heads. We reason that we shouldn't be so direct because they might become too proud and self-satisfied. Another reason often heard is that we might make others feel embarrassed or that we ourselves may feel embarrassed.

When we are direct and honest, we make ourselves vulnerable. Letting others know how we really feel inside would give other people an edge in terms of understanding our true and honest expressions. Therefore, people are often less direct and honest because they feel they would be putting others on the defensive, or they wouldn't know how to accept an honest expression of positive feelings. These reasons may be justified but it does make it more difficult for us to be positive with people in a direct, frank and honest way. How often have we heard people say, "I really can't take credit for that", "you're just saying that", "it was just luck"? These are all defensive reactions borne out of uneasiness and discomfort. They are words that we say often and we have heard said often but they are words that do not really express an open form of honesty.

Being honest is evaluation, it is an evaluation and a value, an attitude and a trait that I believe all people appreciate and honor. Honesty implies qualities of trust and merit, responsibility, moral and spiritual excellence. We cannot have solid relationships without it. Being honest is also an evaluation of a product or of a behavior, an evaluation of a feeling or of a relationship. We want the truth but we want it so that it doesn't upset our own evaluation. We want direct honesty but we are given to the temptation of not being frank for fear of the evaluation it may bring on us.

When you and I are honest we are sitting in judgement of what has just transpired. We are evaluating or giving our true judgement or true feeling about the matter. Our honesty becomes an evaluation as much of ourselves as it does of the other person. People are very different in how they were raised, in the background they came from. So when others express things to us in a less direct way we often wonder whether indeed it may be a matter of their custom or training than in not holding to a value of honesty. It is also for this very same reason of difference in custom that open, true and frank honesty has almost disappeared.

If we are to develop honesty, what are we to do? First, I believe we need to establish personal credibility and integrity. If we are credible and believable, as well as trustworthy, our statements will be accepted even when they are not positive. For honesty to be accepted for what it is, we need to be credible. People need to come to believe that our word is to be trusted, and when we say something we have good reason to say it. In some cases our honesty can put people on the defensive and make them suspicious as well as feeling threatened. Sometime we need to say it anyway. In other cases we have several choices: we could just listen and not say anything; we could give reasons or explanations for what we say and why we say it; we could use words and phrases that are honest but not an evaluation. Sometimes saying things with carefully selected words is the best alternative. We often do this by speaking to the behavior and not to the qualities of the person. For example, if you say "You're a good boy", that is an evaluation of the person. But if you say "I like the way you sat down quietly", that is speaking to the behavior and not to the person. There is a big difference between the two. The latter will not make a person as defensive. Finally, we need to be honest in the language we use. We don't need to be brutally frank and hurtful. What we say should motivate and it should make people feel free of our control, free of our judgements as well. Let's be much freer in focusing on the positive. Let us listen much more before we say things, and let us ask questions to try to understand the other person's point of view. Let's talk and say things and let them know how we feel. In all we do we should let people know that we can be counted on. Let's follow through with our promises.

Honesty brings not only freedom but also a positive self-image, because it focuses on the behavior, not the person. Honesty is the only way to build positive, healthy relationships. Honesty allows one to see the real you, a person of worth, a person worthy of love, a person who can give and receive love. And when love is given and felt, the result is always a positive self-concept. To build a positive self-concept requires love, love made visible.

Making Love Visible

For now, let us assume we agree on what love is, there being so many intricate and complex definitions. Let us assume that love is caring, is confidence, is learned, is thought and emotion, is selflessness, is sacrifice, gives freedom to the other and that when it exists it is a force of healing. When we accept this definition of love it is apparent to me how this can be made visible in daily practical ways. At its simplest level, love made visible is to trust, even in the face of doubt. Love made visible is to give of oneself. Love made visible is to encourage and not to discourage. Love made visible is to free and not to hold or bind for selfish gain. Love made visible is to discipline oneself and others. Love made visible is to be virtuous and live by spiritual and universal principles of goodness and peace. Love made visible is to sacrifice. Ultimate love is to give one's life for another. This is the highest and most important form of love. It is AGAPE, Godly love.

I believe we can see this kind of love around us everywhere. It is there and I'm glad we have it. I have personally experienced it in my own life. I have seen it in how the listeners have responded. I know what love is by having experienced it. I have seen love made visible. Yet, we need to stress it, we need to encourage it in each other.

Because I do not believe that love is automatic nor instinctual, it is possible that many people do not know what true love is, nor do they know how to experience and practice it. Anthropologists tell us that there are entire societies in which love is absent. But this doesn't prove the rule that love is not possible. Indeed, it challenges us to show that love can be learned, is learned and needs to be taught, modelled, believed in and practised.

Our society seems to give us many more examples of love made INVISIBLE. What do we hear of or see most of in the television and news reports? We hear of wars and conflicts, murders and power struggles, robberies, divorces and separations, scandals, graft and abuse. We are beset by forces moving us more and more to a view that love, real love, is either impossible or at the very least difficult to have and practice. We are parent-bred with all their insecurities and defenses, competition-bred, to get rather than give and fed philosophies of hedonism, individuality, complacency and apathy. In such a world, love is invisible, at least to the naked eye. So we become quite critical and sardonic. We fall prey to making love invisible. What are we to do?

In making love visible we need to first have LOVE OF SELF. To make love visible requires that we love ourselves. This is seen in the confidence we have in ourselves, in the self-esteem and the value we place on ourselves. Love of self is knowing and understanding ourselves, believing we are worth the price of loving. Simply put, we need to love ourselves without personal arrogance. If we have that self-love we can accept criticism and not be overwhelmed by setbacks and problems. We can allow or accept differences in views. Love made visible is loving oneself.

Secondly, love made visible is experienced through RECIPROCI-TY. To make love visible requires giving to others, whether in romantic love or in altruistic forms, that is, helping, sharing, complimenting and giving. The reason love has to be reciprocal is that to give allows us to receive. Our own human resources are frail and limited and most of us do not have the highest form of love, that unconditional love, that allows us to give without wishing anything in return. To give or love without receiving it is difficult for us, but it is possible, if we believe the idea of reciprocity. Most of the time we do experience this reciprocal love and in that we see love made visible.

A third form of making love visible is to practice the principle of NON-RESISTANCE. Love made visible is possible if we do not use an eye for an eye philosophy to guide our life. Research supports the tenet that even if we don't actively aggress or hurt others, they perceive it as acceptance and understanding. In practical terms, love is made visible by not taking revenge, not fighting back, not playing one-upmanship, not competing. This is love expressed through non-resistance. Indeed, if we support or just not respond we become a passive bystander and we will further the cause of harmony and peace. Remember, it always takes two to have an argument. If we resist the urge to defend ourselves, even in the face of the greatest temptation, we will have made love visible.

Why do we need love or need to love? Writers tell us that the causes of love are the needs for security, sexual satisfaction, self-esteem and belonging. If this truly causes love, then all of us should have love and be able to give it. Being "in love" makes it possible to have guilt free sex, to marry, to view oneself as normal, healthy people, to have safety and acceptance as well as security. These are the stepping stones to the solution and resolution of all the problems and illnesses that beset us daily. A person that is beautiful is one who loves and is loved. Love alters psychological processes themselves and allows us to reach the heights of self-fulfilment - the highest personal goal we can set for ourselves in this earthly existence. In this sense, love conquers all and without it we are but an empty shell. Life in this world has no meaning or purpose without love. Let us make love visible and thus fulfil the greatest task and commandment of all. Love builds a positive self-image. It never fails. Love of self always precedes love for others. To love is to believe in one's own worthiness and when that evaluation is fully believed, the self-concept is strengthened.

Positive Misery or Positive Happiness

Up to this point in this chapter we have focused on the development and qualities of the self-concept. A positive self-image is no accident, as is a negative self-concept. We have stressed repeatedly that changing the self-concept is no easy matter. In our discussion we have stressed openness (dare to be you), belief in oneself (worthiness), the value of love (self-love precedes a positive love of others), and the value of honesty (realistic self-appraisal). Within each section we have offered ideas as to changing the self. We will end this chapter with further strategies, but before we do, there is another important matter to consider.

A positive self-concept should be everyone's goal. We have shown its value and effect in everything we do. Most people today are aware of this. If this is so, why do so many people suffer from a negative self-concept, or from the effects of a negative self-concept? And why is the self-concept so difficult to change? Part of the answer may be found in the evolution of man on this planet. There is a belief by social scientists in the philosophy of *hedonic asymmetry*. This belief holds that the net quality of life tends to be negative. Life was designed by the evolutionary process of survival, not for happiness. People who survived did so because they overcame obstacles and problems. Survival of the fittest may not be accepted by some as an explanation of the evolution of man, but it fits in well with man's social and personal growth. From infancy, man has competed for survival, whether it be for attention, love, recognition, grades in school, employment and finding a marriage partner. Those who won felt satisfaction. Their loss of misery created a positive self-concept. The positive self-concept turned their life, by and large, into positive happiness. Those who lost, felt misery. Their loss of satisfaction created a negative self-concept. The negative self-concept turned their life, by and large, into positive misery. You see, the net quality of life for those who do not survive among the fittest is truly negative. The end result is positive misery, a stressful life and a constant search for positive happiness. Because the self-concept is so stable, the search for happiness is no easy task if the self-image is negative.

Many people can remember or know of truly happy individuals. These happy people feel a sense of satisfaction and pleasure in life. They exude joy and confidence. They think positively of themselves and praise it in others. Are these people real? Are these people hard to find? The answers are "yes" and "no". Happy people are real and they are not hard to find.What is it that they have that makes them happy? To be sure it isn't their health, wealth or walk in life. Everyone, absolutely everyone, is beset with problems. Happy people have problems too! Then what is it? We believe the answer is very complex, but one thing happy people have is a positive attitude to life, self and other people. They are often upset, angry, frustrated, irritable and annoyed, but they can and do work through these miserable feelings. Their attitude to life is that happiness doesn't come automatically, it is hard work! Happy people commit their abilities to making life enjoyable. Think of this concept in the framework of a marriage. A happy marriage is not an automatic result of falling and staying in love. Happy married couples work hard at their marriage. Building a positive self-concept is directly connected to finding satisfaction and subsequent happiness in life. Hedonic asymmetry theory may be right! If we do not work hard at building a positive self, the net quality of our life may indeed be negative. Happiness is not an accident and not a biological given. We have to make every effort to find it. Our Charter of Rights and Freedoms may grant us the right to be happy, but unless we work at it, it will not be ours to have. A positive self-concept becomes the key to unlock the doors of positive misery and enter the kingdom of positive happiness. The process is a complex one, to be sure. If you take the attitude that it is worth the effort and are willing to work hard, you can change your net quality of life to one of positive happiness. What follows next are some typical and creative suggestions for building a positive self-concept and entering the kingdom of positive happiness.

Strategies for Building a Positive Self-Concept

Maintaining a positive self-concept is as difficult as changing one from negative to positive. If this thought hasn't hit home yet, you've been half asleep reading this chapter. Although we have given a few suggestions already in this chapter on changing self-concept, we have ten more that may be of help. Another thought! Developing and maintaining a healthy, positive self-concept requires first and foremost a changed attitude to life, an optimistic, positive outlook. Here is how one listener to 930 CJCA's "That's Living" radio program put it:

> "...I find I need to be told, things need to be stated and heard by me, then even the obvious becomes "common sense reality about living"...I'm getting out of a depressed state I have been in for years, not really realizing I was in it...Then I think after our 18 year old came out ok from a traffic accident I make up my mind to quit feeling sorry for myself and LIVE; and LIVE HAPPY. I really *heard* what these people said to me. Life is much more rewarding now. It took me 42 years to realize it!..".

Sometimes it takes a traumatic event to make us realize our good fortune. But traumas can also make us withdraw into helplessness and pessimism. The strategies we are going to suggest all require hard work and practice. Even in the darkest night, a small dim star can cheer us up. When our feelings are depressed, it is hard to think logically; it is hard to mobilize ourself to action. To begin our journey to a positive self, start with the first suggestion, then slowly try some of the others. And do not give up!

By Hook or by Crook

This phrase is well-known, I'm sure, to many of us. I must give credit to Dr. Robert Schuller, however, for putting this phrase into another perspective for me, and hopefully for you, the reader. The words "hook" and "crook" refer to fishing and shepherding experiences. Just as the fisherman needs a hook to catch a fish, a shepherd uses a crook to guide his sheep. Neither the shepherd nor the fisherman could do without this equipment. When times are difficult, when feeling down, when crises overwhelm you, begin to "hook" in the resources. John Donne wrote "No Man Is An Island". We need each other. I know it is often in the darkest hour that we need help the most. At such times we cannot stand alone. As hard as it may seem, be willing to ask for help. Admit your frailty. People do rally around us during difficult times. How true this was for me! It is not so much that people don't care, but that they don't know what your needs are. One person's weakness is another person's strength. Being asked to help is not an imposition, it is a privilege. So use that "hook", the hook of a voice asking for help.Use the resources that are there, whether neighbor, friend, family member, medical doctor, social service worker, pastor or priest. It is the first and vital step when the "bootstrap" methods are hard to implement. Call that friend right now. Let others help "picture you positive".

Pamper Yourself

Dr. Peter Hanson made this suggestion in his best-selling book *The Joy of Stress*. Dr. Hanson's view was that to relieve stress one must learn to pamper oneself within one's budget. The idea is not new. What happens when you do something wonderful for yourself? You feel good. You relax. Your mind empties of fret and worry. You begin to reflect on your needs and likes. As you do this, you take on another perspective of your worth as a person. Everyone is allowed some time for oneself, to do the things one enjoys. Taking time out for yourself takes planning. It won't happen by itself. As you plan it, you become sensitive to inner needs and wants. But the major impact of pampering yourself is the belief in your worthiness of it. You deserve it. Think of the tag on your shirt, ILAC. You are a loveable and capable person. Believe it and act that way. Every person wants and deserves at least some of the simple pleasures in life. So pamper yourself. Write down those things that would bring you happiness, whether it be playing games with your children, going for a walk, taking a hot bath, reading a book, going to a movie, watching television, going out with spouse or friend, working on a hobby, exercising, or any other thing. The end result will be a belief in yourself as a worthwhile person, deserving of this respect and fun. As you do this, begin to "picture yourself positive".

Broaden Your Horizons

Failures, indeed, repeated failures cause us to lose confidence in ourselves. As you lose self-confidence you become afraid to risk or attempt any task, let alone a new task. Parents and teachers already know that if you build "success experiences", the self-concept slowly changes to positive, at least in those areas of success. Behavioral scientists believe that it is best to act or respond first because action changes emotion. Cognitive scientists believe just the opposite. Change the thought and you change the feeling. Both views, however, are correct. Both action change as well as thought change will affect one's subjective appraisal. You act as you feel, and you feel as you act. Getting someone to do something different is as difficult as getting him to think differently. Just as thought-patterns change, so do emotions. We believe that action, or change in action, may be somewhat easier. We suggest that to build a positive self-concept, attempt a small task that is guaranteed success. With one small success you gain the confidence to try another task. We know that feelings will change over time. Just think of how the feeling of first love gradually loses its magic unless you change and work at it. Continued pleasures wear off just as much as the pain of loss. To build a positive self-concept, broaden your horizons by attempting a new task. With time, plan to attempt some new project every two years. As you do this, you begin once more to "picture yourself positive".

Altruistic Egoism

When stress is high, when failures pile up, it is natural to feel self-pity. People with a negative self-image are wrapped up in their own failures. They cannot see the light at the end of the tunnel. How does one begin to change this self-contemplation and self-imposed misery? Dr. Hans Selye believes that as we begin to reach out to help others our own troubles begin to vanish. Concern and care for others gives rise to bringing one's own negativism into focus. Helping others brings meaning and purpose to life. As one finds meaning, as Dr. Viktor Frankl wrote, depression, hopelessness and negativism change to positive thinking. Altruistic egoism simply refers to a concern for others over self. It is unselfish actions in the interests and welfare of others. Dr. Robert Schuller once remarked "you can't judge a person's life by its duration, but by its donation". Giving your time and talent in the service of others changes your perspective on your problems, your failures. But more importantly, it makes you feel good. Every act of kindness begets kindness in return. You begin to feel needed, valued and respected. We suggest, therefore, that you look for opportunities to help others in need. There are a number of agencies such as Big Brothers, Big Sisters, Uncles at Large, Volunteer Nursing Aides who would welcome your help. Schools as well as hospitals and churches need your help. Get to know the needs of your neighbors and offer your services. As you do this, you begin to "picture yourself positive".

Personal Freedom through Goal Setting

In the seventeenth century the philosopher Spinoza wrote that freedom consists in acting according to one's own goals, rather than those imposed by others. Lack of self-confidence erodes the ability to not only fulfil other people's demands, but also one's own aspirations. In fact, in the low ebb of the negative self-concept, motivation is lost. The only starting point at this stage is to set immediate, short-term, achievable goals. One small step of success leads to a large step toward a positive self-esteem. If you don't set your own goals, others will set them for you. The sense of personal control slowly slips away. Young children, even adolescents, need parental and teacher guidance. But even for children, setting personal goals, allowing choices in activities, gives them a feeling of freedom. A sense of freedom instills personal responsibility. Have you ever wished you were free to do what you want? I have. Personal freedoms are limited by rules and responsibilities to be sure, but choice of personal goals beyond those imposed by need moves you to the belief in freedom. To gain that internal focus of control, take time to think about what you want to accomplish. Begin on a week-by-week schedule, then move to a month-by-month and finally a year-by-year plan. As you do this, you will begin to "picture yourself positive".

Reframing and Refocusing

Co-hosts on "That's Living" radio program repeatedly use this strategy to ameliorate a problem. The radio program is "problem-oriented", but a "problem" can be shifted in such a way that allows solutions to be accepted. Reframing and refocusing simply refer to "seeing this situation from another angle or point of view". Naturally, you have to be open and flexible enough to allow other views in your mind.

Let me give you a few examples of reframing. Can you see "fear" as a method of response that saves you the effort of trying to overcome risks? Can you understand "anger" as a way to instill docility? Can you accept "guilt" feelings as a means to move you to a higher moral standard? Do you believe that "grief" is your right to cry for help? If so, you are open to reframing your own problems and negative feelings. To begin, write out a specific problem. Then write down the worst possible case resulting from this problem and the least possible outcome. In the middle column, write down all creative possible alternative ways to view the situation. Read what you've written. Circle those thoughts that are reasonable alternatives to your present feeling on the matter. Can you accept it? If so, you have refocused and reframed a problem. Dr. Schuller once said that "every exit is also an entrance". You have just entered into the world of beginning to "picture yourself positive".

Write, Read, Burn

Dr. Steve de Shazer, in his popular book on brief therapy, suggested this idea. When feeling blue and lonely, when the pain won't subside, this exercise may bring you relief. Once relieved of the pressures of stress you can try one or several of the other strategies. For now, find a quiet place in your home or apartment. Take a note-pad and write down as many negative feelings and thoughts as you can. Close the pad and continue your usual activities. The next day, pick up the pad and read what you've written. Add any new thoughts. Allow the words to sink in. Feel the mind and body sag as you look at your list of troubles. Close the pad again and continue your usual schedule. On Day 3, bring along a safe metal container and some matches. Re-read your list, light the paper and watch your negative thoughts and feelings burn to ashes. As Dr. de Shazer puts it, see your troubles literally "go up in smoke". The literal act of writing, reading and burning symbolizes what will happen in your mind. It helps to be a strong visualizer, a person who can imagine and fantasize. Nevertheless, the exercise has been found helpful. Once again, your negativism dissipates, burns up, and you begin to "picture yourself positive".

Worry Efficiently

Once again, I would like to credit Dr. Peter Hanson for this idea. It is described in detail in his book *The Joy of Stress*. All of us worry. Some more, some less. I don't think it is possible to get rid of the worry activity altogether. So let's keep on worrying but do it efficiently. To worry efficiently one must think about the issues in a realistic and logical fashion. If you can do something about the situation, then think about what you can do. Call it worry, if you like. But many people worry about things that just cannot be changed, things like the weather, or the world economic situation, or even about the fact that your son isn't home at midnight, or later. People have all sorts of worries. The list need not be repeated here. To worry efficiently is first to think about whether you can do something to change the situation. If you can, do it, and act quickly. If you can't change the unchangeable, pick another worry. Some therapists suggest that you designate a worry time, a worry chair and a worry room. Take thirty minutes of each day, find that chair, sit down and begin to worry. When thirty minutes are up, get off that chair and resume your duties. Keep all your worrying to the set "worry time". Try it. It has been found to not only reduce the stress of worry, but find useful solutions to your problems. You will now find it easier to "picture yourself positive".

Offensive Denial

The word "offensive" is meant to imply a positive action much as is understood in sports. Go on the offense. The best defense is a good offense. Denial is a defense mechanism whereby we block out negative feelings or experiences. We don't think about them. In fact, we may even literally deny that we have them. Taken to an extreme, this strategy can lead to a hindrance in seeking solutions to your problems, because denial won't let you own the responsibility. But the context of the technique is in controlling the negative thoughts about the self. Simply do not dwell on the negative. Block them out. When they appear in your mind, shift your thought to a positive one. Some people find it helpful to talk to oneself. Literally say, "I'm not going to think about this negative thought anymore. Lets see, what happened today that was good?" Dwell on the positive. If you can't see through a difficult problem, look around it or over it. See it as a challenge, not a roadblock. Entertain hopes. Suppress the negative and displace it with an offense that is good-oriented and positive. Used in this way, this strategy will allow you to "picture yourself positive".

Depersonalization

This word has specific meaning in the psychological literature. It means an alternation of consciousness, identity or even motor behavior. At the extreme, depersonalization is an experience for those with sleepwalking, amnesia, fugues (cannot recall one's previous identity) and multiple personality disorders. We are suggesting a mild form of this alteration of consciousness whereby one's sense of immediate reality is temporarily changed. Think of it as a form of daydreaming, but daydreaming with a purpose. Many actors, athletes and performers take ten minutes a day to "visualize" themselves having success. The daydreaming can be very specific. See yourself going through the entire "activity" with success and applause. Picture yourself positive. This has been the ending phrase of each strategy because it is so powerful. People who can emphasize the positive, visualize the success, act that way in the real situation. As you depersonalize and imagine an anticipated task, strive at all times to "see" a positive outcome. Notice the feeling inside your stomach when you visualize success. Concentrate on that feeling. Continue the exercise. As you picture yourself positive, you literally fulfil the prophecy that as you see the positive, you experience it. This is a self-fulfilling prophecy.

In this chapter we cannot hope to discuss all the issues and strategies. Much has been written on this subject. This brief sketch, however, has been full of important ideas and suggestions. We know that it is hard to break your negative self-images and thoughts. Recognition of one's need for change and for assistance is the first and vital step. That is how infants learn to walk, and that is how you can learn to change the negative self-concept to a positive one. As a measure of prevention, lead your life so you wouldn't be ashamed to sell the family parrot to the town gossip. After all, the best defense against a negative self-concept is a good offense. All of us will experience failure, some people more so than others. But everyone can win. Believe this, and you will "picture yourself positive."

CHAPTER 3

Fears and Phobias

FEARS AND PHOBIAS

In the early days of "That's Living" there was considerable interest about the impact of this radio show on listeners, and one day
there was an observer from the *Canadian Medical Journal* sitting in on the program. The original topic did not seem to be evoking
much listener response, but in the answer to a question, an inciden-
tal mention was made of phobic reactions. The switchboard lit up.
The same phenomenon has been happening ever since. It is our belief
that many people suffer from phobias, but few of us have any idea
how widespread and common these fears are among the general
population. For some reason we "suffer in silence". When the topic is
discussed publicly, everyone wishes to participate.

Advice to listeners on questions about phobias is always very
different then advice on any other topic. Most people who have developed phobias already have a great deal of information on the subject.
Most questions about child rearing or other aspects of psychology can
be answered with information. With phobias, answers are harder to
discover or accept. Reasons have to be found for the development of
phobias.

Anxiety Disorders
Generalized Anxiety

"...other times, Doctor, when something just bloody awful
has happened and I feel the concern but don't know about
it? I can't even tell you what on earth is the matter. I just
feel as if a catastrophe has happened to me or my family
or somebody, I don't know what's going on, I have physical

and mental symptoms, yet no matter how hard I work at it I don't even know what's bothering me. I should tell you my doctor is almost getting tired of seeing me, he says I'm not having a heart attack, although at times it certainly feels like it."

This is an excellent example of someone suffering from generalized anxiety. Sometimes it is difficult to find differences between fear and anxiety. If we think of fear as being normal and having a cause, anxiety is generalized fear without a specific cause. However, anxious people usually have some base for their anxiety. When a person has no idea at all what is causing grave concerns, then we can speak of a generalized anxiety disorder. In these instances, people suffering from anxiety disorders are not aware of the reasons for their concerns. The anxiety can persist for weeks or months and doesn't seem to be related in any direct way to current or recent past experiences. People with generalized anxiety are difficult to help, because problems are not readily uncovered. Physicians can treat symptoms, in fact Valium is one of the most commonly prescribed drugs in Canada. Yet often, even under medication, patients continue to have a vague uneasiness that something has happened or is about to happen. Sufferers from generalized anxiety disorders usually have both physical and emotional symptoms. Medical or psychological treatment is usually indicated.

Panic

Those readers who have suffered from a panic disorder will certainly know all of the symptoms. A panic attack is similar to an anxiety disorder except the symptoms in this case are much more severe and the onset can be sudden and dramatic. Imagine, if you will, just walking down the street on your way to a routine assignment, when you are stricken with emotional and physical distress of an immense magnitude. You are terrified and there is no reason for it.

Symptoms such as a rapidly beating heart, a feeling of dizziness, faintness, desire to run, etc. are so severe that very often individuals who suffer from panic disorders will adopt all kinds of strategies to avoid such a frightening experience again. Particular streets are avoided. Sometimes people will even stay indoors at certain times of day, to prevent another attack from happening. The problem of a panic disorder is not necessarily the symptoms experienced, it is simply that the amount of anxiety is totally disproportionate to any known cause, internal or external. Women appear to suffer more from panic disorders than men.

Obsessive-Compulsive Behavior

Another common anxiety disorder results in people utilizing "rituals" or fixed patterns which intrude into their daily life patterns. These obsessional ideas may often start with a phobia, or a panic disorder, but when avoiding times or places does not solve the problem, a person can become obsessed with the idea. This almost becomes a circular pattern where a person seems to have to think constantly about whatever it is that causes the most fears. Common obsessions include ideas about safeguarding cleanliness, or health, or in more severe and dramatic cases obsessive fantasies about doing something shocking or hurting someone.

The obsessive-compulsive person is often in an unhappy conflict state, on the one hand almost forcing unwelcomed thoughts and secondly performing ridiculous actions or rituals to calm the situation. The interesting feature of compulsive obsession behavior is that these rituals are not unknown to many of us. Sometimes we can mask obsessive-compulsive thoughts by calling them "superstitions". Almost all of us at some time or another have stopped ourselves from checking and double checking and even triple checking, whether or not doors have been locked or taps turned off. Many of us have thought about washing our hands one more time immediately after the act has been performed. Many quite normal individuals avoid public restrooms or phone booths. Psychologists working with students are aware that some individuals never hand in assignments until the last minute because of checking, triple checking, reworking.

"...Will I ever be satisfied? I clean a room and then reclean it then once again I clean it. I dust tables when they have been dusted five minutes before. I'd like to be normal and have fun and see messy things without hating myself. What now?"

Tuning Out Life's Anxieties

Like all problems, anxiety disorders come in stages. The person with a panic disorder or full-blown obsessive-compulsive rituals often has major problems coping with fear and anxiety. Most of us, though, have strategies so that we can "tune out life's anxieties".

"...Our brother in law has emphysema and is on oxygen all the time. He gets spells of being terrified, he says he can't seem to explain to the doctor just what he is going through. He feels the doctor thinks he's losing his mind...He takes a lot of pills...but I do wonder if one of them is giving these upsetting times..."

It's hard to know. In this instance we advised the author of this letter to check back immediately with her medical source. Rumination of possible causes are likely compounding rather than solving the problem. In this instance we had a positive response on radio. After advice from a physician, this anxious situation was alleviated.

Many times we have heard people say "I don't even want to think about this" or "I don't want to know". There are many situations in life that cause pain and anxiety for people. When problems are small or when there is little we can do, taking an optimistic view has been found to be very helpful. It lowers one's anxiety and helps one cope day by day. Psychologists have known this for years.

Our brain sorts out problems just the way we sort our mail. Junk mail gets thrown out before we even open it. Our mind also censors information. We repress, that is, we don't let something into our awareness; or we deny, that is, we say it isn't true; or that it doesn't exist. Sometimes our mind projects, that is, we say the other person has the problem and not us. There are times when we rationalize away our problems, or we talk ourselves into an acceptable solution. Yet, repressing, or not letting our mind become aware, can sometimes be helpful. It is helpful if we also tend to look upon the positive in the situation. We know, for example, that before surgery, people who are the repressers, who think of the surgery and going into the hospital as going on vacation and have the positive thought that it will make them better, recover much more quickly. The unconcerned do recover better after surgery. This has been studied and researched. It has been found that the people who deny or repress their anxieties have fewer medical problems, fewer complications, and were discharged much earlier. This form of self-help can be called a filtering of information that we let into our consciousness, a repression of information.

Many popular writers like Norman Vincent Peale, Dr. Robert Schuller or William Glasser write about positive thinking and positive addictions. These things do work, but the question is how do they work? Where does one start?

First of all, start by thinking of positives and look forward to the good things that come along each day. Just in planning our day in such a way that we can look forward to one positive thing that can keep our mind off our anxieties is important. This has worked in the case of my spouse who was ill with cancer and it has worked for me as well. Next, we can start by blocking out the negatives. If we stop ourselves by not thinking them or even saying them then our mind will not dwell on them. Literally saying "Stop" helps our mind cope with the anxieties. We must then start thinking about a positive thing, something small, something that we can anticipate. If need be, the literature does suggest that if we can set aside time for worry, so that we can still have the luxury of worrying, certainly we should do this. We suggest that setting aside a particular half hour of a day for worrying is often the best strategy. We then would tend to spend that particular half hour each day thinking about all our troubles and anxieties and when that half hour is up we say "Stop" and go on to an enjoyable activity that we have planned right after it.

There are other things that can help in tuning out life's anxieties. One is to look for alternatives. There are always alternatives. Think about what other things we can get involved in, or think about, or do;

then choose the one that is the most enjoyable and least troublesome. Set a plan in motion and work towards it. We can also look for positives in other people. There must be something positive in what other people bring to the situation. It is also helpful to tell others that they have been helpful to you, or supportive of you. Just saying that helps other people respond to you more favorably and thus they share in the common caring and concern.

All of us are capable of deceiving or fooling ourselves. For centuries we have known about mechanisms such as repression or denial. We can deliberately censor information flowing through our brain before it enters our conscious awareness. This can be very helpful to us. When there is nothing one can do to change the threat that one faces, one is better off denying that danger by blocking it out of one's mind, at least temporarily. This helps one stay calm. Of course, this tuning out can also involve risks. We cannot avoid the danger signals like chest pains; a bleeding mole; always feeling tired. At these times we must go and see our doctor. Even in marriage, deceptions exist. Some spouses refuse to accept the trouble their marriage is in and don't let a single suspicion enter their mind even when the clues are there. Modern psychology explains this as repression. These people wish to have their marriage intact and they don't look at the dangers that are lurking. Evidence from neuropsychologists suggest that the brain can censor information before it reaches conscious awareness. This mental censorship is possible because the brain sorts through an immense amount of irrelevant information and lets into awareness only a narrow slice. People have been found to have tremendous ability to control what they see and hear. Highly anxious people seem to do this best. We all do it, though. This is how we "tune out" life's anxieties.

However, physiological measures show that the body does react to anxiety through perspiration or increased heartrate. What is found is that people process negative information in the right half of the brain's cortex and process verbal information in the left. There is a neurological mechanism used to repress or to deny threatening infor- mation. Most of us try to obscure our problems. Sometimes we even call it stubbornness. When pressures are high, we tend to repress. When the repression is on physical things that may need medical attention, then I think it is a danger to us. However, when the repression is to keep negative thoughts away so that we can enter positive thinking into our mind, then we can learn to live with life's problems much easier. We know that to tune out really big problems is a mistake. We know that people such as victims of early childhood traumas are more likely to suffer from diseases such as hypertension, ulcers or even cancer. People who talk about their problems early are less prone to these diseases. "Tuning out" should be done only in so far as it may not result in further disease. The ability to speak the truth and to face it is indeed a remedy, but it must be a gentle confrontation and always with a positive thought or some pleasant event planned for the future that keeps us continually improving our own mental and physical well-being. There are no easy solutions, but in a small way positive thinking and planning for the positive and not overdwelling on the negative can be a tremendous help.

Handling Common Fears

From strategies about tuning out life's anxieties, let us now turn to information about fears and in particular normal developmental fears. Anxiety disorders are very difficult, and most parents do not like to see children afraid. It should be pointed out, though, that fear is very normal and very necessary in the learning process. In any discussion of abnormal fear, it is often wise to look at fears and concerns which our children have now and most of us have had in the past.

Normal Childhood Fears

So many parents are concerned about their children being frightened. It just makes sense to assume that some fears might be part of growing up. Perhaps it is worthwhile sometimes to talk about some of the normal, age-related fears, which, although common, can still be a real concern to parents.

Let's start out with the obvious. First, most children do experience specific fears. One study that I read recently showed that 43% of children ages 6 to 12 had multiple fears (7 or more as reported by mothers). What are these fears? Well, they can take many forms from specific, such as fear of animals, strangers, and water; to the abstract, getting lost, death, being kidnapped. Both boys and girls have these fears. In a study by Bauer in 1980 it was reported that these fears are more common with girls.

Now some fears can be the direct result of learning. The famous psychologist John Watson taught us about conditioning where a child becomes afraid of a white rabbit. The innocent rabbit had become associated with a loud noise. Also, we can expect children will become afraid through modelling. Parents must be very careful if they have phobias about heights, cats, or spiders. We don't need to tell children that we are afraid if we fear thunderstorms. The effect is very noticeable.

Most of these childhood fears are usually quite transient. One study showed that 6% disappeared after one week and 54% after three months. A year after a fear was noticed, that concern was cured in almost 100% of cases. The point here is that age-related fears disappear without intervention or treatment. Advice to parents is not to pay undue attention to them. Avoid letting fears become methods of attracting attention.

It seems worthwhile to put a list of many common fears along with typical ages at which they appear. All parents will know that this list might be as good or bad as some others; it will never be totally accurate. One of the nice things about children growing up is that they grow up at different stages. With that caution in mind let's try some typical ages when fears occur.

AGE	FEARS
0-6 months	Loud noises, loss of support
6-9 months	The fear of strangers
lst year	Separation, injury, toilet
2nd year	Imaginary creatures, death, robbers
3rd year	Dogs or cats, being alone
4th year	Dark
6-12 years	School, injury, natural events and peer-related social fears
13-18 years	Interpersonal relationships, injury, social
19+ years	Injury, natural events, sexual

The best treatment for these fears is perhaps no treatment at all, except modelling. If, though, a child has a fear which becomes excessive, is beyond the child's control, or lasts much longer than one would expect for the age, if it results in panic or avoidance behavior, then we may have a phobia, and that is a different story.

In summary, many childhood fears are normal and age related. A parent's responsibility is to treat these situations calmly, promoting confidence between parent and child that these very real concerns will pass. Sympathetic listening is a trait all parents should possess.

Fear as a Motivator

This topic has really been used as a follow-up rather than a preamble to discussion about phobias, with both adults and children. When we talk about fears, often listeners will respond by talking about the value of punishment and the usefulness of frightening people into a prescribed course of action. It is true that many people are concerned about standards. Often we feel that perhaps too soft an approach can lead to children becoming spoiled and difficult to control. In one instance a listener actually recommended to other people on the air that we could teach children by using very dramatic examples. Her belief was that throwing cold water on the faces of two and four year olds would stop tantrums. She also indicated that burning a child's hand would keep him away from stoves. The stove lid example was a useful one for the incredulous psychologist host. Mark Twain once indicated that "if a cat was burned by a stove lid it would never go near a hot stove lid again, or for that matter a cold one."

So the question comes up, *how is fear* or *fear of consequences* a motivator for better behavior? At first glance this would seem to be a very good way of influencing behavior. Certainly many societal rules are based on this concept. For example, if you break the law you are punished. The ultimate use of fear is, of course, capital punishment. Why not, then, teach fear of consequences as one excellent way of instilling values or knowledge in a child?

There was a psychological experiment some years ago in Maudsley Hospital, England. There were four groups of rats in this experiment, three of them were in experimental groups, one group of rats provided the control. Three different treatments were prescribed for the experimental rats. One group of rats was decorticated, one group was drugged. Finally, one group of rats was simply frightened. The interesting results of this study included the finding that the control rats were easy to spot, they were different from the experimental rats. However, no one could tell the difference among the brain damaged, drugged and frightened rats. The behavior was the same. If the rat made a mistake, it would be repeated. The experimental rats had lost the ability to learn from experience. Sometimes we assume that if a child is afraid or has failed, he or she can repeat the task differently. Actually in most instances it is success that frees us to try new approaches. Our decision-making strategies are not good when we are frightened.

Is fear ever useful then as a motivator? Of course it is. A child must be afraid of traffic. It doesn't help to explain all the reasons. The wise parent just keeps the child off the highway.

However, terror, or real fear, can stunt a child's emotional growth, resulting in continuing nightmares and repressed feelings. If restraint or fear is necessary to protect the child from greater danger, then use it. Thomas Gordon, a psychologist, stated that rigid rules and standards are necessary for the protection of those who cannot protect themselves, such as the very young, ill, or disturbed. These methods, though, are very much less helpful when we are dealing with healthy individuals. We all need the freedom to be involved in decisions that affect us.

The point, then, of discussing fear as a motivator is to simply point out that it is important for parents to know a child's strengths. It is easy to motivate through strengths. Let's not overreact to normal developmental fears, but if these fears continue, then is the time to seek professional assistance.

Negative Thought Patterns

Now it is certainly normal to feel anxious before important life events. We expect anxieties to occur when a child starts school, college, or embarks upon marriage. Chronic anxiety, though, can be a real problem. For a person who suffers from continuing anxiety, he or she must learn to live with tension. Even very young children can show symptoms of anxiety including things like insomnia, nervous mannerisms, stomach aches, blinking, yawning and headaches.

Right now many of us are sure to have some real anxious moments. Most of us are worried about jobs, exams, relationships, successes, or failures. Yet almost all of us know other people who are anxious all the time. These people live with the prediction of probable failure. Think of a person you know who always seems to be negative. If he or she is a sports fan then the home team will be knocked, to avoid later disappointment. Sometimes for the anxious person an excellent strategy is to look ahead for negative results, or the worst possible scenario. It must be very scary for the individual to be frightened every day. When any of us are unsure, we try hard to please others, thus we need reinforcement for our self-image, many of us always have a nagging fear that we're not performing, we're not doing enough for ourselves or others.

The strategy now might be to take a look at a common "what if?" situation. What if you fail the exam? What if she turns you down when you ask for a date? What if your marriage fails? What then? What plans or strategies will you adopt? Then, after having looked at what the worst possible scenario might be, try a time tested remedy which psychologists advocate for many situations - use thought substitution. What we are attempting to suggest here is that you might replace anxiety and nagging worries with short term goals. Admit that you might fail, that things might become more difficult, then substitute the negative thought patterns with positive short term goals. This is something each of us can do for ourselves.

Admit negative possibilities, then substitute positive feelings.

Thought substitution, a behavioral technique used to disturb negative thought patterns, is often associated with "thought stopping", discussed earlier in this chapter. One interesting thing about us is if we're asked to stop in an authoritarian tone, most of us usually do. Anxiety or negative thought patterns, when they become a feature of your life, are indicators that action is necessary. It is time to turn negatives into positive thinking.

Nightmares

When a psychologist discusses fears it doesn't matter whether we are discussing normal developmental fears, phobias, or anxiety attacks - the topic of nightmares does come up. It is indeed terrifying for a parent in particular to hear and view a child reacting in absolute terror to something we don't understand. A nightmare can be a frightening experience. We should not think of nightmares as problems that affect only children. Many adults have nightmares and/or night terrors.

The field of dream research is also rapidly expanding. By means of REM's (Rapid Eye Movements) psychologists have traced sleep patterns and can tell when a person is dreaming. It should be noted that researchers have confirmed what we already knew, that is, all sleep is not relaxing. A person can be quite tense when dreaming. For example, when we are ill we often have a type of "fitful sleep".

What then, is a nightmare? Perhaps the best theory is that a nightmare consists of a real fear that we are able to repress, or shut out of our consciousness, when we are awake. Like most events, nightmares bring out this fear in a type of disguised form in a dream. Without the disguise, the fear becomes intense. However, when the dream appears so real, when the emotions are so intense, when the sleeper is so afraid, then he or she does waken, many times screaming and crying. Bad dreams and nightmares are useful symptoms for the physician in diagnosing some other illnesses. One example of this would be early morning waking, as a sign of some types of depression.

While there are many ways to help with nightmares, one common way is to learn to relax. An attempt should be made for the sufferer to go to sleep in good humor. If we know what is bothering us, then the problem should be dealt with when awake and conscious. It is recognized that this is not always possible.

If the problem can't be solved readily and often it can't, nightmares can involve inconvenience and tension with other family members. A failure to quickly solve a problem should result in alternate treat-

ment strategies. These may consist of medication through your doctor, or hypnosis and relaxation therapy through your psychologist, or other professional. If the problem can't be solved, maybe a person can relax and learn to live with a difficult situation.

When a child has a nightmare it is important that the parent should be exceptionally supportive. Talk in a very calm reasoned manner. Try to get things back to normal as quickly as possible. It is important when we are dealing with children, that we don't allow this waking and crying to become some form of an attention getting device.

If you're curious as to the source of your bad dreams, one way to monitor dream behavior is to write down all you can remember about the dream upon waking. Don't wait. These thoughts disappear very quickly. When writing down one's feelings, it is important to deal with emotions perhaps even more directly than content. A content of a dream is often not as important to the dreamer as the emotion experienced and the question "When did I feel this way before?" is often a valuable one to ask yourself upon waking.

Very often repressed memories are not terribly frightening when they are brought out into the open and we remember what it is that scares us. As with all serious situations, if nightmares persist, get professional help.

Understanding Phobias

It is generally thought that approximately 30% of people have phobias to the extent that these fears interfere with a normal happy life. For those people then, here are some ideas.

In the first instance, we all know people who have phobias. The young boy or girl who is frightened of snakes would be one example, but some men and women can also be frightened of caterpillars. Many people have a fear of heights, and we all know individuals who are uneasy or even terrified about the thought of flying, or in some instances taking a long trip by car.

The term phobia comes from the Greek word "phobos" - the Greek God of Fear. The likeness of phobos was painted by ancient warriors on masks and shields to strike terror in the hearts of enemies. So a phobia is a fear. In reality, though, not a real one. Not only is the fear "not real" it is totally out of proportion to the amount of danger that could be evident. A person who is phobic cannot explain the fear, even to himself. The emotion is beyond any kind of voluntary control. The degree of fear is very real. Some people can become so terrified that they will go to great lengths to avoid cats, snakes, dogs, or even downtown in some instances. There are people who are not phobic that can understand this fear, as all of us can be more afraid than expected of natural phenomena such as typhoons, tornados, violent crime. These fears can be intensified while familiar fears such as the automobile, which may pose much more danger, are commonplace and therefore less frightening.

There are many kinds of phobias, in fact so many that classifications are not used much anymore. To keep track of all phobias that people can develop would require so many words that we just don't have a specific label for a specific illness. Most people, though, have heard about vertigo which comes from acrophobia, or a fear of heights. The term agoraphobia literally means "fear of the marketplace" and has come to depict a fear of open places, crowds, or unfamiliar settings. Many adults and some children have aquaphobia, a fear of water. As indicated earlier, it is just not possible to list all the possible combinations of phobic reactions but two more. (1) xenophobia - fear of strangers and (2) the very familiar claustrophobia - fear of closed places.

Many phobias can begin with an anxiety attack, as discussed earlier. In extreme cases these are called panic attacks. The anxiety then becomes focused on an object or situation such as a snake, or an elevator. People with phobias develop ways of coping with these fears, and often these coping mechanisms do not work as they involve cumbersome procedures or avoidance. On the positive side, phobics don't usually require hospitalization. Outpatient treatment is often successful. Common ways of treating phobias include psychological techniques such as hypnosis, relaxation, or systematic desensitization. Often medication prescribed by medical doctors can be helpful. Newer techniques involve biofeedback.

There has been some research on the prevalence and types of phobias. People at approximately age 50 seem to have developed the most irrational fears, but there are very few with children under 10 or adults over 65. A fear of snakes is most common in late teens or early 20's. People fear crowds in their late 50's or early 60's. Many of us have had children who were afraid of injections. Age 10 seems to be a particularly good time to note this fear. Perhaps the most common phobia of all is a social phobia -fear of appearing before a crowd, or public speaking. There are very few modern phobias, such as fear of pyjamas or electric outlets. Some modern phobias include flying, or driving in cars, but these often have a rational base.

Well then, how can one help oneself? The key is relaxing. Familiar treatments not too long ago would encourage people to climb a ladder one step at a time until they felt relaxed at a certain height. Later it was found that the process could be speeded up through hypnosis or relaxation. People with agoraphobia seem to find real reassurance and assistance in working together with others who have the same problem. Agoraphobic groups are common in most cities in Canada and the United States.

Don't become angry with yourself, it doesn't help. Perhaps the first step in "curing" a phobia is to decide whether the fear is rational or irrational. If it is irrational then a person should stop using his good mind to solve the problem, and simply admit that you have an irrational fear. Once admitted, you can invent strategies or develop techniques to divert your attention.

School Phobia

Psychologists and psychiatrists are not the only professionals who work intensively with school phobics, but all three of the authors of this book have spent considerable time working with families where school phobia is a severe and threatening problem. Each September, the hosts of "That's Living" recognize that a substantial percentage of calls will be from parents whose children can't or won't attend school. Because the problem is such a serious one for so many families, we'll deal with it in a separate section.

"...Dr. Paterson, you're a school person, help us. What is wrong with our kindergartens? This is the second child I've taken to kindergarten myself, and the same thing is happening. He hates the teacher, cries from the time I put him in the car. I've tried to help, but the school people don't even seem to want me there. I'm battling a screaming, frightened child every single morning. What are they doing to make him this way? At home he is the nicest person anyone would ever want to meet."

It would be nice if this situation was uncommon, but it isn't. There are many research studies looking at the prevalence of the problem. One dramatic study showed that school refusal was estimated at about 5% of child psychiatric referrals, but represented nearly two thirds of those identified by the Doctor as "phobic". There are in every city and town many children that do not go to school and utilize extraordinary methods to keep parents from enforcing attendance. One example happened to this writer. In the course of my psychological duties, I served as a consultant to a children's institution working with "emotionally disturbed children".

The child in question was twelve. He had been to school twice out of eighty some days. His strategies for avoiding school were excellent. He had seen medical doctors, psychiatrists, psychologists, social workers. He had run the gamut of treatment in the city of Edmonton, Alberta. My treatment strategy was hypnosis. The boy and his social worker arrived at my office at approximately 8:00 a.m. I utilized relaxation. When he was very relaxed I made the suggestion that school for him today would be a positive experience. The session seemed productive. At the end of the session his social worker indicated to me that he certainly hoped that when the boy returned to school the next day, it would be a fruitful experience. I queried this "next day bit". It was explained to me by the social worker that it would not be a good idea to send the lad to school right after hypnosis, as there might be a treatment effect. After I debunked this notion, the social worker, not the child, then intervened to say it still would not be a good idea because on that particular day all of the children were bringing lunches and they had not prepared a lunch for this child. My thoughts ranged from anger to pity for all those parents who put up with excellent reasoned excuses which on the surface makes sense, but taken with the entire picture, show an entirely different syndrome.

The mother in the first letter about school phobia is probably involved with the problem rather than the solution. The social worker in this second example matched wits with this lad and lost.

Most professionals divide the term, school phobia, into at least two categories. The first type of child who refuses to attend school is afraid of the school itself. These cases are probably very rare, although this is the common reason presented by many parents. In these instances children really fear the school and become anxious whether or not a parent is present.

More commonly the fear is not of the school situation but of separation. This is called "school refusal". These children may be receiving mixed messages. You know the situation, "You must go to school. It will be good for you to go to school, you'll learn things and you will be reading. Mommy will get along at home - somehow - without you." Please, allow the writer to apologize for the sexist tone of that quotation. It was not a direct quotation, and of course could apply to a parent of either sex. The point though, and it is a valid one, is that as parents, we very often give the child a mixed message. We tell him in the same statement to go to school and imply that we need the child to stay home. These are interactional problems, the cumulative effect prevents either parent or child from taking positive action. The major reason for the school refusal or school phobia is not so important as the fact that positive action is stymied. If the major problem is an anxious parent, or if the major problem is an anxious child, or if the parent really fears the school will harm the child, or if the child really feels that school is a frightening place; the problem still remains.

In a school phobia situation, the parent should examine his or her motives. If we believe that the child is too young, or not prepared for school, the child will pick up this interpretation consciously or unconsciously. If we overreact to tears in early school experiences, the result will be the same.

Regardless of the therapist's point of view, all experts in this field believe that the longer the child is prevented from attending school, the more serious the problem will become. The trick is to continue attendance, work with school professionals behind the scenes to make a more pleasant environment, but "get the child to school".

The news in this instance can be good news. Most young children do return to school and this is a temporary situation. With older children who have this problem, the situation definitely requires professional help. Sometimes we even get results like these.

"...Thank you so much, doctors. Your few suggestions showing me I was part of the problem have helped immeasurably. Sandra is happily back in grade one."

Summary

We've established in this chapter that fears and phobias and anxiety syndromes are very common. We've also established that many different professionals can be helpful. Group therapy for agoraphobics, educational assistance for adults, medical help for some types of panic disorders are only just a few examples of the different kinds of treatment that are available. Because there is often a very good success rate with phobic patients, many professionals are anxious and eager to try to work with people with these types of problems.

Whether or not one has a more traditional view of phobias and looks towards helping a patient discover a cause, or a more recently developed strategy of eliminating symptoms, some practices are similar. Patients must not spend time berating themselves or downgrading the seriousness of the problem. Feeling guilty about being phobic, does not cure the phobia.

The first sign of positive growth for you is when you are able to be relaxed in a normally tension producing situation. Enjoy the feeling, try it again soon, so you reinforce the different connections. An early method of treating height phobia (acrophobia) was to have a person take one step up a ladder at a time and remain until he or she was comfortable. Now this can be done through relaxation right in your therapist's office. Treatment strategies recently developed do include medication, relaxation and hypnosis, plus biofeedback. They all work well, and often working with other people in the same situation through a group is exceptionally helpful. There is little in the literature as yet, but apparently discussing phobias with professionals through radio and television talk shows can be beneficial. At least this would be suggested by our mail.

Because part of the treatment of phobias is often related to not feeling guilty and being able to laugh at yourself, one more story about one of the authors of this book. The program was on fears and phobias and the questions were coming "hot and heavy". Two separate callers phoned about "escalator phobia" and the host psychologist tried to put this in the same category as other simple phobias, including claustrophobia. Finally the host was called by a former department store manager who was in retirement. The man indicated that he thought everybody knew about "escalator phobias". He said in his work in a department store he had seen people become frightened of escalators time after time, particularly older people going down from one floor to another. The host was, of course, interested as that was exactly what the calls had been about. The ex-manager explained that very often people start on an escalator by grasping the handrailing. As your arm is pulled ahead, people lose balance and have a sensation of falling. He suggested one cure for this "phobia" was simply to step before you grasp the handrail. Well this sounds almost too simple to be true. For the last several years the hosts of "That's Living" have received calls and letters indicating that this is one of the best single pieces of advice ever received from the program. Nobody knows everything.

CHAPTER 4

Love and Marriage

LOVE AND MARRIAGE

Relationships and Roles

Today's family, as we once knew it, is on the brink of extinction. Nobody seems to know what love is anymore, nor if it is necessary in relationships. Men and women are confused about their roles and responsibilities. Marriages occur as frequently as before but they don't last. Families are fragmented, separated, disenfranchised, pulled apart from within and without. Although polls indicate that people still consider marriage and family the most important element in their lives, nearly half of the individuals polled believe that family life has deteriorated in the past fifteen years.

The situation was deemed so serious and important that the Government of the United States held a national White House Conference on Families in June of 1980, at Baltimore. What could have been a valuable meeting of informed and concerned citizens, became a battleground for confusion. President Carter wanted to know how the government could help strengthen the family, a noble cause. As is typical in today's society, the conference disintegrated into arguments over abortion, rights of homosexuals, women's rights and roles, pro-family and anti-family issues. Within this context, the traditional family, as we once understood it, had no chance of survival. This traditional family with working father, housewife mother and children present, represents only 8% of all families today. Instead, we have to consider that over 40% of all families are fragmented through separation and divorce. One in five children lives with a single parent. The single, most important change in the family today is the emergence of the working mother. Women are not satisfied with their family lives. Only 20% of all parents today regard having and raising children as the most satisfying part of their marriage. Drug abuse, alcohol consumption in excess, unfaithfulness, decline in religious and moral values, serial affairs, individuality are but a few of the problems facing families today. Higher incomes for many, poverty for others, shorter work hours, dual-career families, labor-saving technical innovations, changing attitudes to self, marriage, love, relationships, work and children threaten the stability of the family. Although people become impassioned when the future of the family is discussed, few know the answers to the complex dilemma of love, marriage, relationships and family. This chapter recognizes the problems and struggles in love and marriage. The issues are complex and serious. We hold to a pro-family position, while recognizing the myriad of forces that can undermine the marriage and the stability of that unit. We may not have definitive answers, but we do have a position. We hope this chapter will provide some insights that will be helpful to you as you deal with the concerns in love, relationships and marriage.

Problems and Power Struggles

In the 6th century, Pandects wrote the following "For a man's house is his castle. One's home is the safest refuge to everyone".

Surely this must be true. Yet it is very interesting that the highest percentage of personal problems dealt with on the radio program "That's Living" have to do with home problems. Surely home is where a person should be able to take off his mask and become what is innately there. This unmasking allows any of us to be what we really are - to let go - to say or do what we like. If this happens at the end of the day, then fears and worries can fade, anger can drain away, tensions can melt.

On the other hand, and equally as true, if members of the family are worried, if we are resenting each other, if we can't understand what the other person is saying, then stresses can mount and home can be a place of misery. If this ever happens, it is vitally important to try to interrupt the vicious stress circle at an early stage.

It must be obvious to all of us that we need a storm-centre, a haven, a refuge. If this is not a part of our daily life, then our tensions very likely will spill over into the outside world. It is recognized of course that all family problems can't be solved. People go through life with differences of opinions, but problem solving techniques within the family are important; if an entire problem can't be resolved, we can be helped to learn to live with it, or pieces of the puzzle can be put together. There are few families that live in perfect harmony. In fact, maybe there aren't any.

When we are young, we look for magic, a sense of fulfilment, perfection; we think of a permanent relationship, marriage, or parenthood. Of course, these magical moments exist, but through a lifetime there are perhaps more times where we must face disenchantment, a natural state of affairs, but often deeply disappointing.

When the family is in disarray, when there is crying, when there are accusations, to the point where even the family pet is involved, try to break the stress cycle. In a crisis situation it is never helpful to ask impossible things of either other people or yourself. Try to work on those behaviors of yours which are most annoying to other people, ask your spouse or children to do the same, look for improvements and they will happen.

It must be that humor is a problem solver. These comments were started with a 6th century quotation, perhaps it is wise to end with another, this one from the 5th century B.C., Herodotus said:

> "If a man insisted on being serious, and never allowed himself a bit of fun and relaxation, he would go mad or become unstable without knowing it."

Herodotus also taught the value of patience in every endeavor when he said:

> "Haste in every business brings failure". This is true for problem solving in all other areas.

Perhaps one of the things to remember about the 1980's will be the way our society has confronted the serious issue of family violence. When we talk about family violence, the idea of power struggles seemed to surface over and over again. If arguments, discussions, fights and even violent altercations are the result of power struggles, it seems necessarily advisable to know something about these situations.

Now all of us have been in situations where the argument is not as important as who wins. Examples of this phenomenon are easy to find. We can have an owner versus a manager in a sporting situation. Very often George Steinbrenner exerts power over his field manager, Billy Martin, who is fired over and over again. Sometimes we can have a star player versus a coach in a power struggle, like Babe Ruth versus Miller Huggins. The truth of the matter is that one player really can't be bigger than baseball, basketball, hockey, or whatever.

In a classroom situation very often a new teacher, a practice teacher, or a substitute teacher will be tested by the class. Children at most ages love to see how much power they have.

Power struggles are also common in marriage. Sometimes parents can fight each other through the children by over-ruling each other. This can be very confusing, not only for marriage partners, but for the children as well.

To some extent our society encourages power struggles. In the 1800's, Saxe wrote about *THE GAME OF LIFE*, recorded as follows:

> In battle or business, whatever the game,
> In law or in love, it is ever the same;
> In the struggle for power, or the scramble for self,
> Let this be your motto-Rely on yourself!
> For, whether the prize be a ribbon or throne,
> The Victor is he who can go it alone.

1. Power struggles are very natural

This may seem hard to believe but it is indeed part of human development. As a youngster the child finds that he or she can influence parents by actions, actions like temper tantrums, smiling, or chuckling. If these behaviors work (reinforced) they are repeated. If the behaviors work often, the child can be in control. We may even think of him or her as a spoiled child and we will receive lines like "you don't love me unless..."

2. Don't engage in power struggles with children

The reason I am suggesting that we don't engage in power struggles with children is we already have the power. Sometimes this is not the case. Often power struggles occur between adults and children in second marriages. Children will respond to the natural parent, the other parent in the family has little power, being seen as the usurper of the missing parent's former role. The natural mother or father then can hold power like a referee. It doesn't work. There is no need to make a point that has already been made. In jest I have often said in training teachers that it is a good idea when a child is testing for power, to advise that we will find out who the teacher is at the end of the month. The person getting paid is the teacher, those who do not get paid are the pupils.

3. In adult battles, make rules

The first rule I would like to suggest in any power struggle is that there must be no violence, not ever, no matter who is at fault. Fighting fair is a counseling technique taught to couples. This involves sticking to the topic under discussion. Other rules for problem solving include listening to the other party, trying to see if you can understand even if you don't sympathize with the other point of view. Another suggestion would be to recognize a power struggle when it happens. It's difficult to engage in a power struggle, if both parties recognize what is happening.

Does it mean, then, that because one is a parent or one is a teacher, that person is always in power in a family or classroom situation? Of course not. The best groups we have found are ones with rotating leaders. Certainly children in some matters have expertise and should assist in family decision-making. Often the teacher will relinquish power to children in the classroom for various reasons.

In summary, power struggles occur in most real life situations, avoid them if possible, when they happen they should happen in an atmosphere charged with determination to resolve problems, not an electrically charged situation leading to conflict and possible mental or physical abuse of other people.

Just a Housewife

Conflicts and power struggles are commonplace in every home. Less common today are the traditional families where the husband works out of the home, the wife in the home. Concerns can arise out of role changes or demands placed on each partner within their role in the family. A young mother described her feelings as follows:

> "...I have tried to cope with my situation for quite some time now but have only managed to dig myself into an unbearable depression. I desperately need to sort out my emotions but have been unable to do it myself or with my

husband's help...I'm 25 years old and have been married
to my husband for three and a half years. We had our first
baby...and now, after having been employed the past ten
years, I'm at home with the baby. I don't feel I'm adjusting
particularly well to this but, on the other hand, perhaps
I'm going through the same emotions that any new mom
goes through. At the same time, I feel our marriage is
breaking down bit by little bit...I'm confused about myself,
how can I possibly expect (my husband) to understand?"

Do you often feel besieged, bored or frustrated? Do your greatest
satisfactions and pleasures come from satisfying the needs of others
and pleasing your spouse? Do you feel that your true worth and
pleasure come from meeting your own needs and that you need some
other, more fulfilling career other than being a housewife? Does
meeting household chores dissatisfy you? Is your self-esteem wither-

ing because you are "just a housewife"? Does your husband remind you of Archie Bunker? Do you often feel like an Edith Bunker?

The television series "All In The Family" is often taken as an example of how one should *not* treat a housewife. Betty Friedan in her book *The Feminine Mystique* made people aware that a career at home is difficult - and difficult to enjoy. She said that many women of middle and upper class homes felt trapped. However, women whose husbands had blue-collar jobs didn't feel that badly about staying home. When they compared outside jobs of carting heavy trays, cleaning other people's homes, standing up all day selling hats, they did not covet their husbands' jobs at all! But women whose husbands had more glamorous jobs often felt alone, uncomfortable and unhappy at home - besieged by heavy demands and lots of work.

There's plenty of research on job satisfaction that shows that work, even low status work, plays an important part in a person's self-image. Women at home, women who are ill and incapacitated, unemployed women and men begin to see themselves as useless. Outside work gave them social contact, a wider perspective on life and a more active life. This variation added pressure but also much more enjoyment. It gave them a new confidence. For men and women alike, friends made their work very pleasurable. In addition, the research showed that twice as many housewives as opposed to employed wives were dissatisfied with their lives. Twice as many housewives claimed their husband's work was more interesting than theirs. Twice as many housewives claimed that they did not have a fair opportunity in life and wanted their daughters to be quite different from themselves. Today parents encourage their daughters to get educated and get a good job. This is not what it was like in the 1950's, at least not in my own family. There, the daughters were encouraged to get to work. A high school education wasn't even deemed important.

It is true that many women who are housewives are certainly not confused at all and are very competent homemakers. However, the research shows that a good 33 percent do not feel competent or even enjoy their housework. Interestingly, women who worked outside the home felt they were not good at homemaking. Is outside work the answer?

The answer is No. Housework doesn't make you happy or unhappy. The difference lies elsewhere. Those individuals who want to work outside the home and don't are the most unhappy. It isn't the outside work that is the answer, it is whether you feel happy in the work that you're doing in the home. The answer is in really what you feel you want in life, how you see yourself and what you feel you would like to be and do. In other words, what picture do you have of yourself? If you have a picture of yourself as a housewife, then you will be happy there and quite comfortable, seeing to the needs of your children and your spouse as being the primary and most important role in the world. These women are not confused. They enjoy their work. They see it as the most important work in the world - the cornerstone of our society. They feel in control of their lives and they're in good physical and mental health.

So the confusion for the wife lies in the fact that she must be doing what she feels she would like to do. If outside work is desired, then some effort ought to be made to move in that direction. One has to remember that employed wives have double burdens, a burden in the home as well as in the job. Women in the work place, therefore, report more stress than men. It isn't all sweetness and light to be working and caring for a home.

Today, our families move so often that networking of social relationships, often a major part of the housewife's enjoyment, is easily eroded. The contacts and social support are not there. Women who stay home are lonely. Many take to watching television, cleaning, cooking, feeling worthless and in despair, staring at four walls. One woman commented, "it's like being in jail". They miss others and they miss the social life. When their husbands come home from work, they are tired and want to stay home whereas wives may want to go out.

Whether or not a woman should take a job over her husband's opposition to it is a different question. In the research, 50 percent of the females said "no" - women should not take a job outside the home over the husband's opposition. Given this attitude, many women feel trapped and confused. Either way, whether they stay home or whether they go to work, they are unhappy. If she takes the job her marriage may be in trouble, but if she stays home she's unhappy. I feel that it is so important for the women to fully come to grips with what they really enjoy in life and what they would like to do. They should then take the time to fully discuss these things with their husbands. If her husband is unhappy with her taking a job outside the home, then a compromise could be reached whereby she may do some volunteer work, or perhaps take a one-day-a-week job that wouldn't interfere with the home. At any rate, this should be settled in a manner that would be pleasing to both sides.

Men and Fathers

Not only are some housewives confused and unhappy, but also men and fathers. Men's roles with the family are changing rapidly. Movies like "Mr. Mom" are scoffed at by some men who adhere to traditional roles for fathers and wives. Shifts from rural to urban living, predominance of dual-career marriages and increasing pressure from women's groups have forced men to change their self-image. The "confused housewife" can easily be replaced with "the confused father". We examine this issue next.

What is a man? Who is a father? Is he the person who spends seconds per day interacting with a child, or 2.7 encounters daily of 10 to 15 seconds with his spouse? Man, the man we know is in a rat race of life, living and working. A man is a person with responsibility for leadership, showing his children his family and spouse the way in education, in social spheres, in spiritual and emotional development. Children look to their father for decisions and for discipline and support. This we call authority. Most men, most conservative men at least, see themselves in this role. But men are in an identity crisis today. The feminist movement and the women's liberation movement have given rise to new thinking about who we are as men and what it is to be masculine, authoritative and disciplined.

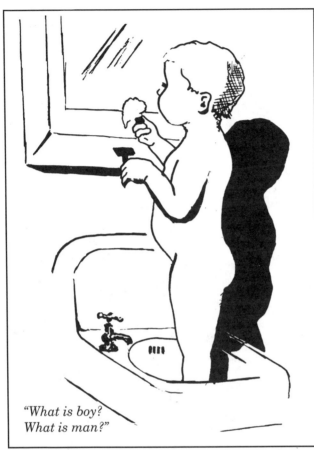

"What is boy?
What is man?"

The image of man, and who he is, is being dismantled as is the image of "woman". A decade ago, women who were caught up with the image as presented in television through *Wonder Woman*, *The Bionic Woman*, or *Charlie's Angels* developed a new concept of who they are. Men need to have a very careful look at who they represent and what they represent.

The concept of what is man becomes even more important for us when we realize that men commit 90 percent of the major crimes, 100 percent of the reported rapes, 95 percent of the burglaries, 94 percent of drunken driving charges, 70 percent of suicides and 91 percent of family offenses. It is true that whereas these offenses are caused primarily by men who are single, the family man and the man of marriage and parenting is caught in a crisis of identity when few resources exist to tell him exactly who he is and how he is changing. Men's satisfaction with marriage or with work, if it lasts, is in the later years whereas for women it is in the early years. Most men have a change of attitude and values in their late 30's and 40's. At this stage he becomes very disillusioned with his life. This disillusionment often forces the woman in the family to go back to work, become liberated, aggressive, angry and depressed. Men are often caught up with an affair, or turn to alcohol. Some men become depressed and attempt suicide. Separation and divorce is often a common by-product.

"What is man?" is often answered by "what is boy?" Our boys are to be aggressive, play rough sports, not play with dolls and not help around the house. Boys should be active, get dirty, love spiders and frogs. In the picture of the traditional male we find him doing average or even poorly in school (although not all men do), skip classes, love fishing and hunting, chase girls, love cars, wear a cap, act macho and be popular. Most of us believe this. We don't see man as a poor athlete, a lover of classical music, a piano player, or a homemaker who cleans rooms and cooks, sews and knits. We don't see man as an expresser of feelings who cries at weddings and funerals, or as a decorator who loves colors, couches and capes. No, we see man as strong, the protector, an outdoorsman, a provider, a protector of women, a fixer of cars and appliances. Man, true man, must be a worker, have the ability to support as well as protect his family.

This image of man is changing today. The hero soldier and the breadwinner image is no longer the view of experts. Is this right or indeed is this good? The overemphasis on hyper-masculinity has given rise to the rape and violence towards women and other men, as well as to spousal abuse and pornography. Men, today, who hold the traditional image may involve themselves in inconsequential roles with children and child rearing, with an overemphasis on sexual prowess. I believe that most men do not want the hyper-masculine role, and are not born that way.

There are a few areas in which the male-role strain is showing up. One is in the area of physical size. Men do not like to be short. With size comes the image of power, authority, and strength. Small men are unhappy. Culture devalues smallness. Clothes are made for the average or taller. Man has had to learn to cope with his own physical size and physical appearance. Today that picture is changing but this has caused a strain quite apart from the other stressors that men face in their life.

The second role strain is found in men's attitudes towards their families. Many men are becoming more immersed in their families and children, but this was not so years ago. In the 1980's, over 30 percent of men did household chores, a 10 percent increase since 1965. Even so, today's men are almost ridiculed, if not poked fun at, if they ever show that they like the family role, like to do household chores, play with children, or stay home and let the women take an outside job. The movie *"Mr. Mom"* is still a comedy, not a serious drama.

Another role strain is found in the attitudes that men hold towards education. Who helps with the child's school work or who goes to parent teacher meetings? Very few men show up at these meetings. Where are they? They're home working, repairing or watching television. They're not interested in assisting their children in education, even though they realize that education may be a form of self-enhancement for themselves and for their children. Today many more men are taking an active interest in their child's schooling beyond just checking on report cards and disciplining to have the homework done.

Men have difficulty in dealing with emotions. How many men talk about feelings, show tears or discuss emotions with their children, their spouse or other men? Happily, many more men today do attend marriage workshops, listen to radio programs about family issues, or attend workshops on self-development. Men are not men they believe, if they show a great interest in emotional aspects. Fortunately, this attitude is changing, but many men still do not discuss their feelings. Rather, they prefer to discuss politics, religion and sports. Men look at and admire cars, tractors, motorbikes and trucks. Feelings are so messy.

The final issue of role strain in men is the participation in fatherhood. Today there is an increasing social trend for fathering, that is, being a parent or a childcare worker, even a babysitter or a player with toddlers. This was very difficult to express years ago. Men's jobs did not give them time to be involved. There were no employer-sponsored leave programs for men to assist in the care of children. Men did not have the option to be more involved as fathers. Today, more men are wanting custody of their children. Men are slowly accepting a fathering role.

Today, the question is not "HAVE MEN CHANGED?" but, "HOW DO WE WANT MEN TO CHANGE?" Being a man, yet wanting to be able to express emotions and loving the beauty of colors is not being gay. How many children are being mercilessly teased as being gay when they do not do the boyish things? Many! I hear many women express fears, or at least concern over a man who likes to be with women in the kitchen, or who loves to pick out clothes and curtains or who talk about cooking and recipes. Many women express concern over a man who is gentle, sweet and emotional, or who dresses in beautiful pink and pastel colors. This is not what makes women, women; or what makes man, man. Man does not need to be woman, but he needs to be both mother and father. Man is born with a history of both mother and father. He is what he is, due to the influence of both mother and father. To be truly a man is to be both like mother and father. To be man is to be father and friend. To be man is to be compassion and integrity. To be man is to be strong and weak, emotional and controlled. To be man is to be leader and servant. To be man is to be provider and recipient. To be man is to be person, sexually different from woman, so that the two can be one. The issues are not resolved and we will need to look further to our changing image and role as to what it means to be both man and father. Habits change slowly. One listener wrote us the following letter:

> "...I am a working mother and I have a very demanding career. When I get home after work I find I am doing all the household chores without any help from my husband. I have tried discussing this with my husband and it doesn't seem to help as he still believes it is the wife's job to look after the children and do all the household chores. I find that I am building up a lot of resentment because of this and it also causes a lot of strife in our marriage..."

No, role-change in today's family is a slow, laborious process. Unless men can accept the new responsibilities, resentments will continue to build up, resulting in separation and possibly divorce. Resolving the role-conflicts is as important for the wife as the husband, let alone the children. Traditional roles and traditional families are slowly disappearing and new concepts evolving. The change to a new family-role system also forces change in other family relationships.

Mothers and Daughters

A young mother shared this concern about her relationship with her mother:

> "...I'm having a problem with my mother. We are first time parents with a 14 month old baby and...our baby is the centre of the problem...we decided to watch our son's intake of what kind of food you feed to a 9 month old baby, especially sugar and salt. My mother seems to think that giving a baby any quantity of sugar or salt in his diet will not hurt him...There seems to be a lot of tension with my folks on this issue. I've tried everything to alleviate the tension, but I'm also holding my ground. My mother is a very domineering person and she's not very open...There seems to be some sort of power struggle with my mother, she apparently doesn't like the idea of me having authority because I'm a mom now and my mother feels she doesn't have as much authority as she used to ...My relationship with my mother is diminishing considerably..."

How do you get along with your mother? You may be a whiz at your job, wise in dealing with your children and womanly with your husband, yet it may take only a mere five seconds in the presence of your mother to make you feel like a teenager again. Is there a tug-or-war with your mother? Does mother still boss you around? Do you clean the house furiously when she comes over? Do you get annoyed at her suggesting that you should wear this or that, lose weight, rest more, or not talk to the children that way?

Psychologists tell us that the mother-daughter bond is most lasting and profound. Many women, regardless of age, still cling emotionally to their mothers. At the same time mothers seem to never let go of their daughters. Most of us don't really like growing up, unless, of course, we're in our teenage years. Daughters hang on to the approval and protection of their mothers.

Recent research has indicated that daughters tend to have a more difficult time with the passage to independence and freedom than sons. Usually this is so because the mother-daughter relationship is much closer emotionally than the father-son relationship. Emancipation or independence is much more difficult to obtain. This psychological breaking free isn't always completed until the daughters are well into their 20's or 30's. Today's economic times makes it even more difficult to break free from the parents because we seem to be more dependent on parents for babysitting services, help around the house or lending money. Women are also staying single longer or raising children on their own. Mothers mean well and they want to help. You are their daughter, after all! Single mothers do lean on their parents to make a complex dual career role work for them.

Not long ago a daughter was considered "turned out" when she got married. Today there are fewer markers to tell you when you're an adult. Even the 16-18 year olds have similar independent behaviors as a 25 year old does today. Economically, we're not doing as well as our parents. We're leading less stable lives, so parents are often involved financially longer with their children and grandchildren. Parents and especially mothers are more involved in our lives than ever before.

It is important that we not give up relating to our parents. It is a significant aspect of our growth and development, as well as an attainment for freedom in our own lives. All of us can learn from our mothers. Dr. Benjamin Spock's book on *Baby and Child Care* sold more than 28 million copies. In an interview on April 8, 1985, Dr. Spock said "I really learned it all from mothers". The relationship may change over time and circumstances. Mothers, as well as daughters, have a responsibility to reframe their roles. If they don't, conflicts and crises will appear as sure as night follows day. Although there is a special bond between mothers and daughters, there are times when mother and her husband just want to hole up somewhere, eat, drink, make love and pretend they were born sterile and raise Dandie Dinmonts. A mother should love her daughter enough to accept her as she is. Daughters should love mother enough to accept her as she is. Relationships are always two-way streets.

Fathers and Sons

Bonds between mothers and daughters are different from those between fathers and sons. Same sex bonds are less complex then cross-sex bonds. Thus, there are greater differences in mother-son relationships, than mother-daughter relationships. Similar contrasts are found between father-daughter relationships and father-son bonds. For a woman a son offers the best chance to know the mysterious male existence. For a man, the same mystery holds true, a daughter helps him learn of the female existence. For the purposes of this chapter, however, we will restrict our discussion on the father-son relationship. Since Drs. Paterson, Blashko and I have 9 sons among us, our discussion may be somewhat more subjective.

Until recently, sons have been in a preferred position in the family. Young couples frequently wish that their first-born would be a son, especially if one asked the father. Sons were needed to continue the family genetic pool, carry the family name and take care of the parents in old age. Sons worked on the farm behind their dad, learning all they could. Fathers wanted to have sons to take fishing, play ball, roughhouse and run the family business. Very little has changed in this regard, although today the attitude to a daughter's ability to carry out these roles is accepted. It is increasingly apparent that modern fathers do not want to be peripheral figures in their child's life. They want to be integrally involved, especially husbands of working mothers. Fathers do spend less time with their children than mothers, but their influence is still felt indirectly. In fact, fathers' influence may have a greater impact because of the relative novelty and greater punitiveness of their paternal responses.

Each father is different and so are the children. Fathers can be as close to daughters as to sons. Nevertheless, fathers do reward feminine behaviors in girls, as a rule, and masculine behaviors in boys. Social learning theorists implicitly believe that fathers have a greater impact on sex-role development in boys than in girls. In fact, children (boys or girls) will imitate both of their parents, unless one parent is more nurturant or powerful. In this case, children will imitate preferentially. This has given rise to all kinds of worries of girls becoming too "masculine" and boys too "feminine".

Father-son relationship is a complex issue. Attachments and preferences change over time. Infants prefer mothers up to 2 years of age, and girls shift preference from one stage to the next. Research is clear on the fact that fathers do have greater interest in their sons and are more directly involved in the rearing of sons. Furthermore, several studies have shown that fathers have a great impact on their son's moral development, achievement and intellectual development, social competence and psychological adjustment. Anti-social, unempathic and hostile fathers risk the development of delinquency in sons. Fathers tend to facilitate intellectual development in sons more than daughters. In fact, both parents tend to emphasize achievement and competition in boys more than in girls. Fathers increase their time and companionship with sons when they imitate father and when they are high achievers. Underachieving boys have inadequate relationships with their father.

Paternal nurturance has been shown to be closely linked to social competence in sons. A strong attachment and love between father and son leads to a son's increased self-esteem, greater social adjustment, and happiness in later heterosexual relationships. Some writers go so far as to suggest that a disturbed father-son relationship is a precursor of homosexuality.

There are few verified facts in the father-son literature. Two things do seem to stand out as significant. First, a happy marital relationship by and large leads to happy, well-adjusted children. Secondly, a parent's impact on the child must be taken from a child's point of view. The significant factor is clearly the importance of the parent in the child's life. This importance, or salience has greater impact overall, than the particular techniques one uses in raising children. Many fathers are not "masculine". Similarly, many fathers do not wish their daughters to be "feminine". We need, instead, to take account of the parent's goals and values. Today's blurring of sex-roles has made the situation more complex than ever before. Our view is that kids value both parents and learn from each of them. When circumstances separate parents, both mom and dad can fulfil the parenting role. The institution of marriage was intended not just for procreation but for shared responsibilities. Single parents can raise children quite adequately, if they find the inner strength to cope with the stresses of single life.

If there is one major difference in father-son to mother-daughter relationship, it is in the emotional bonding styles. Fathers and sons seem connected more so on an analytic and cognitive plane, mothers and daughters on an emotional-nurturant plane. Sons are encouraged by dads to use logic and reasoning, to pursue intellectual routes, to use mind over emotion. Father-son love is very strong, but it is linked by a cognitive style, lending to the son's earlier emancipation and independence, to think for himself. Fathers find it easier to "let go" of their children. This doesn't mean that fathers are not nurturant and the mothers not interested in abstract, intellectual pursuits. Indeed, today's mothers, especially middle-class mothers, actively encourage all children, regardless of sex, to pursue academic careers. The child with a non-nurturant father may be better off if the father is not available. There is consistent evidence that father-absent children often are better adjusted than children with passive and ineffectual fathers. Conversely, maternal overprotection and over-dependency are frequently found when father is absent. Father has a role to play. Research shows that children do not form as intense a parent-child relationship when both parents are present. Father's role seems to produce greater independence and aggression. When father is gone the mother needs or actively seeks a close-binding relationship. This intensity can create later emancipation difficulties. Fathers love their children, as do mothers, but father-son relationship appears to be more critical than mother-son relationships when the father is present. This is an important conclusion because it reinforces father's role in the son's growth and development. Sons do need fathers, as husbands need wives, or wives need husbands. In all family relationships, the effects are reciprocal. A significant effort should be made in community mental health programs to support fathers in being effective parents. A vast number of children do not have consistent and meaningful contact with their fathers. This is a serious situation and must be remedied if the children, whether sons or daughters, are to take advantage of their developmental opportunities.

▌ Partnership in Marriage

The original ideas for this concept came from a paper written by Gary Emery, Director of the Center for Cognitive Therapy in Los Angeles. His ideas about dependence and independence of partners in a marriage were fascinating, but I have been unable to find his paper to give him credit. Nor am I aware now which are his ideas and which examples are taken from my own experience. In order to give credit where it is due, it is my belief that the original ideas for this topic were discovered at a Canadian Guidance and Counselling Association conference in Quebec City, in May, 1985.

The theme of this section has to do with a relationship where one partner is independent, the other is not. It is probably not a radical idea. Some people like to be looked after. Many times in developing parenting skills, we find parents who have real difficulty helping their children to assert independence and become decision-makers. The result of this type of upbringing is that the adult now has a very low self-esteem. A child who has not learned to be a decision-maker grows up looking for a mentor, who will make decisions for him or her. New problem solving strategies are never developed without assistance.

On the other hand, there are many people who like to be rescuers. One might even categorize all professionals in the helping professions as having some of these characteristics. Surely it is good in any family for one person to be excellent in a crisis. Other family members will automatically look to this individual for help and assistance. In some family situations this can be the negative situation if one family member is always giving rather than receiving support. That person may have problems if he or she cannot consistently fill the role.

A major problem can develop when a "take charge" or independent person marries someone who needs constant support. At first glance this would seem to be a union "made in heaven". However, there are trouble spots. Where you have the scenario of Jack as the helper and Jill as the helpless, the union may be in serious trouble. May I hasten to say that it could just as easily be the other way around with Jill as the independent rescuer and Jack as the helpless partner.

Let's start, though, with our original example and say that Jack needs to help in order to bolster his ego, so he takes over most of the decision-making in the relationship. This works fine for awhile, until he beings to resent Jill's helplessness. For example, she doesn't write cheques, make major purchases, etc. On the other hand Jill needs support, so perhaps she makes him feel constantly guilty for not helping enough. The logical conclusion to this scenario is that Jack could begin to resent Jill more and more and actually he does less, changing from a helper to a critic and finally a persecutor. It is not out of the question to see this kind of a relationship resulting in some form of family violence. It could be a dangerous combination.

The point of this example is that "clinging vine" relationships don't work very well. In a permanent relationship or a marriage where one partner is very dependent, the relationship is heading for a breakup or the divorce courts. Why can we not have two independent people in a relationship, two partners, each with his or her own life space? We then have cooperation and the constant daily bringing of new ideas and meaning into the marriage?

There is hope for "Jack and Jill". Through marriage counseling or some kind of professional assistance, perhaps Jack can be helped to stop blaming, maybe he can be taught to realize that his behavior was what made Jill so dependent in the first place. Jill, on the other hand, must learn that while she is not responsible for the way her personality has developed she can do things to learn to count on herself, to accomplish. It is not necessary to blame Jack for not being of more assistance.

There are ways of spotting and solving problems in a dependent relationship. Some suggestions are as follows:

1. **Recognize and admit the problem**

2. **Handle and work through negative feelings** you have both towards yourself and towards your partner.

3. **Make use of your own resources** to change both your own thinking and your own behavior. Strike out in a new direction, hopefully your partner will do the same.

A marriage is a 50 - 50 relationship. Each partner has feelings of independence and dependence. It is in the blending of these needs that the problem is solved. Independence is not a license for personal freedom in a marriage. Dependency is not an invitation for exploitation and abuse. Each partner in a marriage has opportunities for manipulation. It is when the manipulation is consistent and denigrating that the marriage eventually falls apart.

Independence and dependence are important factors, but there are other traits that can help or hinder a marriage as well. Some of these have been discussed in other chapters. We now turn to a discussion of marriage, affairs and divorce.

Extramarital Affairs

Extramarital affairs do occur and in most but not all circumstances cause eventual marriage breakup and divorce. For a variety of reasons, extramarital affairs to not enhance a marriage as some therapists claim and if found out, destroy a family, with the resulting conflict, negative feelings, distrust, anger and feeling of loss and neglect.

Extramarital affairs usually imply sex outside the marriage, a practice condoned or even agreed upon by a few, but not sanctioned. Religious people will not condone it because this is simply adultery. People with high moral standards will not condone it because it is unfaithfulness. Others do not condone it for psychological reasons because their temperament and character will not be able to accept or allow extramarital affairs. It produces guilt. One's background and upbringing may also not sanction extramarital affairs because of past family and social conditioning that has preached against it.

Extramarital affairs can be just as destructive without having sex with someone other than your spouse. An affair can be platonic, based

on needs or interests, career or work, that brings you in close and frequent encounter with members of the opposite sex. Time spent together seems downright pleasant and fun - a dimension not experienced with the spouse. Although you love your spouse, you enjoy this other person without necessarily having sex with that individual.

Not too many spouses are open-minded, trusting and self-confident enough to think that their spouse should do this kind of thing. Not too many spouses feel comfortable with the idea that their spouse interacts, even without sex. Why is it that extramarital affairs, with or without sex, simply cannot be accepted? The reasons reside inside the person and in the situation. Extramarital relationships, even without sex, mean that the spouse must have the ability to accept that their most intimate friend, their spouse, must be shared. The spouse must also feel that his/her own personality, life and behavior are not sufficient to satisfy that spouse. The spouse must feel that their marriage must be shared on one or several grounds with a person who becomes a potential rival. Not too many individuals can accept the fact that her spouse must look elsewhere to find greater fulfilment and happiness. Even those who think logically and rationally, who would realize that one person may not be able to satisfy all of one person's needs and desires, still find it hard to live with a person for a long period of time without conflict when extramarital relationships are there. A marriage, even a happy one, is at times conflictive, with partners left with unfulfilled needs. Yet our nature is to believe in marriage as the fulfilment of oneself and life. When anything we do suggests otherwise, the spouse and the marriage need reworking and change. It seems to me, however, that occasional visits and chats, games and sports or career meetings do *not* detract from a marriage or disrupt it. It is only when the extramarital-non-sex related activities are frequent and take time away from a spouse, family or children that they will destroy the marriage.

A spouse, each spouse should develop other interests and activities. When these activities involve the opposite sex, however, and occur too often, then the relationship between spouses speaks of unfulfilled needs and leads frequently to resentment, doubt, fear and uncoupling. Uncoupling is gradual. Uncoupling refers to the fact that something is separating the intimacy and bonding between a husband and wife. When marriage partners begin to uncouple they will find themselves having more conflict and more arguments. Spouses with temperaments of low self-esteem, jealousy, possessiveness, insecurity, lack of personal resources will react very strongly to a spouse spending an inordinate amount of time with a member of the opposite sex.

Extramarital sex, when infrequent and *not* found out, will not destroy a marriage, unless guilt causes one to confess. Sex outside marriage, whether it is for curiosity, an antidote for boredom, a desire for variety, or a belief that it causes personal growth, usually widens the gap of personal intimacy between marriage partners. As one begins to uncouple, the conflict increases slowly but surely. Even though the spouse is a great provider and a wonderful father, is kind and hardworking, when extramarital sexual relationships are found out, they will lead to conflict, psychological distress and possibly divorce.

A leading American psychotherapist, Dr. Arnold Lazarus, says that having affairs is not proof that something is lacking in a marriage. I disagree! Having an affair is proof that your self-control is not adequate. Having an affair is proof that you do not believe in faithfulness. Having an affair is proof that you are willing to risk your marriage. Having an affair is proof that your spouse does not meet every need. Having an affair is proof that no one can meet every need but that doesn't turn us into entrepreneurs or nymphomaniacs. Having an affair is proof that moral integrity can be sacrificed, even if discreetly, because you know what you did.

I don't think it helps to rationalize away extramarital affairs. If religious convictions don't stop you, you have to consider the bond, the unity that marriage represents. Just because couples don't work at their marriage sufficiently to make it entirely possible to be faithful, doesn't make outside sex right. Psychologically it destroys the feelings towards the other spouse and slowly erodes the intimacy, friendship and union that marriage represents. Whenever an opposite sex relationship occurs with some regularity and frequency, intimacy is damaged. Extramarital affairs are a risk and a danger to a good marriage.

Jealousy in Touch

The human touch, the hand, as it reaches out and touches is the most important and significant aspect of human relationship. In some cultures there is training of children and adults to touch, to shake hands, to hug or kiss. This is normal and expected in most cultures. However, it has been found that in North America there is less touch than in other cultures such as in the Mediterranean, French or Puerto Rican cultures. Touching is intricate and complex. Touching can have several meanings and can be done in many different ways. There is the touch of parents as they cradle a child. There is the professional touch of counselors and doctors as well as barbers and hair stylists: there is the social polite touch of greeting or separating showing appreciation and reflecting cordiality without intimacy; there is the friendship and warmth touch of family and friends or close workmates which shows warmth and affection; and then there is the love and intimacy touch of close family and friends showing deeper affection and caring. Finally, there is the sexual arousal touch which is erotic and physically stimulating. Touching always means something. We need to be aware what the touch means. The key to knowing what a touch is, is not just in the mind of the person being touched, but in the mind of the person doing the touching. What is your motive when you grasp

someone, hug or stroke someone? Remember the power of the touch. It can create relationship, bonding and heal friendships. Touch can create anger and jealousy by a spouse or a close friend and can signify acceptance as well as forgiveness. The key in the touch is in how you touch and where you touch. Often, the interpretation of the touch is in the place of the touching, in the quality of the touch and whether it is reciprocal. For example, in most cultures it is quite acceptable to have people touch on the arm, hand or shoulder. It is more intimate to touch by placing one's arm around the other person or to kiss on the cheek or the lips. Then, there are the erotic zones such as the neck, legs, lips, knees, breasts in which the touch represents a physical intimacy, or a desire for physical closeness. It is important, therefore, to know how and where to touch because often your message and intention can be misinterpreted and your spouse, seeing the touch, can be quite jealous.

Men and women respond differently to touch. To a woman a doctor's touch is reassuring and the reaction is very positive. Research shows that lowered blood pressure and anxiety result when doctors touch women but for men this is not so. Apparently, men touched by doctors feel more anxiety and withdrawal. Women may have been touched more than men as children and this may very well account for the differences. Women also tolerate closer personal space than men and therefore desire or enjoy touching more. Women greet each other more physically than men. For men, being touched or watching their friend, spouse being touched causes them to feel awkward, uncomfortable or ill at ease. Of course, your personality has something to do with your comfortableness in touching. The more authoritarian and rigid you are, the less likely you are to feel good about touches or seeing others, especially your spouse, being touched. Research shows that frequent touchers are less afraid or suspicious and less likely to be jealous or suspicious of your intentions. Frequent touchers seem to have less anxiety and tension in their everyday lives and are more satisfied with their bodies and physical appearance. For some people, words and feelings are enough to show intimacy. For others, touch and physical closeness is needed to express love and intimacy.

Society differs in response to touch and opinions whether it is helpful or not. For example, people who are perceived as being of higher rank or status do more of the touching, indicating power. People of higher rank do not like to be touched by lower ranked people. Higher status people use touch as a status dominance. Most people see the touch as not the thing to do, especially if it involves touching higher status people such as your boss, a teacher, therapist, or any other superior.

Touching someone is increasing today. A world without touch would be cold and rational, distant and mechanical and mostly verbal. We need touch for survival. Healthy infants deprived of touching for long periods of time become emotionally upset, depressed, withdrawn and unstable. Touching someone in a appropriate way, knowing the person you touch, can be a very meaningful experience and can lead to greater friendship and intimacy. Just be careful about where one touches, who one touches and when one touches. Be careful about how long and how often one touches. Spouses and lovers may see the touch and wonder what it means. It can lead to problems of suspiciousness as well as jealousy.

You may recall in your own past experiences how jealous you became when you saw someone touch you spouse or lover. What was the feeling inside you? It's important that you talk about these feelings to your spouse. It is important to let them know what kind of sensitivity you have to this act. For most of us, we tend not to think about it unless we become jealous of the way someone else is touching our spouse. It is important that you watch reactions. I find myself watching my very dear close friends touch others so as to read their intent. When people I love or my spouse touches someone I pay attention to who it is they touch, where the touch was, how long it was, what the reaction was during the touch and whether eye or body contact was made. If I see this touching more than an expression of social greeting, more than just friendship, I could get upset. Even if my wife disagreed with me on what her touching meant, I would argue that it isn't in her intent, but in the other person's perception of that touch. If touch is seen as intimacy and arousal then you become responsible for the other person's reaction. Therefore, try to discuss this with your wife or friends so as to prevent problems. Try to control and understand the nature and value of the touch as it affects others. Children use touch and like to be touched. With children, don't hesitate to hug them or hold them often. Friendships can be deepened through touch but be careful that your friends enjoy and appreciate your touch. If they don't, simply refrain from touch and use verbal means to express your caring. Try not to touch your superiors because this is often misinterpreted and can lead to difficulties. It is important that one be touched after a failure experience. Winners seem to get touched more than losers. Touching after failure is an affirmation that you still care.

Divorce and Beyond

Widowed, separated and divorced adults have many adjustments to make. Their life as they once knew it is changed. For the widowed, it may be a sudden change, whereas for the separated and divorced it is a slower period of transition. New responsibilities appear with the children, family income, work, meals and housekeeping duties. Probably the biggest change of all is accepting the fact that the old goals which were well laid out at one time now are dramatically altered. The hopes and dreams of a once good relationship have disappeared. Past experiences often bring back both positive and painful memories. The future may look bleak and barren, especially at first. Life without a partner to share and comfort, to console and discuss is lost, at least temporarily. Life from the separation onward must be planned anew. Often panic and anxiety set in with depression being the most common result.

Normal joys and experiences once fully expected and counted on, no longer are there. This may include a sex life, the usual pleasures of each other's company, the laughter, the humor once shared, the tiny secrets once discussed. What was once a happy life with the normal pleasures taken for granted and enjoyed together, no longer is there. Life becomes a constant search for partnership and happiness and for a return to those things you once enjoyed.

After divorce comes a search for a new life and new responsibilities. The relationships are changed within the extended and immediate family. There are small changes to be expected such as whether

one should send birth-
day cards to uncles and
aunts, or to his or her
brothers and sisters, or
to the parents-in-law
with whom you were
once intimate. There
are changes with re-
spect to attendance at
weddings,   anniver-
saries or graduations.
There arc changes with
respect to going shop-
ping or going to eat at
the old places, fearing
to meet the old friends
with whom you once
spent time. There are
changes with respect to
how you relate to the
children and how the
children relate to you.
There are changes with
respect to accepting the comments of people you both knew who still
want to be friends. Since the relationship is changed, those friends no
longer may be available. The changes are not just your doing. They are
brought about by others you once rubbed shoulders with, or cared about.

After divorce, a partner may seek new relationships, a new partner
and possibly remarriage. When children are involved, this new change
in relationship brings with it other problems as well. There are questions with respect to whether the children will accept the new spouse, or
whether that new spouse will accept the children. There are changes
with respect to how the new spouse will accept any communication and
relationship with the former spouse. When conflicts have been intense
and bitter, entering into a second marriage can bring very special problems. The new partner cannot really stay clear of this conflict and is
often caught helpless in the middle. Disputes affect everyone, often
widening to the larger extended family. Relationship with the new partner often starts well, then ends with disputes so that the new partner
may at first begin to withdraw from this new second marriage. As a
result, remarriages are often on shaky ground. Research does show that
upon first divorce other relationships tend to fall apart more easily, pri-

"The Blended Family"

marily as a result of trying to cope with all the changes that occur in a divorce situation. There are other issues one could cite such as problems with stepchildren and stepparents, legal custody problems, economic and job problems and lowering of the standard of living. These stressors change a person. The unravelling of these complex situations takes more than effort and will. Ultimately, it takes a change of personality and a change of mind, a change in the inner core of being - a conversion experience if you will. Sometimes careful management of the situation can bring happiness to a second marriage, but not without a strong commitment to that person and a willingness to communicate, to give and take. Personal goals may need to be sacrificed for the good of the new relationship or for the children. There must be a willingness to forgive each other and forget the past and establish new goals. There must be a resolution of the hurt and guilt within, a willingness to accept the past pain and provide for a setting that brings about new memories and a new attitude to marriage.

Research has shown that boys are more affected by their parents' divorce than girls, especially if contact with fathers is limited. Boys in divorced families appear to be more exposed to conflict than girls and react more strongly to the diminished contact with the father than girls. Boys also desire more contacts. Researchers have noted the frustration that mothers have had with their sons because they reminded them of their ex-husbands, at whom they were angry. This implies a double rejection for some of the boys. A striking finding in some recent research was that children living in the custody of the same-sex parent were better adjusted than children living with the opposite-sex parent. Father-custody boys and mother-custody girls showed significantly more social competence, maturity, cooperativeness and self-esteem. Mother-custody is not always the best and may in some instances create a negative outcome. Traditional mother-custody arrangements, in which children visit their fathers every other weekend or four days a month, has been found to create intense dissatisfaction among children, accompanied in many instances by profound feelings of deprivation and in some instances, reactive depression. Research does suggest that joint custody in which a child spends at least 35% of the time with one parent, and the remaining time with the other parent, often leads to more satisfied children and adults.

In today's society, one is desperately trying to normalize divorce because it is so common. Divorce is always a transition to another type of family unit. There is a lack of clear roles for divorcees which often makes them unsure of what to do and how to react. Divorced people are very vulnerable. The changes are many. Professional assistance should be sought to assist and support.

It Hurts To Love . . .

At the time of this writing, it has been three weeks since my dear wife and my children's mother passed away from cancer of the colon and liver. She had been ill for a very short time. The cancer was not discovered until May 5, 1987 and she passed away on October 7, 1987. She underwent a lot of pain and suffering but fortunately the the doctors were able to control most of her pain and she died quietly and peacefully on Wednesday, October 7, 1987 at 7:00 p.m. Myrna loved life and living, she loved people and parties and she loved me and her three children. I feel saddened and depressed in the loss of this dear friend and wife because I know how much she would have loved to live and be with us and because I also miss her a lot. Without a doubt this is the most difficult experience of pain that I've had to live through. It will take time to finally heal. Marriage is a unity, a union of two people one being in "the other", one becoming the other. When that union is broken, the heart is ripped inside and the pain is real. There is actual physical pain and suffering.

There is a cost to us in really loving someone, just as there is a cost to *not* loving. Without love we walk alone, our world is made up of grey and gloom, of rain and cold, no one to give us warmth, share our feelings, help bear our burdens. Not to love bears a heavy cost to us. On the other hand, to really love someone and to lose the one we love also has its costs. Whether we lose that person through death or divorce or through conflicts and disagreements or by separation of distance, the pain is there and it is a heavy burden to bear.

I will never regret the love that I had for my dear wife Myrna, even though the cost of losing someone you love is very high, the pain very deep and the memories for now painful. People we love, though, deserve to be remembered. The pain and sorrow that memory brings is worth the price of loving. Love is everlasting and even though we may hurt the rest of our lives I would not trade it for never having loved someone so much at all!

We love because we have learned to love ourselves. Love of self shows us the worth of others. Scripture tells us that we "love our neighbor as ourselves". If we do not love ourselves, we cannot love others. Any measure of self-hatred, self-disrespect leads us to love others less and lessens or limits the bonds of love, the support, the encouragement. It limits the joys of living. Love of self also gives us the strength to carry on in the face of adversity because we that remain have a responsibility to ourselves and to others.

The sorrow and anguish we feel in having lost a loved one is deepened not only by the extent we have loved, but also by the giving in to feelings of self-pity. My pain was the strongest when I thought certain kinds of thoughts: "I miss her, I'm lonely, I need her company, I'm all alone now, no one to help me as she did, I can't enjoy others because she's not with me, I wish we could love each other again, I'm left all alone". Myrna's dad once remarked, "We'll never be able to show her our love again". Are these thoughts familiar to you? I think so. From time to time they return, often and unexpectedly, and we break down and have a good cry! When I feel the worst, when I hurt the most, it is because I feel so sorry for myself, for my boys, or for our families who loved her so much. Myrna knew and understood what this pain would bring for us once she was gone. She said to me that she felt badly in leaving us because she knew we would hurt and she wouldn't be able to help. But she's gone to another place with new memories and a new existence and in my mind we can connect with her at least in that hope that our faith gives us. Our faith, therefore, is a strong sense of comfort and security and lessens the self-pity even though our sorrow is very great. That even now and I'm sure for time to come when I'm all alone in the house I do miss her deeply and then I feel sorry for myself. That emotion breaks down any sense of rationality that I may have.

When someone you love dies so does a part of you. That part can never be replaced and so the grieving in various degrees and stages carries on after the death. What also dies are the goals and plans you have made with that person, the future goals that would have been. This is the second hardest aspect to accept for me. Our boys are still at home. We were in midstream of our life planning a lot of events together for the future. Myrna wanted to see her boys married and love those grandchildren. She wanted to plan a big Fiftieth Golden Wedding Anniversary for her mom and dad next summer. We were going to relax more, get the mortgage paid, travel and plan early retirement with lots of fun things to do together. Now these plans with her cannot be realized and in that there is a great sadness. Everything is changed. Nothing is the same as it once was. Change, any change, is hard to cope with, but this is a major change. Unless those plans can be altered the cost will be very high. Unless you can eventually work out a future that you would still enjoy in some measure, the cost of grieving can weigh you down for the rest of your earthly life. I talked about the future with Myrna. She gave me guidance and suggestions. She, in essence, already knew what my future, my plans would look like and this gave me comfort. Those plans may change somewhat, but when they can be made in this way, the road to recovery will be easier with less pain and sorrow ahead.

Losing someone you love brings many other feelings such as anger, denial, depression, anxiety, frustration, and pity. This is the high cost of loving! Myrna said to her parents and me in the hospital "It wouldn't hurt so much if I didn't love you so much". But think of a world without love. Without love there would be no happiness ever and no real joy to living. Without love there would be no support for each other. Without love there would be conflict and hatred and destruction of self and other. Without love there would be no joy in seeing beauty or colors and sunsets. Without love there would be no love for self or for children. Without love there would be no positive purpose in living or working. Without love there would be total destruction of society in the long run and in the end we would all self-destruct or destroy each other.

Because we love, we become people with a purpose in living. Love is eternal because it never forgets. Through love we maintain a meaning for future. Through love we gain power to overcome every trial. Love is stronger than any enemy that will oppose it. Love is what gives us hope. Love's opposite is not hatred but apathy. Apathy is to give up. It does not face reality or make choices. Apathy cannot and does not love because it kills the spirit - it kills life and liveliness and in the end it promotes the opposite of "LIVE", which spelled backwards is "EVIL". The opposite of love destroys the essential attributes of life itself.

There may be a number of people we know that have chosen not to love, who have in the end destroyed themselves if not literally than certainly in their own spirit of liveliness and living. In doing so, they have deeply hurt others who have loved and they've become unable to control their own lives. What do we do, those who experience or have felt the pain of separation through death? We must continue to love and in doing so we will receive love. Christ said, "I am come that they might have life and that they might have it more abundantly".

Have you noticed that it is the people who loved and have experienced the pain of loss through death that are able to understand and help others who are bereaved? They can be more effective than any professional because they, more than anyone else, through their love of son, daughter or spouse or any other loved one, understand the spirit of life. They know what it is by having experienced its loss. Their love to others restores vitality to their life - the vitality that brings back the essential attributes of living. They are, by helping others through their pain and suffering, more capable of perceiving and feeling life again and the numbness of their own pain goes away. There will be a time in our life when God will call each one of us home. In having loved and in being loved we can give back life and its abundance to ourselves and others. In doing that we may bring back its vitality to our own life which at present may be dreary and depressed. Those who have died, also loved us and others. Their love for us should not die with them but should be given over to those of us who remain. This makes love eternal. This is not an easy task but with the support of a family and a community of people who love each other, we can get back what we feel we have lost and so deeply mourn.

The Bond of Love

There isn't a relationship or marriage that can last a lifetime unless love is there. What is this thing called love? Love is a key ingredient of bonding between individuals. It is not there in real or full measure at the beginning of a relationship. The first growth of love may begin with a conscious choice of seeking out a specific person, or it may be fortuitous, that is, it just happened. If it was fortuitous, there is usually an emotional link, a feeling, call it romance, liking, an arousal, passion and infatuation. The love in a relationship goes beyond friendship. It requires at least three major things:

1. Emotional bonding and intimacy

This part of love involves close sharing and an emotional link between the partners that does not involve just sexual attracting. Bonding and intimacy occur when partners empathize and anticipate each others moods and emotion. They do things together. They enjoy each other's company.

2. High emotional drive

Love does involve a motivation towards each other physically. Although it is possible to have love without sex, it is more difficult and it is rare.

3. High cognitive involvement

There has to be a decision to love and a commitment to maintain it. Couples who truly love each other reach each other through the mind and not just through physical attractiveness or emotional bonding. Couples can agree to disagree, can deal with ideas and content and talk about things in a casual and intensive way.

These three aspects of love go beyond friendship. The sharing is close and the ties that bind go beyond the activities of living together.

Even though they may be physically attracted to each other and sexually involved, this will not in itself be true love. There has to be a decision to love and a commitment to maintain it.

People in a love relationship are not just friends or even best friends - they are a bonded, sharing, intimate unit attracted to each other and committed to love each other faithfully. If there is too much "emotion" in a marriage, it likely won't last because sex does not hold a relationship. If there is too much "mind" the marriage would stagnate and the couple would tend to ignore each other. If there is no "arousal", the partners tend to look elsewhere. If there is all "romance" and no "bind" then the thrills end after a few years.

Love needs constant nurturing. Whether you believe me or not, it takes effort. I know other experts disagree. I've been married almost twenty-five years, others much longer, who would agree with me. I believe in one marriage for life. That kind of marriage takes great effort. However, I also know that some circumstances such as alcoholism, drugs, death and loss experiences, homosexuality, illnesses, physical and sexual abuse, mental disorders and certain career patterns where one partner is never home create difficulties. If these were the only reasons for relationship breakups, our statistics for divorce would be significantly lower than they are today.

A lot of little things tend to pile up over time and if not dealt with cause uncoupling. This uncoupling distances the marriage partners mentally, emotionally, and sexually. The motivation to love and the commitment begins to fade. Partners slowly do things to uncouple and then wonder why.

Love will bond your relationship. It is the glue that makes marriages last a lifetime. With love comes shared values, a willingness to change, a willingness to tolerate flaws and a match in values. These are the most important factors in holding a marriage together. How interesting your partner is, how much education, what they have or how much money they make, or what kind of inlaws they have, or even whether one can listen attentively to each other are found to be less important factors in bonding a marriage. Love is emotion, motivation and cognition. Each component is needed. Each takes work. When one partner wanes, love lessens and the danger of a breakup is there.

Therefore, it is important that the triangle of love be matched to some degree. Where one partner begins to look for sex and the other for mind then the triangle will not match as closely, the bonding will not be as intimate and the commitment will not be as strong. People need similar emphases, similar interests and values in their marriage. Researchers show that opposites do not necessarily attract. There must be a movement toward developing similarity and congruence. In addition, I think that a marriage needs some degree of involvement of partners in activities that both can enjoy. It is true that one person can't be everything to that individual, but there must be a significant amount of involvement of the couple on activities. It is important that couples work on matching emotion, mind and arousal as often as they can. Work on the ability to make love in a variety of ways; work on physical attractiveness and develop a high degree of empathy. And then, blend and compromise on attitudes and values so that there is a bonding at the cognitive level as well.

In the end, love means to trust even in the face of doubts; to give of oneself, of things, to encourage and not discourage. Love is to free the other person and not to hold or bind for a personal or selfish gain. Love is to discipline oneself and others. Love is virtue. That is, to live by spiritual and universal principles of goodness and peace. And finally, love is to sacrifice. Ultimate love is to give one's life for another. That is the highest and truest form of love. Love in a relationship is the key to making it work. There can be no other ingredient that can create the bonding and intimacy that makes a union last. This kind of love is not easily found. It needs to be developed and nurtured. Most of us think that this kind of love just happens. We wait for something and it never comes. Search in your own mind for those aspects of love that need developing. Continue to strive for these things in your relationship so as to bond you for an intimate lasting union.

CHAPTER 5

Human Sexuality

HUMAN SEXUALITY

Normal Sex

This section is about the male and female sex organs and how these organs work. I utilize the medical names for the sex organs. I also use other "well known" words for describing the sex organs. I am writing this section for those individuals who are normal and want to improve their sex life.

This section is not about morals or ethics. It is not about who can have sex with whom, when a person should have sex, how old a person ought to be to have sex, whether sex is used for enjoyment or simply to produce children, or whether sex should be between married partners only. This section is to assist you in knowing about the sex organs, how these sex organs can be used to give you the most pleasure, plus ideas about emotions and relationships in the sex act.

In the first part of this section, I talk about "how to get the most out of sex". Although we have liberalized attitudes towards sexual behavior, I find that few people know enough about the anatomy and physiology of good sex.

This section is about normal individuals who would like to learn more about sexual pleasure.

It is important to have some knowledge about the anatomy of the sexual organs. Please note the diagrams of the anatomy of the male and female sex organs. Try and remember the names of the different parts of the sex organs because I use these terms to describe the role of these sexual organs to the sexual act.

Anatomy of the Male

The external male organs include the penis, scrotum, testes, epi-

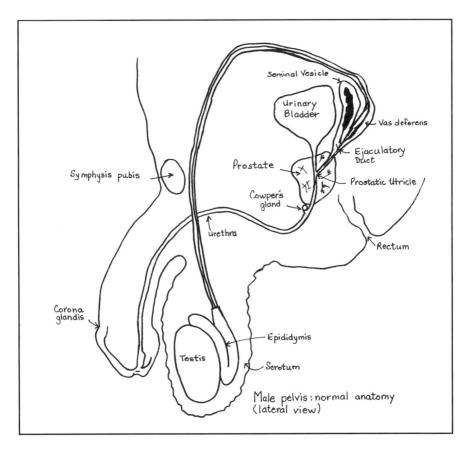

Male pelvis: normal anatomy
(lateral view)

didymus and parts of the vas deferens. The internal parts of the human sex organs are the vas deferens, seminal vesicles, ejaculatory ducts, and prostrate gland.

It seems that all men in all societies are preoccupied with the size of their penis. It has been shown by medical and scientific studies that good sex is not related to the size of the penis. Good sex is a result of two people knowing how to use their sex organs properly.

The erect penis measures 14 to 18 centimeters in length. When the male is stimulated physically or psychologically, the blood vessels in the penis increase in size and the penis becomes erect. The parsympathetic nervous system is responsible for producing the erection. The sympathetic nervous system is involved in the orgasm (ejaculation; "making a person come"). When the prostrate contracts, the man "comes" (ejaculates). Urethral contractions propel the ejaculate ("come") through the penis. Each time a man ejaculates, he produces

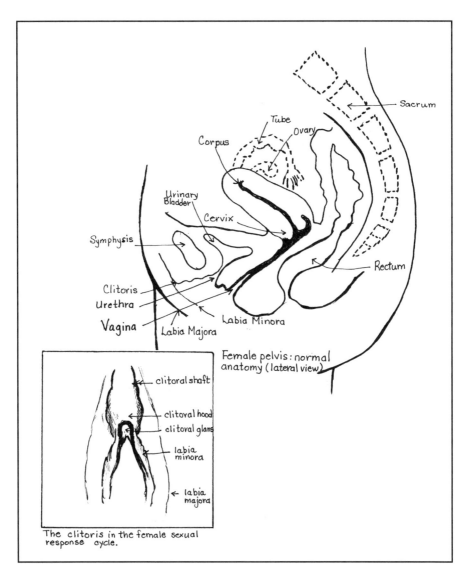

Female pelvis: normal anatomy (lateral view)

The clitoris in the female sexual response cycle.

one teaspoonful (2.5 ml) of fluid which contains 120 million sperm cells.

Anatomy of the Female

Please look at the diagram carefully and remember the medical names for the different parts of the female sex organ. I would like you to learn about these parts because I discuss how these parts work.

The external genitalia of the normal female is also called the vulva. The vulva consists of the major and minor lips, clitoris, glans, vestibule of the vagina and vaginal orifice.

The internal systems consists of ovaries, fallopian tubes, uterus, and vagina.

The vagina is usually in a collapsed state. When the penis enters the vagina, the vagina gets longer and wider. The clitoris is the main female sexual organ that gives the pleasurable feelings. Orgasm occurs when the clitoris is properly and adequately stimulated.

When women masturbate (play with themselves) they prefer to rub the shaft of the clitoris. Women find the glans of the clitoris too sensitive. The glans of the clitoris becomes painful.

During the sex act, the penis does not touch the clitoris directly. During the sex act, and especially when the woman is on top of the man, the clitoris is rubbed by the man's pubis. The "woman on top" position is one of the best positions for the woman to reach orgasm.

Let me state it again, the most important sex organ in the woman is the clitoris. When the clitoris is properly stimulated, the woman may reach orgasm. It does not matter how the clitoris is rubbed. It may be stimulated during the sex act; the woman may stimulate it by herself; the woman could stimulate her clitoris during the sex act. Orgasm in the woman is not produced by a large penis, "fast sex", "hard sex", etc. Orgasm occurs only if the clitoris is properly stimulated.

The Male Sex Response

In this section, I describe what happens to the man when he is sexually aroused and experiences an orgasm.

It is generally believed that there are four phases of the male sex response: excitement, plateau, orgasm, and resolution.

Phase 1 - Excitement (several minutes to hours)

The male can develop a sense of excitement and erection when he is physically stimulated (stroking or kissing). The man could also be excited by thinking about a woman, fantasizing, looking at pictures, watching a video or by being close to a woman. Erection occurs within ten to thirty seconds. The erection may "go down" very quickly if something distracts the man such as a loud noise. The scrotum and testes tighten and lift. Sometimes the nipples become "hard".

Phase 2 - Plateau (30 secs. to 3 mins.)

The male may then develop a sexual flush. This means that there is a reddening of the skin, almost like a rash, that starts on the stomach and spreads up to the chest, face, and neck. The glans, penile shaft and testes increase in size. Muscles of the face, stomach and chest tighten. Heart rate increases up to 175 beats per minute. Blood pressure and breathing rate increases.

Phase 3 - Orgasm (15 secs.)

During ejaculation, there are 3 to 4 contractions every one second of the vas, seminal vesicle, prostate and urethra. Then, some minor contractions of these organs occur at irregular intervals. The muscles then relax. The heart rate may go up to 175 beats per minute, blood pressure increases greatly, rate of breathing goes up to 40 per minute. The young person can give a spurt of "come" up to 18 inches. This spurt decreases with age until there is only seepage at age 70.

Phase 4 - Resolution (10 to 15 mins. but could last up to 1 day if there was no orgasm)

The flush goes away. Perspiration may occur over the body including the soles of the feet and palms of hands. The penis gets back to normal size after 5 to 30 minutes. The testes descend 5 to 10 minutes after orgasm. The male often has a sense of well-being at this time. Further sex is not usually possible during this period.

The Female Sex Response

Phase 1: Excitement

The female can become excited by physical stimulation or psychological stimulation as I described for the man. At this point, fluid forms in the vagina which will lubricate the vagina. The nipples become erect, the clitoris becomes hard, and the minor lips become thicker and bright pink in color. The vagina becomes lubricated and bigger.

Phase 2: Plateau (30 secs. to 3 mins.)

The woman develops a sexual flush which looks like a mild red rash starting on the abdomen and going to the chest, neck and face. The nipples remain erect and the breasts enlarge. The shaft of the clitoris withdraws deep into the prepuce. The clitoris moves a lot under the prepuce during the thrusting actions by the man. This occurs because the penis produces traction on the minor lips and the prepuce. The major lips, in the woman who has not had a child, almost disappear. The major lips, in a woman who has had a child, become very large. The minor lips suddenly turn bright red to burgundy red. As stimulation continues, orgasm will follow in 3 minutes. The vagina produces a great deal of fluid at this time to increase lubrication. The upper two-thirds of the vagina balloon out to a diameter of 3 ins.

Phase 3: Orgasm (3 to 15 secs.)

During this phase, the sexual flush continues, the nipples remain hard, the breasts continue to be enlarged, and the clitoris remains hidden under the prepuce. Then 3 to 15 contractions of the lower third of her vagina occur at 1 second intervals. Blood pressure, heart rate and breathing rate increase. The woman often has many facial movements and movements of her arms and legs including tightening of her toes.

Phase 4: Resolution Phase (10 to 15 mins. If no orgasm, up to one day)

The woman experiences a sense of well-being. However, if she has been stimulated but did not reach orgasm, it may take two to six hours for her to settle down during which time she might be irritable and feel discomfort. If the woman has experienced orgasm, she will often have perspiration (sweating) over her body. The breasts return to the normal size. The shaft of the clitoris returns to normal position in 5 to 10 seconds. If there was no orgasm, the clitoris may remain hard for several hours. In a woman who has not had children, the major lips return to their larger size. In a woman who has had children, the major lips then decrease to their normal size. The minor lips return to their normal color in five minutes. The vagina returns to its usual state.

Whoa! Let's cool it. Let's take a break. Let's just discuss one more time what we are trying to do in this chapter.

I told you that we are going to be talking about normal sex. You have now looked at the diagram and the names of the different sex organs. I also talked about what happens to the men and women when they are sexually excited and reach orgasm.

Remember the title of this chapter "Human Sexuality". Let's start talking about how we, as people, can go about getting good feelings out of sex. Let me remind myself and you that sexual behavior is a very complex thing. I am sure that you know there are libraries full of books about sexual behavior. Obviously, I cannot cover all the topics that are possible in relationship to sex. If I were to talk about everything that is related to sexual activity in people, I should write a very thick book.

I am sure that you know the word masturbation. Masturbation means that the person stimulates his or her own sex organ. When people stimulate their sex organs, they may just do it to get a nice sensation, or may stimulate the organ to the point that they reach orgasm. We are all embarrassed about talking about masturbation. I don't know why. Without doubt, it has something to do with our upbringing and the morals of our society. It's quite easy to talk to a friend and say that you had good sex. I am absolutely positive, that "No one ever talks to their friend about what a nice way was found to masturbate and how good it felt".

As far as I am concerned, sex can only occur properly between two people who trust each other. Good sex usually occurs when there is the highest regard for each other. Good sex occurs when people feel positively towards each other.

Researchers have shown us that good sexual feelings and orgasm can occur between people who are not in love. I am somewhat worried about giving this statement. I know that I will be open to criticism. People who criticize me will often think that I am recommending sex between anyone and everyone. That's not what I am saying. I am simply saying that two people can have good sex as long as they have enough trust in each other that there will be no harm.

If anyone is reading this section and thinks that they can have negative feelings such as hostility, anger, or aggression and have good sex, I would ask them to immediately quit reading and throw this book away.

Let me state my ideas again. Two people do not have to be madly in love to have good sex. Good sex can only occur if people have good feelings about each other. Negative feelings such as hostility never lead to good sex.

In humans and the rest of the animal world, the male seems to be ready and wanting sex. Think of the male pigeon who is always strutting around puffing out his feathers and cooing loudly. He is putting the "make" on the female pigeon. She doesn't seem too disturbed. She walks around, eats and frequently flies away from him. Think of the peacock that we have so often seen in the zoo raising and spreading out his wonderful feathers and "constantly" trying to "make out" with the female. Again, she seems quite disinterested. I remember watching a television show about some antelopes in Africa. The males fought each other for three days; penis extended and flinging back and forth; to show that they are strong and worthy of the female. Meanwhile, the females "hung around" eating grass, looking up occasionally to see the silly boys banging their heads together. If you happen to be from a farm or ranch, you'll notice the bull going with anticipation from cow to cow hoping that he would "get lucky". Enough of this. I'm simply trying to emphasize that males become sexually excited frequently. It seems that the male is constantly looking for a female who would be receptive.

This also seems to be true in humans. The male seems to have a greater need for sexual activity than the female. I have read books which state women have a higher sexual drive. I don't think this is true. It is true that women who have decided to have sex can carry on for longer periods of time and have more orgasms than men. I have read that women become much more sexually active when they reach 40. This is not true.

Let's now talk about the relationship between a man and woman so that "each will get the most out of sex".

First, the man and woman should "mutually decide" that they would like to have sex. This means that "both" want to have sex. Now, it is true that sex can occur when one desires sex but not the other. However, I don't think that this generally leads to good sex. On the other hand, the man may stimulate the woman who is not interested in sex to the point that she gets excited. The opposite is also true. That is, if the woman has a desire for sex and the man doesn't, she can seduce him to be excited sexually.

Let's imagine that the man and woman have now agreed to have sex. What should happen at this point? I think that it is very important that the setting is appropriate. Let me give you an example. If a husband and wife agree to "make out" and go to their bedroom, which is next to their children's bedroom and does not have a lock on the door, then they probably won't "get the best out of sex". The couple will be trying to remain "quiet" so that they would not be "heard". "Bad for good sex". Privacy is very important. If you are expecting your child to awaken from a dream and come rushing into your room, there is a good chance you won't be giving your full attention and energy to doing the things you ought to do to have good sex.

Let's try this again. In general, for you to get the most out of sex, you should find a private and secure place. Aside from having a private and secure setting, it should be "sexy". I really don't know how to define "sexy". You define it. You decide what a sexy environment is like. Everybody has their own fantasy. If you think that a sexy setting means fur rugs and furs on the bed, then let it be. You decide what's best for you. You make the setting which you think will turn you on.

Couples seek sex therapy but tend to forget common sense. For example:

Doctor: "When do you have sex?"

Answer: "At the end of the day when everything else is done. Just before we are about to go to sleep."

Doctor: "Are you tired when you are about to go to bed?"

Answer: "We work hard and are exhausted by the end of the day."

How can you get the most out of sex when you are exhausted? Do you run a race when you are exhausted? Do you write an important test when you are exhausted? Do you go for an important interview when you are exhausted? My statement is quite clear. Let's have sex when we are not exhausted.

Two opposite emotions cannot exist at the same moment. If a person is angry about something, then that same person cannot be smiling and happy at that same moment. This is true to any two opposite emotions. Sex is a nice, positive, pleasurable experience. If you are trying to have sex when you have negative feelings such as fear or anger, forget about sex. I simply can't understand how a couple can go to bed, argue about the kids or finances and then plan to have good sex. If you want to get the most out of sex, tickle each other, have fun during the day, make jokes, cook a meal, put icing in each other's face and lick it off, but please don't fight.

The man and woman must be in a positive mood. This means that the couple should work on developing good communication and a strong positive relationship. Enjoy each other. Learn to see the good points in each other. Accept each other's limitations and imperfections. Give your partner your deepest interest and concern. Give your partner the feeling that you really like him or her. If your partner has a problem, give suggestions to help out. If your partner has some behavior that you would like changed, talk about it gently. BE GOOD TO EACH OTHER.

Okay, we're set. We've been getting along. We had an excellent day. We have security and privacy. We've set up a sexy little place for ourselves. Now what?

It's important to have an adequate amount of time for the sex act. It's not a good idea to say to your partner, "Gosh, look at it, it's nearly 12:00 o'clock". This means that it's late, that it's time to go to sleep, morning will come very quickly so "let's get it done". Bad! Yes I know that we can have a "quickie" now and then. Sure it could be fun. But we're talking about getting the most out of sex. Sooooo, let's give lots of time if we're to fool around properly.

Let's not forget about our personal hygiene and general grooming. If I come back from a fishing trip and smell like the fish I caught, look like the fish I caught and am as slimy as the fish I caught, I don't think I'll turn my partner on! I guess the message should be clear. Let's be sure that we shower, shave, put on some makeup, etc. It's probably best to throw the baggy red woolen underwear into the clothes hamper and put on something nice and sexy.

Let's now make love. Sure, we can just do "straight hard sex". However, it's nicer if we make "warm love". Let's read a book together. Let's give each other a back rub. Did you think of going to the sex shop and picking up some oil that smells nice so that you can rub your partner down; make her feel good on her skin, muscles and bones. And vice versa. Do you know where your partner likes to be touched and rubbed? (Erogenous zones)? Ask your partner. Tell your partner to make some sounds when there are good feelings. Explore a bit. It's fun. Sex therapists talk about "erogenous zones". This refers to different parts of the body which really feel good with certain kinds of touch, pressure, and massage. What is good for one person may be terrible for another person. For example, some women have extremely sensitive nipples and feel terrible when the nipples are touched. Other women like their nipples touched and rubbed. Some individuals love to be tickled on their sides and others simply hate it. Some individuals like to have their head massaged but others find this annoying. Some individuals like to have deep massage pressure on their foot but others feel nothing. We are all different. We have to explore each other. We must try different techniques. We have to tell each other what feels good. We must explore and communicate!

How I would like to write a recipe for good sex. You know what I mean. Fifteen rubs here. Five pressure points there. A good dose of tickling here. A dash of kisses on the neck. One hand full of breast rubbing for three minutes. Kiss the forehead lightly four times on three different occasions. Well, just forget it. There is no one recipe which will lead any given person to sexual excitement; just as there is no one flower arrangement that is pleasing to everyone. There is no one lasagna that everyone loves. We all have our tastes. We all have different ingredients that make up the total recipe. This means that we have to explore, practice, and teach each other about what feels good to us. Also, after eating the same lasagna and having the same flower arrangement for a while, we need a change. The same is true for sex. If we repeat ourselves with the same sex recipe, then we will quickly get bored and not get sexually excited. We need something interesting and unique in our life. This refers to all aspects of our life and not only to sex. You've got the idea. Be innovative! Be daring. Sometimes you'll get into trouble because it doesn't work. Well, that's okay. Now you know it doesn't work. If I hit a golf ball once and it went all the way to the right, I don't quit golfing. I just try and swing a little differently. So if you swing and hit terribly, try again. AIM TO PLEASE!

Well, let's hope that we're getting a bit hot and bothered.

In this chapter, I do not describe the many different positions that there are to have sex. There is a nice book called *The Joy of Sex*, edited by Alex Comfort, that has lovely diagrams about the different positions.

Now let's discuss the male and female sex organs and how they respond to stimulation.

It is well known that men reach orgasm on almost all occasions that they have sex. It is also well known that it is much harder for a female to reach orgasm (climax). In general, the sex act has to occur in such a manner that the male tries to inhibit his orgasm and the female tries to stimulate her orgasm. The opposite is sometimes true. It is infrequent that there is a couple where the woman reaches orgasm very quickly and the man reaches orgasm very slowly.

At this point, it might be best for you to look at the diagrams of the sex organs again. Also, read the part about the plateau phase and orgasmic phase for the woman. I would like you to pay special attention to the fact that the clitoris retracts (pulls away) and seems to hide under the prepuce during these phases. Also remember that it is the stimulation of the clitoris that is the most important factor in producing orgasm in women. Therefore, during sexual intercourse the focus must be on stimulating the clitoris in the woman.

It is my suggestion that the woman is best stimulated when she is on top of the man. Sometimes this is not possible because of physical problems. Also, some women don't like this particular position. When the woman is on top, the weight of her body brings her down on the man quite well. The penis usually enters deepest in this position. In this position, the woman has total control of movements and activity. She can then move in such a manner that would give her the best stimulation of the clitoris. When the woman rolls her hips forward (towards the man) two things happen: (1) the penis goes in further, pulls the minor lips, and the minor lips then pull the prepuce. This causes stimulation to the clitoris; and, (2) the prepuce and clitoris are rubbed against the man's pubice (hairy area). This also causes a great deal of good stimulation to the clitoris. With the woman in this position and controlling the body movements, orgasm can usually be reached.

It is common for women not to be able to experience orgasm

through normal sexual intercourse and therefore they masturbate during sexual intercourse. Women may be embarrassed about this and not want to suggest it. Men may get upset about this because it somehow affects their "manliness". Let's forget about embarrassment and manliness for a while. Let's just do what works. If masturbation during intercourse works, do it.

Unsatisfying Sex

Up to this point, I talked about the anatomy of the sexual organs as well as the reaction of sex organs to stimulation and excitation. I also described the changes that occur with orgasm. This part of the chapter focuses on problems in sexual activity which I have described as "unsatisfactory sex".

This particular section on unsatisfactory sex relates to heterosexual relationships.

Unsatisfactory sex is divided into eight disorders including:
1. Inhibited sexual desire
2. Inhibited sexual excitement
3. Inhibited female orgasm
4. Inhibited male orgasm
5. Premature ejaculation
6. Functional dyspareunia
7. Vaginismus
8. Atypical psychosexual dysfunctions

There are many factors that can prevent an individual from having satisfactory sexual experiences. Some of the difficulties that can lead to unsatisfied sexual experiences are:

1. Physical problems - An individual who is physically ill cannot perform well sexually. This refers to short term physical illnesses such as severe colds. Severe and long-standing disorders such as diabetes can impair sexual feelings.

2. Emotional problems - Emotional problems may be short-lived such as those that occur with stress. For example, an individual who is working a double shift for a number of days may not be able to function adequately sexually. Other emotional disorders may be more severe such as depression. Until the depression is treated, the person may not be able to function sexually.

3. Interpersonal difficulties - The husband and wife who are arguing over a problem such as finances may not be able to function sexually.

4. Lack of sexual knowledge - I am always amazed by the large number of "skin magazines" there are on the market every month. One would think that in this liberated society with a great deal of attention to sexual matters in the media including radio, television, and magazines that individuals would have good knowledge about sex. In fact, studies have shown that individuals have very little knowledge of basic sex organ anatomy and sex organ physiology.

Inhibited Sexual Desire

Inhibited sexual desire refers to a lack of desire to participate in sexual activity. There is usually no problem with the sexual organs, sexual physiology or the knowledge of sexual activity. Simply, the person does not seek sexual activity. There is no desire.

There are several reasons for this lack of desire. Some individuals have a very high desire and others a low desire. This does not mean that one is normal and one is abnormal. It just means that we are made differently.

When a person does not have sexual relations for a long period of time, the desire decreases. Sexual organs must be used for there to be a desire. This is especially true for women. If you let the sexual organs go to sleep, they simply don't awaken.

Lack of desire may occur during periods of stress, anxiety, depression or some other severe physical or mental disorder.

Studies have shown that men have a decreased sexual desire when they experience certain kinds of pressures which may be related to work, finances, or family relationships. The man may be so involved with his job and the problems in the company that sexual desire disappears.

It seems that women are more affected by problems of their relationship to their husband. If women feel dominated, not given a chance to make decisions, or not get the affection they hope from their husbands, they will show less sexual desire. When there is lack of privacy, sexual desire will decrease. For example, in-laws staying at your place for the weekend will decrease the desire for sex. Probably one of the most common reasons for lack of sexual desire is conflict within the marriage.

Inhibited Sexual Excitement

In the man, this is experienced by an inability to maintain an erection (hard on). This disorder is experienced in the woman by an inability to attain or maintain lubrication. Studies show that 33% of women have difficulty maintaining sexual excitement. Lack of sexual excitement (impotence) is the most common sexual disorder in men. In this disorder, men have the desire to experience sex, but are not able to maintain an erection.

Table I lists the drugs that may cause "inhibited sexual excitement".

Table II lists a number of diseases that may cause "inhibited sexual excitement".

Lack of a desirable sexual partner may lead to impotence. In other words, a man may be able to have an erection to masturbate or to have sexual intercourse with a certain partner but not with his wife. He may not view his wife as desirable. Similarly, women may not find the husband desirable and therefore not be able to maintain the excitement.

Many emotional disorders such as depression, drug abuse and alcoholism can lead to this disorder.

Inhibited Female Orgasm

In this disorder, the woman may feel the desire and become excited but is not able to reach orgasm. This disorder refers to women who cannot experience orgasm during sexual intercourse or during masturbation.

Many women cannot experience orgasm during sexual intercourse unless they masturbate at the same time. This may be related to a lack of knowledge as to how to stimulate each other. In fact, it requires a great deal of knowledge and practice for the man to be able to stimulate the woman's clitoris adequately during sexual intercourse.

Before the age of 35, 75% of married women have not yet experienced orgasm. 40% of unmarried women over the age of 35 have never experienced orgasm.

There are many physical disorders that may interfere with orgasm. These disorders are listed in Table I and II.

Psychological problems leading to an inability to experience orgasm include fear of impregnation, rejection by the sexual partner, anger towards the sexual partner, feelings of guilt about sexual activity, fears of experiencing pain during sexual intercourse.

Inhibited Male Orgasm

This disorder refers to men who have a desire for intercourse and do get sexually excited during intercourse but cannot achieve a climax (orgasm).

This disorder occurs because of medications (Table I) or physical diseases (Table II).

TABLE I

Pharmacological Agents That Cause Sexual Dysfunction

Psychiatric Drugs
    Tricyclic antidepressants
        Tofranil
        Pertofrane
        Anafranil
        Elavil
    Monoamine oxidase inhibitors
        Parnate
        Nardil
        Marplan
    Other mood-active drugs
        Lithium
        Amphetamines
    Major tranquilizers
        Mellaril
        Trilafon
        Stelazine
        Haldol

Antihypertensive drugs
    Aldomet
    Aldactone
    Apresoline
    Ismelin

Commonly Abused Drugs
    Alcohol
    Barbiturates
    Cannabis
    Cocaine
    Heroin
    Methadone
    Morphine

Miscellaneous Drugs
    Antiparkinson agents
    Digoxin
    Inderal

TABLE II

Diseases Causing Sexual Dysfunction

Infectious
    Mumps

Cardiovascular Diseases
    Atherosclerotic disease
    Cardiac failure

Renal and Urological Disorders
    Peyronie's disease
    Chronic renal failure
    Hydrocele or varicocele

Hepatic Disorders
    Cirrhosis (usually associated
    with alcoholism)

Pulmonary Disorders
    Respiratory failure

Nutritional Disorders
    Malnutrition
    Vitamin deficiencies

Endocrine Disorders
    Diabetes mellitus
    Hyperthyroidism
    Hypothyroidism

Neurological Disorders
    Multiple sclerosis
    Parkinson's disease
    Temporal lobe epilepsy
    Spinal cord disease
    Central nervous system
        tumors
    Peripheral neuropathies

Poisoning
  Lead

Surgical Procedures
  Perineal prostatectomy
  Sympathectomy

Miscellaneous
  Radiation therapy
  Pelvic fracture
  Any severe disease

There are many psychological reasons for not being able to reach orgasm including anger at the partner, and loss of sexual attraction to the partner.

Premature Ejaculation

This refers to the man who ejaculates too quickly. The man may ejaculate as soon as he develops an erection or as soon as he enters the vagina. About 40% of men treated for sexual disorders have premature ejaculation as their chief complaint.

There are a number of factors which may lead to this disorder. The novelty of a new sexual partner may lead to such excitement that ejaculation is reached very quickly. Excessive stimulation during the excitation phase may lead to orgasm prematurely. That is, partners who are "playing with each other" for a long time may reach such a high level of excitement that ejaculation may occur at the moment that intercourse is attempted. Some men have such anxiety about performing adequately that they reach ejaculation too quickly. A stressful marriage may lead to premature ejaculation. This is probably due to the fact that the man may have sexual desires and is able to attain sexual excitement but wants to ejaculate quickly so that he may have the pleasure of orgasm but not have to relate to his partner for a long time.

In most cases, it is difficult to find the cause for premature ejaculation.

Functional Dyspareunia

This disorder refers to pain during intercourse in both men and women.

Surgery to the woman's genital tract may lead to dyspareunia (pain during intercourse). There are a wide variety of physical disorders of the vagina that may lead to dyspareunia.

If the woman has intercourse before she is in a state of readiness, she may experience dyspareunia. Many psychological problems such as fear of sexual intercourse, fear of pregnancy, stress, and depression can lead to dyspareunia.

Pain during intercourse is a relatively uncommon disorder in men.

Vaginismus

Vaginismus relates to muscle spasm at the entrance of the vagina preventing penile insertion. This disorder may be caused by fear of pain, anxiety about sexual intercourse, a strict religious upbringing with associated feelings of sex as a sin, and problems in the relationship between partners. This disorder seems to occur more often in educated women and those in the higher socio-economic groups.

Atypical Psychosexual Dysfunction

This refers to a wide variety of sexual disorders that cannot fit in the above seven groups. Some individuals compulsively masturbate. Some men and women may not have a pleasurable sensation during orgasm. Women and men may describe a total lack of feeling during sexual activity. Couples with unsatisfactory sexual experiences may be placed in this group when one member prefers morning sex while another member of the couple prefers evening sex.

Treatment of Unsatisfactory Sexual Behavior

As you can see by Table I and Table II, there are many physical causes for unsatisfactory sexual activity. Physicians must diagnose and treat any physical disease that exists. There are sexual therapists who specialize in assisting couples to develop satisfactory sexual relationships. Many of these sex therapists use the treatment techniques that have been originally described by William Masters and Virginia Johnson.

In the Masters and Johnson program, therapy is viewed as a problem between the two people. That is, if the male is having premature ejaculation, or the female is experiencing vaginismus, the therapist sees the problem as a result of the interaction occurring between the two people. Usually, there are dual-therapists. That means that the couple visit a male and female therapist. Usually the male therapist meets for at least one interview with the man and a single interview with the woman. The female therapist meets for a single interview with the man and then the woman. The couple then meet with the male and female therapist to discuss methods of curing the unsatisfactory sexual experience.

A great deal of emphasis is placed on discussing the marital relationship. Discussions are held in respect to attitudes that the couples have towards each other, work schedules, decision-making about a variety of family problems such as finances and child rearing and discussions on other daily family experiences.

Discussions also focus on methods of exciting each other. Too often, therapists find that couples will complain bitterly about unsatisfactory sexual experiences but are unwilling to spend time and energy on improving their sexual relationship. It is not uncommon for couples to rush through their day of work, relate to their family, do a variety of household duties and then plop into bed exhausted. When they are exhausted, they spend only a small amount of time on themselves in terms of showers, colognes, special lighting effects, stimulating each other and guiding each other to a high level of excitation and orgasm. They simply do not have the time or energy to do this. Then they "bitch" about not having adequate sexual feelings!

If there is some physical disease such as diabetes or psychological disorder such as depression, anxiety or alcoholism, these disorders must be treated first.

The therapists also focus on sexual anatomy and sexual physiology. For example, if a male does not know how to excite his partner, then the woman cannot reach the excitement phase. Also, if the male thinks that rapid long movements of the penis in the vagina lead to orgasm in the woman, then the woman will always experience unsatisfactory sex. The man must have good knowledge about female anatomy and the fact that the clitoris must be stimulated.

Therapists give exercises to the couple so that they may excite each other through touch, sight, sound and smell. The therapists encourage the couple to give and receive bodily pleasure but not to have intercourse during this phase. This is a very important technique. I'll repeat myself. The therapist educates the couple to give and to receive pleasure. They ask the couple not to have intercourse during these exercises. Through knowledge and communication, sexual foreplay is taught to be as important as intercourse and orgasm.

The therapists encourage the couple to fantasize during foreplay, intercourse and orgasm. Couples know that certain fantasies give them a great deal of pleasure. However, they also feel that to have these fantasies during foreplay, intercourse and orgasm is somehow bad or should not be allowed. Common sexual fantasies in men and woman include having sexual activity with another partner, observing sexual activity, fantasizing that they are being forced into sexual encounters, fantasizing group sex or fantasizing sex with a same sex partner. It is my experience that couples feel upset when I recommend this technique of fantasizing. I guess they feel that they are betraying their partner if they fantasize.

Couples are encouraged to try different sexual positions. During this phase of therapy, they are encouraged not to reach orgasm.

If a woman is suffering from vaginismus, she is taught to open her vagina with her fingers before intercourse. Women may purchase vaginal dilators to increase the size of the vagina and prevent vaginismus.

Premature ejaculation is successfully treated with sex therapy. The "squeeze technique" is used to treat premature ejaculation. In the squeeze technique, the man or the woman stimulates the erect penis until the earliest sensations of orgasm occur. At this point, stimulation is discontinued and the woman squeezes the coronal ridge of the penis for several seconds. The coronal ridge is that part of the penis between the "head" and the "shaft". This may be repeated several times. The couple can then go on to have intercourse and ejaculation will not occur prematurely.

For a woman who has anorgasmia (inability to reach an orgasm), she is taught to masturbate or use a vibrator.

In summary, the goal of treatment is to educate the couple about sexual activity, facilitate communications, and improve relationships within the marital unit.

My following comment, to the best of my knowledge, is not to be found anywhere in textbooks or manuals on sexuality. My comment is quite simple. We are all different. About this fact there is no doubt. Not all of us can be Olympic athletes. Yet, somehow, we want to be Olympic sexual athletes. I would suggest that we decrease our preoccupation with having the most phenomenal orgasm or the largest number of orgasms. I think our preoccupation should be with making each other feel good! Feeling good may last a long time. Orgasm lasts a short time. To look at, to touch, to tickle, to give pleasure to each other, in whatever manner possible, should be our goals. Let's be good to each other. Let's make each other feel good. I think this is what life is all about. I think this is what will give us a great sense of pleasure and satisfaction. I think this is what will get us turned on to each other and turned on to life.

Variations in Sexual Behavior
Homosexuality

Homosexuality refers to individuals who prefer sexual partners of the same sex. A woman may prefer to have sexual relationships with another woman. A man may prefer to have sexual relationships with another man. It is estimated that 4% of males and 2% of females are homosexuals.

When writing this book, I had some difficulty deciding where to put the topic of homosexuality. As you can see, this part of the

chapter is entitled "Variations in Sexual Behavior". There is a great deal of controversy as to whether homosexuality can be considered a normal variation of human behavior or whether it is a disorder. In 1974, the American Psychiatric Association ruled that homosexuality is not a mental disorder. However, if you should go to libraries to read about homosexuality, you will find this disorder described in chapters relating to abnormal sex or sexual dysfunction or sexual disorders.

The most important feature which defines homosexuality is the characteristic that an individual is sexually attracted to and experiences sexual activity with a person of the same sex. There are different degrees of homosexuality. Some individuals have feelings that they are homosexual but, in fact, act as heterosexuals. Some individuals can have homosexual experiences only in certain situations such as prisons where they are separated from opposite sex partners. Other individuals are bisexual. This means that they are attracted to and have sex with the same sex or opposite sex. I'm sure that you can name some well known entertainers who have openly stated they are bisexual. There are other individuals who prefer homosexuality but could function in a heterosexual manner. Other individuals are exclusively homosexual and find it repulsive to experience sex with a person of the opposite sex.

Some homosexuals develop a very stable and long-standing homosexual relationship. Homosexuals may establish a relationship, purchase a home, and develop future plans as though they were a married couple. Females tend to establish long term homosexual relationships more often than men.

Other homosexuals tend to develop very short term relationships with other homosexuals. These individuals are frequently promiscuous. Because of the new disease AIDS, homosexuals are changing their sexual relationships. Because of the fear of AIDS, homosexuals are establishing long term relationships.

The type of sexual activity that homosexuals prefer varies greatly. As discussed, heterosexuals prefer different types of sexual behavior such as kissing, hugging, holding, tickling, massaging, oral sex and genital sex in a variety of positions. Similarly, homosexuals have their preferences. Some homosexuals prefer to be the active partner. Other homosexuals prefer to be the passive partner. For example, a female homosexual may be considered a passive partner when she prefers that her partner initiates sexual activity, stimulates her, rubs her, and initiates and continues the oral or genital sex. Some homosexuals prefer oral sex. Other homosexual males prefer anal sex.

Although there has been a great deal of research on homosexuality, there is no adequate explanation as to why some individuals prefer sexual relationships with the same sex. There is no treatment program that could change a person from being exclusively homosexual to exclusively heterosexual.

Gender Identity Disorders

When the term sex is used, it refers to whether a person is a man or a woman because of their sex organs. In other words, an individual is called a man because he has a penis and testicles. A person is called a woman because she has a vagina, breasts and other female sex organs.

Gender identity refers to whether an individual feels and believes he/she is masculine or feminine.

A person is said to have a gender identity disorder when he is born as a boy with a penis and testicles but, right from childhood, believes that he is a girl. In other words, the child has the sex organs of a male but believes psychologically that they are female. A similar disorder can occur in a female child.

These individuals seek medical treatment to be changed. The boy persists to the point that he will eventually have a physician remove his testicles, give him hormones to grow breasts, and have hair removed from the body to appear more feminine. He may have the penis removed and a vagina formed surgically. Females might also seek medical treatment to be changed into a male.

These individuals seek sexual gratification with individuals of the same sex. In other words, if a male has a gender identity problem and believes that he is really a female, he prefers to get his sexual excitement by playing the role of the female while with another male. The same is true for the female gender identity disordered person.

This disorder is also called transsexualism.

Fetishistic Cross-Dressing (Transvestism)

This disorder occurs only in males. The male is sexually excited and reaches orgasm by dressing in women's clothes. This usually begins in adolescence.

Fetishism

The person who has a fetishism is sexually aroused by certain objects that are associated with certain body parts. Some individuals get turned on when they see a special bra. A woman may be turned on to a man who wears rings. Some individuals get turned on more easily when they are having sexual relationships with an individual who is wearing a specific garment. For example, a man may prefer sexual activity when his partner is wearing a short nightie. He prefers this to having sexual relationships with the partner totally nude. Some individuals become so preoccupied with a particular item of clothing or jewelry that they constantly masturbate with the item.

Sexual Sadism and Masochism

An individual is said to be sexually masochistic when that individual experiences sexual excitement when in a passive position of physical or emotional discomfort. The person may fantasize this experience. For example, a person may only be highly aroused sexually and have orgasm when pinched or pressed to the point of pain.

A person is said to be a sexual sadist when he/she gets sexually excited by inflicting pain in fantasy or in reality on their partner.

Exhibitionism and Voyeurism

This disorder only occurs in males. Exhibitionism refers to a male who exposes his genitals to a stranger. Voyeurism refers to an individual who is always seeking to look at unsuspecting women who may be disrobing, grooming, or having intercourse. In both cases, sexual excitement occurs and the individual usually masturbates to the point of orgasm.

Individuals who carry out exhibitionistic or voyeuristic behavior frequently marry and appear normal. That is, they have a job, work for the community, etc.

Pedophilia

Pedophilia refers to sexual excitement with children, in fantasy or in actuality. This disorder may be exclusively homosexual or exclusively heterosexual.

Zoophilia

Persons are said to be suffering from zoophilia if they prefer to be aroused in their fantasies or sexual activities by intercourse or masturbation with an animal.

CHAPTER 6

Psychosomatic Medicine

PSYCHOSOMATIC MEDICINE

This section is about the relationship of our psychology to our body. A large part of this chapter is focused on physical symptoms or physical illness related to psychological difficulties. Simply, the body does not work without the mind and the mind cannot work without the body. If a person has a physical disorder such as heart disease, that person will surely also have some psychological problems such as anxiety or depression.

According to the Diagnostic and Statistical Manual - III-R of the American Psychiatric Association, a category is included which is entitled "Psychological Factors Affecting Physical Condition". This relates to environmental events (death of a family member) which may initiate or worsen a physical condition. For example, a patient may suffer heart pain (angina) when stressed or angered. I will also discuss the fact that physical illness can cause psychological changes. For example, an individual who has developed an incurable cancer experiences many psychological changes. I will explain how our Environment alters our Psychology, and how this, in turn, can lead to "Bodily Changes". The key words will be Environment, Psychology, and Body. Let's think of a time in our lives when we have been embarrassed. The arrow, A, leading towards the head represents the embarrassing situation. That is, we may be sitting at a table when we suddenly tip over a glass of juice. This "Environmental Event" is recorded in our brain. This is represented by the arrow labelled B. At this moment, we think to ourselves "Oh, how silly of me. Oh, how embarrassing". Line C represents the link between our thinking brain (cerebral cortex) and our emotional brain. At this point we "feel embarrassed". The emotional brain is responsible for giving us this feeling. Line D represents the nervous activity that

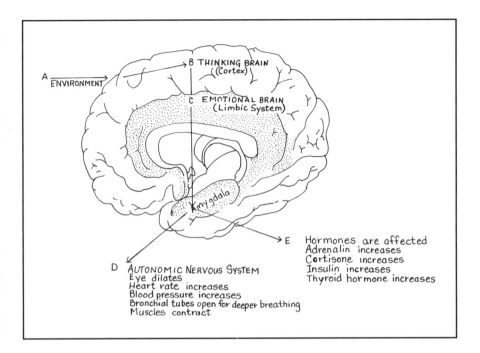

goes from our emotional brain to other parts of our body. This "emotional response" is carried by the autonomic nervous system. In this example, the nerves from the brain to our blood vessels become stimulated. Our face then becomes a beautiful red color. We blushed with embarrassment. Line E represents hormones that are stimulated by our emotional brain. These hormones affect affect various organs. For example, if we should become frightened, hormones will be released. Line F represents the voluntary nervous system which leads to our muscles. During the experience of embarrassment, we may feel "shaky" because of the increased tone of our muscles during this emotional experience.

Every part of our body is connected by the nervous system and the hormonal system which may be activated during certain emotional states. These emotional states are caused by certain experiences in life.

In the next few pages, I talk about the various physical disorders that may be affected by stress. I am not able to cover all the disorders, but instead choose to focus on a few examples. I do not discuss each in great detail.

Physical Disorders

Peptic Ulcer

There are two types of peptic ulcers and they are referred to as gastric (stomach) ulcers and duodenal (small intestine) ulcers. Ulcers are caused by a variety of factors including acid and pepsin which is produced by the stomach. The stomach also produces a protective coating to protect against the acid and pepsin. Acid and pepsin are produced when a person tastes, sees, smells, thinks or expects food to arrive. I think everyone knows of the dog experiments by Pavlov. Pavlov would ring a bell just before he brought food to his experimental dogs. He realized that the dogs start producing saliva when the bell is rung and before the food was given. The dogs were expecting the food and therefore started producing saliva. All of this was caused by the nervous system. In other words, the "bell" meant "food" and the nervous system said "Let's go. Produce saliva".

There are literally hundreds of experiments to show that emotions can affect acid and pepsin production. There is a famous experiment which is sometimes referred to as the executive monkey experiment. A monkey is put into an experiment where he sees a light and then receives a shock. The monkey is then trained to pull a lever as soon as the light goes on so that he does not get a shock. The experiment is then changed and two monkeys are placed in the same experiment. However, one monkey is tied in such a manner that he cannot pull the lever. The other monkey, the executive monkey, is able to pull a lever when the light goes on so that neither of them get shocked. The executive monkey, is in a position of control. He must make decisions. He watches anxiously for the light to come on. The executive monkey develops gastric and duodenal ulcers. It is thought that this monkey feels the importance of responsibility and is highly "activated". Look back at Diagram I. Line A represents the "Environment" - i.e. the light and the lever, Line B would represent the "thinking of responsibility" that occurs in the monkey. Line C represents the activation of emotional arousal of the emotional brain. Line D represents the autonomic nervous system causing acid and pepsin production and the development of ulcers.

This type of stress is experienced in humans and can lead to ulcer disease. A wide variety of stresses could lead to the initiation, prolongation, or severity of the ulcer disease. There is evidence to show that a person who develops ulcer disease tends to be hyperindependent, ambitious, competitive, and constantly striving for superiority. By constantly pressuring oneself to high aspirations, ulcers may develop.

Irritable Bowel Syndrome

It is estimated that of all individuals who seek medical consultation for bowel complaints, 50% are diagnosed as having the "Irritable Bowel Syndrome". Symptoms of this disorder include abdominal discomfort and pain, constipation alternating with diarrhea, and gas. Other names for this disorder are spastic colitis, nervous diarrhea, and mucus colitis.

The cause of this disorder is not totally understood. This disorder tends to worsen with stress. Some patients are diagnosed as suffering from anxiety and others are diagnosed as suffering from depression. It appears that these patients become unduly sensitive to even minor stresses in their environment. Patients with this disorder often use alcohol or over the counter medications to control their bowel functions. The use of alcohol and medications may worsen the disorder. Patients often use large numbers and amounts of antacids, laxatives and other medications to control their symptoms.

Obesity

A person is defined as obese when the body weight exceeds by 20% the standard weight listed in the usual height-weight tables. It is estimated that 75% of North Americans can be called obese or considered "overweight". It is remarkable how animals and humans tend to maintain a constant weight. This has led to a great deal of experimentation and it is now accepted that each of us has a certain "set point" about which body weight is regulated. Weight seems to depend on our genetics. It is very easy to show this factor in animals. Certain strains of mice and rats always produce obese mice and rats.

Obesity is caused by either an increase in number of fat cells (hyperplastic obesity) or increased fat cell size (hypertrophic obesity) or both. This is a very important fact. If a child is obese, there will be a large number of fat cells. Even if they diet in later life, no fat cells ever disappear. It would seem that a child who is fat will have a most difficult time being non-fat in adult life. If slender adults gain weight in later life, they do not have an increase in the number of fat cells but do have an increase in the size of the fat cells.

Another feature related to obesity is physical activity. Physical activity leads to a reduction in weight by virtue of: (1) calorie (energy) expenditure; (2) a tendency to reduce appetite; and (3) increase in metabolic rate. The third feature is important for individuals who diet. As an individual diets, the metabolic rate slows down. This means that the body system slows down so that calories are not burned up. This seems to be a protective feature of the body. That is, if we have a reduction of food available to us, it is very important for our bodies to "slow down" so that we do not lose weight too rapidly and die. This "slow down" of metabolism is easily recognized. Hands become cold, energy is reduced and thinking is impaired.

There are certain parts of the brain that are responsible for producing the desire to eat. Other parts of the brain are responsible for telling us that we are satiated and that we should no longer eat. Hunger centers are found in the lateral hypothalamus, a part of the brain. Satiety centers (satisfaction centers) are found in the ventromedial hypothalamus. I don't expect you to remember these two parts of the brain. I thought I would include these names to emphasize the fact that the brain is responsible for our feelings of hunger or satisfaction.

The society in which we live has a bearing on whether we are slender or obese. There are some societies in the South Pacific where obesity is seen as beautiful. In our society, there is a high value placed on slenderness. Statistics show that individuals in higher socioeconomic brackets such as business people and professionals tend to have lower weights than individuals in lower socioeconomic brackets such as those on welfare.

Emotional disturbances can lead to an alteration in body weight. In severe depressions, individuals may lose their appetite and lose weight. In other depressive states, individuals tend to eat when depressed. Research studies indicate that individuals who are obese tend to have more psychological problems. This is opposite to the myth of the "jolly, fat person".There seems to be a night-eating disorder. This disorder is characterized by excessive eating in the evening, difficulties sleeping, and lack of appetite in the morning. This disorder seems to be related to stress and depression.

We are all aware of the hundreds of diets that are present in the various magazines and books. Many people have become rich from the sale of books about diets. I am sure that there are many types of diets on the market because none of them really works properly. If any one diet would prove to be effective, there would be no room for other competitive diets. Research has shown repeatedly that individuals tend to lose weight when they go on a diet but promptly regain the lost weight. There is no simple and generally effective treatment for obesity that is useful over a long period of time. Obesity tends to be a long-standing condition.

There is no type of drug therapy that is useful for the treatment of obesity. I will say it again. There is no drug therapy that is useful for the treatment of obesity. It is true that certain drugs could be taken to cause a fairly rapid reduction in weight. However, the moment the individual is off this drug, the lost weight is regained. Furthermore, these drugs may produce side effects and are addictive.

Many weight reduction programs utilize behavioral techniques. In general, behavioral techniques involve the use of reward for weight loss. There are a wide variety of manuals detailing the behavioral weight control program.

Tops (Take Off Pounds Sensibly), a non-profit organization, and Weight Watchers, a commercial organization, are successful in assisting weight reduction. Each year, almost half a million persons utilize Tops and more than 1.5 million persons utilize the services of Weight Watchers. These programs depend on the support that is obtained in groups, mutual exchange of ideas, a weekly weigh-in program, behavioral modification techniques with the use of rewards, inspirational lectures, and carefully designed nutritional programs. These organizations are cost effective because of the low cost per session.

Physicians are now hiring nurses and nutritionists to organize treatment programs in their offices. Most large hospitals have developed weight-reduction programs for the treatment of obesity.

A variety of diets are available for weight reduction. Many of the diets are "faddish", "worthless", or harmful to health. Diets which are sponsored by organizations such as the Canadian Diabetic Association and American Diabetic Association are the safest and best diets. Diets should not be utilized simply to reduce weight. Diets should be directed towards a long term change in eating habits. In general, these diets limit simple carbohydrates such as candy, chocolates, cakes, pies and other "sweets". These diets also limit the amount of fat allowable per day. The diets focus on the use of complex carbohydrates such as breads, pastas and rices. There is focus on the use of proteins, primarily in the form of white meats such as chicken and turkey. Emphasis is placed on making the diet colorful, appealing, and unique to prevent "boredom". In other words, diet is directed towards later sensible eating habits.

A weight loss of 1 pound to 1 1/2 pounds per week is adequate.

The commonest type of surgery that is used for the severely obese is the gastric reduction procedure. This surgery consists of making the stomach smaller so that it holds less food.

Weight reduction is often associated with many positive emotional changes. The individual feels good about his or her slender appearance. The person gets excited about the type of clothes that can be worn. With reduced weight, the person breathes and moves about more easily. Individuals show a greater degree of assertiveness and confidence when they have lost weight. Sexual and marital relationships tend to improve. There is a general overall feeling of well-being when a reduction of weight occurs.

A reduction in weight leads to an improved health state. Many diseased states such as high blood pressure, stroke, heart disease, and diabetes can be caused by obesity.

Anorexia Nervosa

Anorexia Nervosa refers to a disorder where an individual is highly preoccupied with body weight and food, limits the intake of food, hides food, loses weight to the point of injuring health including death, fears gain in weight, suffers a preoccupation that the body is large and cessation of mentrual periods. Anorexia Nervosa appears to be more frequent in  the past ten years. This disorder usually begins in girls between the ages of 12 and 18.

Various reasons are given for the cause of Anorexia Nervosa. However, there is no single factor which can explain the development of Anorexia Nervosa. There is some evidence that young females become afraid of becoming mature. They are afraid of developing breasts and having periods. They are afraid that boys will approach them. They therefore stop eating so that they can be very slender, young-looking and not become sexual objects. There is evidence that some anorexics are afraid of educational and social responsibilities that occur with growth and development. They want to maintain their child-like appearance so that they would not have responsibilities as a mature adolescent. Anorexia may develop when there are stressful life situations such as conflict within the family, competition at school or difficulties at a job. Some individuals develop Anorexia Nervosa secondary to a depression.

Studies of children who later develop Anorexia Nervosa reveal that they are frequently "model children", tending towards cleanliness, tidiness, politeness and good behavior. These children often strive to achieve in the school setting and have an unrealistic fear of failure.

The anorexic carries out many unusual types of behaviors. They are often very secretive about losing weight. They are secretive about not eating. They are afraid to eat with their families or in public places. They become preoccupied with reducing food to almost insignificant amounts. At times, they cannot control themselves and have "binges" which are followed by vomiting. Some of the anorexics use laxatives and diuretics to reduce weight. The anorexic becomes extremely preoccupied with exercising.

When the weight goes beyond a certain low point, death can occur from cardiac arrythymias. Death occurs more frequently when the persons vomits and uses laxatives as this causes reductions in serum potassium. Tooth enamel is destroyed by the acid from their stomach.

Anorexics often hide food around the house. The food may rot and produce a terrible odor. When the anorexic is confronted, the answer is "I didn't do it". The anorexic may carry food in pockets and purses. They become preoccupied with recipes, collect books, prepare elaborate meals, and take long periods of time to cut their food on a plate. The Anorexic denies that there is a problem.

The person with Anorexia Nervosa feels that he/she is too fat. They constantly look at themselves in the mirror. They constantly touch their bodies and pinch skin to note how much fat there may be. There is an intense fear of gaining weight and becoming obese. The person with anorexia often becomes preoccupied with other activities such as housecleaning, studying, and exercising. The anorexic often shows a delayed or poor sexual adjustment.

If the weight loss is extreme, the anorexic will often develop swelling of the legs, slow heart rate, low blood pressure, amenorrhea (loss of menstrual periods) and the development of very fine hair over the body.

Many anorexics never come to treatment. The anorexia is either short-lived or the person refuses to accept treatment. It is very difficult to predict whether the person with anorexia will actually become healthy or will continue to have problems with the anorexia. In some cases, the anorexia is severe and the person dies. Some statistics reveal that up to 21% of anorexics die within 4 years of the diagnosis.

The younger the person, the better is the outcome. Other indicators which indicate a positive outcome include normal child development, positive parental relationships, and an acceptance of their disorder and acceptance of treatment.

Treatment of Anorexia Nervosa

Most patients deny that they have a disorder and frequently reject any attempts at treatment. The families are upset because their child rejects treatment. It is important for the psychologist or physician to be supportive of the patient and the family. The physician and psychologist should do everything in their power to make the anorexic feel positive about treatment.

If the body weight is too low, immediate hospitalization is necessary. In the hospital setting, privileges are taken away from the anorexics. They are asked to remain in bed. Visitors are restricted. The anorexic is encouraged to eat and will be given privileges such as getting out of bed, leaving their room, and having visitors when there is a gain in weight. Rewards should not depend upon eating. This produces too much controversy between the patient and the staff. There is too much chance of arguing as to whether a little or a lot was eaten. Rewards should only be offered when there is weight gain. Either there is an increase in body weight or there isn't. Therefore, there will be rewards or there won't be rewards.

In rare cases, the anorexia has developed to the degree that intravenous and tube feeding is necessary. A medically safe rate of weight gain is .25 pounds per day. If too much food is given too quickly, the body's systems may become overloaded.

A variety of drugs have been used for the treatment of Anorexia Nervosa including antidepressants, minor tranquilizers and major tranquilizers. Drug therapy leads to variable success.

Family discussions are necessary to educate the family as to the nature of the disorder. Focus should also be made on any family difficulties and conflicts that exist which may be producing the anorexia or worsening it.

Bulimia

Bulimia is sometimes referred to as Bulimia Nervosa. Bulimia refers to an excessive, uncontrolled, and rapid ingestion of large amounts of food over a short period of time (binge eating). Individuals often experience abdominal discomfort or pain. The binge eating is followed by vomiting. Initially, the individual produces vomiting by sticking their fingers at the back of their throat. Later, they learn to vomit automatically. Patients will often restrict their food intake to such a degree that they may be considered to be fasting. However, they cannot tolerate this fasting and end up binge eating again. The bulimic is highly aware of this abnormal eating pattern but can't seem to stop it independently. The most common method of reducing weight is by vomiting. Less frequently, bulimics will use laxatives or diuretics (water pills) to reduce weight.

Bulimics are of normal weight or slightly above normal weight. They do not experience the severe loss of weight that occurs in anorexia nervosa.

Studies reveal that individuals with bulimia often have difficulty controlling a variety of behaviors. They abuse alcohol and drugs. Other bulimics become sexually promiscuous. Some bulimics have stormy personal relationships. Bulimics may steal. They usually take items such as jewelry, clothing or food.

Many medical complications occur with bulimia. Because of the vomiting and laxatives, low potassium levels develop. This leads to heart abnormalities. Dental problems occur because of the acid from the stomach destroying the enamel. Some bulimics will develop tears in their esophagus. Esophagitis is a common complication of bulimia because of the acid attacking the lining of the esophagus. Mentrual irregularities are common.

Bulimia is most frequent in the young female. There is a history of depressive disorders and alcohol abuse in close relatives of bulimics. Because of this, it is thought that bulimia is related to depression.

The treatment of bulimia usually involves teaching the person about the nature of the disorder. The bulimic is encouraged to keep a diary of their "binge and purge" behavior. Discussions are focussed on self-control. New methods of coping with stress are discussed. This type of treatment is described as cognitive therapy.

The bulimic person is infrequently hospitalized. There is some evidence to show that antidepressant drug therapy may be helpful.

Cardiovascular System Disorders

Anxiety

The details of anxiety states and their relationship to the heart are discussed in the chapter on anxiety disorders. However, I included anxiety in this chapter since one of the commonest symptoms of anxiety relates to the heart.

Every one of us has had some experience with anxiety. Think about a nightmare you experienced. Think back to a time when you were under stress. Maybe you were under stress when you went for a job interview. Whatever your experiences, you will remember that the stress you experienced caused anxiety and a pounding of the heart. You would have had the distinct sensation that your heart was beating rapidly, there was a pounding in the chest and pressure or pain in your chest.

Patients with anxiety symptoms commonly complain of the following: "my heart was really pounding. My heart was beating fast. I couldn't control myself. I had a difficult time breathing. I had some chest pain and I felt that I was having a heart attack".

Cardiologists (heart specialists) know that many patients who are referred with cardiac symptoms may be suffering from anxiety. It may be difficult for the physician to decide whether the symptoms are from anxiety or from a heart disorder.

Depression

Many patients may experience tiredness, weakness, fatigue, difficulties with breathing, and pressure in the chest. These individuals may be suffering from a depression and not from a heart disorder.

Patients who have had myocardial infarcts (heart attacks), may become depressed. They return to their cardiologist or family physician for further treatment complaining that they are not improving adequately because of their heart disorder. However, they do not have a problem with their recovery phase from their heart attack but are having difficulties with depressive symptoms. These patients continually complain about heart symptoms. The appropriate treatment is antidepressant medication.

Drugs prescribed for the treatment of heart disorders may cause depression. The patient may become weak, fatigued, irritable, and depressed. The appropriate treatment is to stop the drug and to prescribe another pill. Once the depression has established itself, antidepressants may be needed.

Sick Role

Some patients complain of heart symptoms such as weakness, tiredness, fatigue, difficulty breathing, rapid heart rate and chest pain because they need to be in a "sick role". This means that the person does not have a heart disorder but has a "need to be sick". You may ask: "Why does a person want to be sick?" There are many reasons. We can generally class these reasons under the concept of stress. If a person is experiencing family conflicts and cannot deal with these problems, it may be easier to simply become "sick". Financial problems may cause a person to take on a "sick role" so that they could receive sick benefits. Others have a great need to be wanted, liked and loved. They then develop a "sick role" to get sympathy.

Anniversary Reactions

Patients who have never had heart disease may develop symptoms of heart disease on the "anniversary" day of the person they lost from a heart attack. Individuals who had a heart attack, re-experience the heart attack one year later.

Psychiatric Symptoms Secondary to Cardiovascular Medications

More and more is understood about the powerful negative effects of drugs. Diuretics, used for the treatment of high blood pressure, often cause individuals to feel weak and washed out. These symptoms prevent patients from functioning socially, academically, or vocationally. Patients may be labelled "lazy".

Many drugs prescribed for the heart can be associated with decreased mental abilities, difficulties sleeping and weakness. Some patients become confused from pills used to treat the heart.

Psychiatric Drugs with Cardiac Symptoms

One of the commonest side effects of psychiatric drugs is to reduce blood pressure. Patients will complain: "I wonder what's wrong. Every time I stand up I get dizzy and feel as if I'm going to black out. This doesn't last long but I'm scared that something is wrong with my heart or blood pressure". When the patient's blood pressure is measured in a sitting or lying position it is usually normal and the patient has no symptoms. However, when the patient suddenly stands up, the blood pressure drops. This is especially true in older people. If the blood pressure drops a lot, the person may have a fainting spell, fall and be injured. Common injuries in the older person include fracture of the wrist or hip.

Stress

Stresses could lead to many different changes in heart activity. Studies of stress on the heart have shown that a variety of changes can occur including high blood pressure, rapid pulse rate, changes in the EKG and angina. Stress could lead to a heart attack and death.

Essential Hypertension

Hypertension is one of the most important factors in the development of heart disease and stroke. A blood pressure greater than 140 over 90 is considered a "high blood pressure". Stresses in an individual's life such as financial difficulties, business difficulties, and job pressures may lead to an increase in blood pressure.

Studies show that up to 50% of patients do not follow the recommended treatment for high blood pressure. It is not known why patients tend not to follow the recommended treatment. Treatment may include exercise, weight reduction, cessation of smoking, and the taking of pills. High blood pressure does not usually produce any symptoms. Therefore a person feels healthy. If the person feels healthy, he doesn't "feel a need" to take a pill. Therefore, high blood pressure is referred to as the "silent killer". It is important for the physician to develop a close relationship with the patient. In this trusting relationship, the physician should encourage and educate the patient to the importance of following the recommended medical treatment.

Coronary Artery Disease

It appears that certain personality types are more prone to coronary artery disease. A great deal of research has been done on the so-called "Type A" personality. "Type A" personalities are driven to working excessive hours. This personality type is different from the so-called "type B personality" who is more relaxed, less aggressive, unhurried and achieves goals in a relaxed manner.

"Type A" persons tend to have higher blood pressure, increased smoking, and increased serum cholesterol.

A common feature of myocardial infarcts (heart attacks) is denial. That is, the patient has the symptoms of the heart attack but often disregards these symptoms or says something like "it's only indigestion". This denial can be deadly! Most deaths from a heart attack occur within four hours of the onset of symptoms. If a person delays medical treatment, he reduces his chance for survival. It has been found that family and friends will often encourage medical care more quickly than the patient is willing to accept.

When a patient is hospitalized for a myocardial infarct (heart attack) a number of problems may develop. Stress is experienced because of the new surrounding of the hospital setting. Patients in these settings frequently suffer from insomnia (inability to sleep). After the third day, patients tend to get over the initial shock of their heart attack. They then begin to think about the long-term implications of the heart attack. This is when depression begins. Some patients reject the controls of the hospital setting and frequently lash out with hostility and anger. Patients may develop confusion because of the severity of their heart attack and the prescribed medications. This reminds me of a patient that I recently examined in the coronary care unit. The internist called me on an emergency basis. When I arrived at the coronary care unit, the patient was running away from the medical staff with a syringe stuck in his hip. The patient had a severe confusional reaction to the Demerol that was given for pain. The patient thought that he was being attacked by a number of gangsters. He ripped out his intravenous, pulled off his heart monitor, jumped out of the bed and tried to escape. When the medical staff tried to give him a sedative by injection he pulled away from the staff and ran down the hallway. This is quite a dramatic example of the important relationship between physical disease, medical treatment, and behavior.

Respiratory Disorders

Hyperventilation Syndrome

Emotions can severely affect our breathing. Our breathing rate can increase in rate and depth. That is, we can breathe more rapidly or more deeply. A wide variety of emotional experiences may lead to changes in our breathing. With stress, patients may overbreathe. This causes them to "blow off" too much carbon dioxide. When this happens, symptoms of lightheadedness, dizziness, faintness, tingling in the hands and feet, cramping in the hands and feet, and even fainting may occur. The rapid breathing is usually not recognized by the patient or those around him.

The hyperventilation syndrome could be stopped by having the patient rebreath into a large paper bag. If this disorder recurs frequently because of long-standing stress, psychological and psychiatric treatment will be required.

Bronchial Asthma

I think everyone knows that asthma is a disorder of the lungs. When the asthma worsens from certain items such as allergies or infections, wheezing increases. Emotions resulting from a variety of stresses may lead to attacks of asthma.

It is extremely important for patients, their families, and physicians to know that stresses may bring on asthmatic attacks. If everyone thinks that it is simply another allergy or viral infection, the true cause of the attack will not be examined. When a patient has recurrent asthmatic attacks, the physician should do an extensive interview to identify stress factors.

Asthmatic attacks are sometimes brought on by pleasant emotions. For example, a person may become very excited about a birthday party. In this state of excitement, an asthmatic attack may be initiated.

Some patients learn to "bring on" an asthmatic attack in special circumstances. Sometimes adolescents do not want to face a difficult teacher or an exam situation. They then develop symptoms of asthma and don't go to school to face the stress.

Endocrine Disorders

An overactive thyroid may lead to symptoms of anxiety such as increased heart rate, shakiness of the hands, excitability, and feelings of anxiety. Low activity of the thyroid (hypothyroidism) may lead to symptoms of depression. The patient feels weak, tired, unable to think and has feelings of depression.

Individuals who have a disorder of their adrenal glands or take steroids, such as Prednisone, may develop a wide variety of psychological symptoms such as depression, anger, agitated behavior or confusion.

There is a long-standing controversy whether menopause (the absence of a menstrual period for one year) leads to depression. Some physicians firmly believe that the lack of hormones leads to a depressive disorder. However, it is probably not the lack of hormones that causes the depression. When a woman reaches the age of fifty, a large number of personal changes occurs in her life. Grey hair, skin wrinkles, reduced sexual interaction with her husband and a change in the "mother" role produce feelings of depression. She realizes her children have grown up and do not need any "mothering". It is these changes in her life that make her aware of the aging process. It is these physical and life changes that cause the depressive disorder.

The Premenstrual Syndrome is a common physical and psychological disorder. It usually occurs in women just before their period. The patient feels a general sense of physical and psychological distress. The symptoms may be mild or incapacitating. Emotional characteristics consist of anxiety, tensional feelings, depression, irritability, inability to control emotions, weakness, fatigue, extreme sensitivity to the comments of others, and crying spells. These symptoms usually disappear when the period begins.

With stress, menses may decrease or stop.

Hypoglycemia (low blood sugar) can lead to a variety of symptoms including weakness, tiredness, difficulties with thinking, fatigue, irritability, anger and restlessness.

Hyperglycemia (high blood sugar) may develop in the diabetic patient and can lead to a wide variety of psychological symptoms including difficulties with thinking, tiredness, sleepiness, and coma. Diabetics may be unable to deal with the stresses of life, and therefore overeat, take in excessive amounts of sweets, or purposely take less or no insulin.

I have only covered a few of the hormonal problems that can lead to psychological problems.

Central Nervous System Disorders

Convulsions

As you know, convulsions or epilepsy is the result of uncontrolled electrical activity within the brain. Some epileptics have a difficult time adapting to the stresses of life and choose not to take their medications. This causes them to have recurrent convulsions as they prefer remaining in the "sick role".

Medications given to control convulsions can lead to a wide variety of psychological symptoms such as tiredness, difficulties with thinking, difficulties with motivation, and a reduced ability to cope with the activities of daily living.

Some patients with a severe disorder of epilepsy seem to develop an "epileptic personality". This means that these individuals tend to have an inability to motivate themselves to attain academically or vocationally, tend to disregard personal hygiene, have difficulty expressing emotions, and may be unable to function independently in life. These individuals often need a lot of social assistance.

Some patients who do not have epilepsy may "act" as though they did have epilepsy. The patient may fall, roll his eyes up, breathe heavily, and move arms and legs. Sometimes it is very difficult to decide whether a person is having a true convulsion or is "acting out" a convulsion. One of the reasons for this difficulty of separating the real from the unreal convulsion is that it is difficult to get an EEG (electroencephalogram) at the moment the convulsion is occurring.

Here is an example of this type of patient. A patient was referred to me one year ago because of a long-standing depressive disorder. She was also treated for epilepsy for the last ten years. She was placed on many different types of antiepileptic drugs. She seemed to continue having "minor seizures". I hospitalized the patient to treat her depression. I consulted another neurologist to help me with the treatment of the patient's epilepsy while she was in hospital. The consulting neurologist requested another EEG. During the EEG, the patient had one of her "minor seizures". She came back to the ward and reported to me that she continues to be concerned about her seizures as she had another seizure during the EEG. The neurologist reviewed the EEG and could not find any abnormality. The diagnosis was quite clear. When the patient had a worsening of her depressive symptoms, she developed a reduced ability to cope with the stresses at her job. She then developed a sense of stress and the "minor seizures" recurred. The depression was treated, the anti-convulsants stopped, and the patient did well.

Headaches

I hate to tell you that "I get a headache when I have to treat a patient with headaches." Why do I get a headache? Well, headaches are one of the commonest complaints that physicians confront. Also, it is difficult to identify the cause of the headaches. Further, headaches may be long-standing and generally unresponsive to treatment. In other words, it is a "headache" to investigate the headache and it is a "headache" to treat the headache.

Magazines, radio and television advertise headache pills. It is quite obvious from this advertising that headache pills are "big business".

Most headaches are very easy to diagnose and treat. However, some headaches are difficult to deal with, both for the patient and the physician. Personal enjoyment, family relationships, social relationships, studying ability and work efficiency are severely affected by the headache. Headache sufferers are always looking for relief.

If anyone should come up with a good answer to our problem of headaches, he should surely receive the Nobel Prize and make bundles of money.

A detailed discussion on headaches would involve many chapters. I will restrict my discussion to cover only a few aspects of headache evaluation and treatment.

Classification of Headaches

Headaches due to specific disease states
1. Infections inside the skull - meningitis encephalitis;
2. tumors;
3. abnormalities of the blood vessels - e.g. subdural hematoma;
4. injury; and,
5. vascular headaches (migraine).

Headaches with no specific cause.

One of the commonest complaints to a family physician by a patient is headache. It is estimated that approximately 10% of patients visiting family doctors will complain of headaches as their major symptoms. Headache is the commonest reason that a patient gets referred to a neurologist.

Patients are often extremely concerned about their headache for two reasons. They are concerned because it may be annoying, and, if severe enough, debilitating. Secondly, the patient is concerned because they fear an underlying medical disorder such as a brain tumor.

The family physician usually takes a history and does a physical examination of the patient. Some laboratory testing is ordered. If no physical disorder is noted, commonly used drugs such as Tylenol, Aspirin and Advil may be tried. Some family doctors may order other drugs on a trial basis. If the patient does not improve, a neurologist is consulted. The neurologist re-examines the patient with a complete history (medical questions which are asked by a physician), physical examination, an EEG (electroencephalogram - this refers to a test where electrodes are placed on different parts of the skull and the electrical waves of the brain are studied), and C.T. scan (computer assisted tomography of the head - this is a special type of x-ray of the head that produces a "picture" of the brain and skull). With the examinations by the family doctor and neurologist, including the specialized tests, the patients may be then given a specific diagnosis such as meningitis, encephalitis, subdural hematoma, tumor, etc. In fact, very few headache patients have identifiable abnormalities of the brain. Most of the headaches are of an "unknown origin" or "unknown cause".

Let me state this again. After the family physician and his consultants examine the patient and order a number of specialized tests, rarely is a specific diagnosis made. The vast majority of headaches are of "unknown origin". Simply put, we cannot find a cause for most headaches.

Most headaches respond to some of the well-known drugs such as Aspirin, Tylenol, and Ibuprofin (Advil, Motrin). If no physical disorder is found, and the headache is successfully treated with Tylenol, aspirin, or Ibuprofin, no further investigation or treatment is needed. Usually the patient and physician are happy at this point.

Unfortunately, some patients have chronic (long-standing) headaches that are annoying or incapacitating. By incapacitating, I mean that the person may be unable to study, work or socialize. It is this person that feels frustrated with the medical profession and, the medical profession feels frustrated with the patient.

I will now outline a few commonsense approaches to assist you with your headache. Caffeine is found in many products such as coffee, colas, hot chocolate drinks, and chocolates. Caffeine and caffeine products are widely used and addictive. A large number of headaches are caused by caffeine. I know a neurologist who refuses to accept a patient in referral for the evaluation of headache if the patient uses caffeine or caffeine products. This neurologist says that so many headaches are caused by caffeine that we are costing the medical health care system too much money examining these individuals. Simply discontinuing the caffeine use can lead to a solution to the headache.

Let's talk about another common addictive drug in our society. Thirty percent of the adult population smokes. A large number of people develop headaches from the nicotine. It is extremely difficult for a smoker to become a non-smoker. It is therefore difficult to decide whether the headache may be caused by nicotine. This becomes a problem because many patients will suffer from nicotine headaches, demand consultation, tests and medications. Patients may become angry with the medical profession for not "curing their headaches".

There are many chemicals that can cause headaches eg. monosodium glutamate. Tyramine-containing foods such as aged cheeses and red wine may cause headaches.

There are many foods and chemicals that can produce headaches. The question then arises, "how do I know whether some thing I am drinking or eating is causing my headaches?" This could be a complex question. At the same time, it can be a simple question. Let's talk for moment about the problem of food allergies in babies and young children. It is well established that babies and young children could suffer from a wide variety of food allergies. Almost any food can produce the allergic response in a child. The pediatrician may recommend that certain common foods such as nuts are excluded from the diet. If the allergic symptoms disappear, then these foods could be slowly added to the diet - one at a time. This same kind of approach could apply to the problem of headaches. That is, discontinuing the use of caffeine, nicotine, alcohol, chocolate and cheeses may lead to the disappearance of the headache.

However, what happens when the pediatrician recommends that certain foods be discontinued but the allergy continues. The answer is a bit more complex but still readily available. The pediatrician places the child on a very strict diet of only a few food products. Then, very slowly, one food product is added every one or two weeks. What I am going to say at this point is not written in any neurological or psychiatrict textbook that I know. I feel somewhat hesitant about giving this recommendation as it may be received with criticism by others in the medical profession. However, I have seen this approach work in a number of cases and I think that it is worth stating. Some of my patients had read a book about food allergies causing headaches. The patients went on a very strict diet of rice for one week. They added one food or drink every ten days. If they were free of symptoms, they now continued this food as a regular part of their diet. If the headache returned, they would stop that food item and ten days later add another food product. Please remember that this is not an established treatment program but one that I have seen work.

Probably the commonest cause of headaches is stress. I would recommend that you read the chapters on the treatment of depression, anxiety and stress.

I have several suggestions for the individual who has chronic (long standing) headaches for whom there is no relief. I would recommend the following outline:

Family doctor — Please stay with your family doctor. Do not doctor shop. If you have trusted your family doctor in the past, continue trusting him at this difficult point in your life. Stay with him. Let him continue guiding you. Verbalize to him that you will stick with him even though you have not had a resolution of your headaches. Ask him whether he would be willing to continue assisting you in whatever way he could. Try and maintain a trusting relationship.

Consultants — The family physician may refer you to a neurologist, internist and psychiatrist. Because you have a symptom for which no organic cause can be found, your family doctor will be asking for help from specialists. Sometimes the specialist will undertake to treat you. On other occasions, the specialist will send a letter to your family doctor who will then guide you through the new treatment program.

Life style — Please try and help yourself. Read about headaches. Know that there are many factors that can cause headaches. Headaches almost never occur because of one single factor. For example, hard work may lead to headaches. However, it is rare that only the hard work leads to headaches. It is often the stress plus the hard work. This may not even be enough. It may be the stress, hard work, and the lack of sleep. That may not be enough to produce the headache. It may be the stress, hard work, lack of sleep, and coffee that causes the headache.

Remove items from your diet such as caffeine, nicotine, chocolate, and alcohol. Don't simply exclude something for one day and say "nothing helps". When you try something like discontinuing caffeine, carry on this way for several weeks. Be intelligent. Be aware. Be a detective. Try and detect what food items or life style activity leads to more headaches. Please be sure that you check your life style and examine how you are doing for things such as rest, recreation, leisure, and adequate sleep. In other words, reduce the stress on your body. One of my patients complained bitterly about his headache. I thought that he was not getting enough sleep and suggested that he go to bed at 10:00 p.m. as he always awakened at 6:00 a.m. He looked at me in disbelief. How could I, his physician, ask him to go to bed at 10:00 p.m. — like a child? My answer was the same that I give to all my patients. The answer goes something like this "I know that you are suffering a lot. I think this approach to treatment would be helpful. You must make the final decision whether you are going to try this type of treatment. It is my job to evaluate and recommend but it is your job to decide." In fact, it was the lack of sleep that was the major cause of the headache.

Use the usual drugs such as Aspirin, Tylenol and Ibuprofin. Remember that no drug is totally safe. Every drug has a potential for side effects. Know these side effects and study them in yourself to see whether they may be causing you harm.

Trial and error — This is an approach that we do not teach properly in our medical schools. This is a good approach but may be frowned upon by some physicians. It appears that physicians are trained to look intensively for a specific cause of a disorder such as headache and then to treat that particular disorder. For example, if a patient presents with headaches and a C.T. Scan reveals a subdural hematoma, then the physician is extremely pleased with himself for finding the disorder. However, if the physician cannot find the specific cause for headache, then he tends to blame the patient for being "neurotic" (whatever that means).

What do I mean by trial and error? This refers to the use of drugs on a trial basis to "see if it helps". There is no crystal ball that the physician can look into and say "Ah, yah, verrry, goood. I zee!" Principles of introducing a drug include: (1) teaching the patient about the drug, (2) giving the patient an information sheet on the drug, (3) starting with very small dosages initially, (4) building progressively to higher dosages, (5) taking a blood sample to measure the level of the medication in the system, and (6) following up (repeat visits) to see whether the headache improves or side effects develop.

The drugs that I am most acquainted with which may be helpful in the treatment of headaches are obviously the drugs used in psychiatry. These drugs are:

1. Anti-anxiety agents
2. Antidepressants
3. Antipsychotics
4. Miscellaneous - Lithium Carbonate, Tegretol, Inderol, Dilantin
5. Addictive Drugs. PLEASE BEWARE!

> It just breaks my heart to see wonderful family members, friends, and patients get severely addicted to "pain killers". The commonest addictive drug that is prescribed is the "pain killer". These drugs include sedatives such as the barbiturates (Fiorinal), and the Opiates such as Codeine, Demerol, and Morphine. Yes, these medications can give short term relief. These medications could be effective. However, they are the most addictive drugs that we have in medicine. So you think you won't get addicted! Forget it! You will become addicted! BEWARE! Please read the section in this book on Addictions.
>
> Let me give you an example of what I mean by addiction. Two years ago a family doctor referred Mrs. J. to me because she was depressed. He told me that she could not get out of bed in the morning, was unable to prepare a meal for her family, never left the house, and no longer talked to her husband and children. The patient was admitted to hospital. A review of the patient's history revealed that she was perfectly well until one year prior to hospitalization. She worked, prided herself in maintaining her house spotless, enjoyed organizing the children and attending their school and extra-curricular activities, and was well liked in her community. However, she had headaches for a number of years and "shopped" from doctor to doctor seeking some solution to her headaches. She eventually obtained "pain killers" to which she became addicted and now she was basically "drugged out". The patient was withdrawn from her drugs. She improved and returned to her previous life style.

CHAPTER 7

Post-Traumatic Stress Disorder

POST-TRAUMATIC STRESS DISORDER

The "post traumatic stress disorder" will be a very popular topic over the next few years. This disorder has become popular in psychiatric circles and will soon become popular in general. This disorder has been known by several names for the last century. However, it is only recently gaining popularity as a diagnosis.

In World War I, a number of veterans were noted to be suffering from a disorder which was called "shell shock". People who had suffered through natural catastophes such as earthquakes or airplane crashes, often suffered certain mental symptoms. Individuals who suffered severe traumatic experiences such as rape were noted to have major changes in their mental state.

Diagnostic Criteria

A person is said to be suffering from a "post-traumatic stress disorder" if the following has occurred:

a) the person has experienced an unusually stressful experience such as an automobile accident, assault, rape, etc.

b) The traumatic event is then re-experienced in the following ways:
   1. recurrently thinking about the experience.
   2. frequent dreams about the experience.
   3. experiencing psychological distress when something or some situation reminds the person of the experience such as the anniversary (re-experiencing the anguish of a child's death one year later).

c) A constant attempt at avoiding all situations that will remind the person of the experience.

d) Experiencing a sense of generalized numbness and unresponsiveness to other life situations. These items are experienced as:
1. the person constantly tries to avoid thinking about the situation.
2. the individual attempts to avoid anything that reminds him of the situation.
3. a tendency to forget the event such as the rape.
4. a decreased interest in daily living. Adults may choose to withdraw and simply listen to records or watch television. Children may withdraw from their parents and choose not to talk.
5. The person may develop a feeling of aloneness or detachment or withdrawal from others. The person "pulls away" from others.
6. The person may have a decreased ability to feel emotions. A person who was deeply in love cannot feel the love emotions and cannot express the emotions of love.
7. The person feels a sense of hopelessness. There is a feeling that nothing will turn out well in the future. There is a feeling everything will go wrong in the future.

e) There is an increased sense of arousal as experienced by the following:
1. inability to fall asleep.
2. outbursts of anger.
3. difficulty concentrating.
4. excessive excitability. The person may jump when the phone rings or get upset if the door slams.
5. anxiety symptoms that recur when something reminds the person of the trauma. For example, if a woman is watching television and observes a rape scene, she may experience all the anxiety and tension that she had at the time of the actual rape.

Mild and Severe Stressors

Stresses (traumatic events) can vary in duration and severity. One of my patients was an air traffic controller. He always experienced stress on the job. He knew that it was a "high stress job". He continued at the job for 20 years. However, the many emergency situations and the "near misses" continued to produce excessive stress. Eventually, his whole life became consumed with his work and he developed all the symptoms that are described above. In this case, he had many mild stresses for a long period of time. He was diagnosed as suffering from a "post-traumatic stress disorder".

The stress could be very powerful as in a military setting where an individual witnesses his buddy killed. In this case, the stress situation is extreme.

Stresses seem to be experienced more severely when a large number of people are involved such as in airplane crashes or tornados.

Stresses become more traumatic when an individual or group of individuals is caught "off guard". In other words, if individuals had a chance to plan for the stress, less suffering is experienced.

A stressor seems to be more traumatic if there is intentional cruelty or inhumanity such as in the German death camps during World War II. Studies of Jewish survivors from these camps revealed many psychological problems that were described above. It seems that people react more severely to the stress situation if they feel trapped, cornered and have no opportunity to escape or fight back.

It seems that some people are much more resistant to the effects of stress. Others seem to be very sensitive to stresses. I don't think that this should surprise anyone. Blond haired individuals are much more sensitive to the sun and more easily burned. Dark skinned individuals can tolerate a great deal of hot sun without burning. Some individuals need only about 5 hours of sleep each night. Other individuals must have 8 hours of sleep. I have given these two examples only to remind you that we are all different. In some respects, we are stronger than other individuals. In other respects, we are weaker than other individuals. Similarly, psychologically some of us can tolerate a great deal of severe stress. Others seem to react even to small amounts of stress.

It appears that the very young and very old can cope less well with severe stresses. Children who have experienced burn injuries, very commonly show symptoms of the post-traumatic stress disorder. Adults with similar burn injuries suffer less.

Also, it appears that some individuals enjoy playing the sick role. They like the attention that they receive when they are "sick".

It appears that individuals who have less support from close family and friends are more sensitive to stress and develop the post-traumatic stress disorder. For example, individuals who are single, divorced or widowed do less well with stress.

Let's look at a short interview of a patient that I had in my office. Bob is 55 years of age and was referred to me because of emotional problems that he developed after a fire destroyed his home. As you read the interview, refer to the items listed at the beginning of this topic. Here is part of the interview.

Doctor: "I have now seen you a few times Bob. How are things going?"

Bob: "I can't seem to get over that fire we had six months ago. It keeps going through my mind again, and again. I can't seem to get rid of the thoughts about the fire. Even with tranquilizers, I can't sleep properly. I still have nightmares. At least I get some sleep now. The nightmares are all the same. They are about the damn fire. I still get up in the middle of the night yelling to my family to get out of the house. The part that bothers me most is about my son. You remember how I told you that the whole family got out of the house except my 18 year old. We all thought that he was trapped in the bottom level. I remember the whole family shouting and screaming. I remember how the family was trying to prevent me from running back into the house to save him. I remember how I attacked the door and knocked it open and flames came shooting at me. I got burned up quite a lot."

Doctor: "Your son is okay?"

Bob: "Yes, he's okay. As I told you, he slept over at a friend's place that night. We didn't know that. We thought he just came home late at night and went to sleep downstairs. These nightmares are incredible. I wouldn't mind if I just simply had the nightmares and suffered them myself. But sometimes I react to these nightmares as though I were re-living that fire. That's when I jump out of bed and start screaming for everybody to get out of the house. You can imagine how upset everybody else gets when I'm raving mad in the middle of the night. My family is pretty good. They awaken and calm me down. A couple of times my wife had to slap me in the face to wake me out of the dream."

Doctor: "Have you been able to get back to work yet? You told me that you had many jobs to do. How's work going?"

Bob: "I still haven't returned to work. I'm not sure why. I seem to have lost interest. Nothing makes a lot of sense anymore. I used to get up at 5:00 in the morning and work till late at night. All of a sudden that doesn't matter anymore. I seem to have lost my spark. I've lost my interest. In fact, nothing seems to affect me as it did before. I get enjoyment from my little grandchildren but I don't seem to be as silly as before. I'm not telling jokes like I used to. I used to be the center of attention at a party. I rarely go to parties now."

Doctor: "You had concentration problems a number of weeks ago."

Bob: "I'm doing a bit better. I can read the paper now. But I can't seem to sit at anything for very long. I seem to have become somewhat irritable and restless. I can't put my mind to anything for a long period anymore. But don't worry doc, I'm doing better."

Doctor: "You used to avoid listening to the radio and watching television."

Bob: "That's getting better, too. I'm not so scared about looking at the television or listening to the radio. I used to get so upset when I would see something about fires or accidents. I still do. However, I've learned to close my ears or close the radio quickly if there is something about fires. I can't look at a paper where it shows a picture of a fire. I just try and avoid everything that will remind me of that stupid situation."

Let's analyze this discussion. I think we would all agree that to live through a house fire would be a very traumatic experience. Look at the first part of the interview and notice how Bob talks about thinking about the fire frequently, having nightmares, and having difficulties with sleep. Bob goes on to talk about his feelings of numbness and detachment. He talks about decreased energy and decreased emotions. He can't seem to get going. This is another major characteristic of the post-traumatic stress disorder. He also talks about his difficulties in concentrating. He is unable to watch a television program where there is a fire because it reminds him of his terrifying experience. He averts his eyes and puts the paper down when there is an article or picture about a fire. He has tried to close off his life so that he does not get reminded of these situations. Individuals who go through the post-traumatic stress disorder may develop severe symptoms of anxiety or depression. Some individuals cannot tolerate this experience and begin using alcohol, prescription drugs such as minor tranquilizers and over the counter drugs such as 222's (aspirin and codeine). Sometimes the post-traumatic stress disorder leads to so many difficulties with depression, anxiety and alcohol use that family relationships may become strained. Conflicts may develop between husband and wife. Problems in the family seem to become augmented. Conflict becomes more severe. Work may be affected and jobs may be lost.

Treatment

Treatment is directed at removing symptoms such as insomnia, nightmares, depression and anxiety. Antidepressants and minor tranquilizers are useful.

One of the most important treatment approaches is to educate the patient about his disorder. The patient must be told that he is suffering from a post-traumatic stress disorder. He must be educated as to the relationship of stress and symptoms. He should be given reading materials to understand the nature of this disorder. Interviews should be held with the family so that each member of the family can understand the problem. In most cases, patients improve with time. In the few patients where there is no improvement, intensive psychotherapy may be necessary.

CHAPTER 8

Personality Disorders

PERSONALITY DISORDERS

More has been written on the subject of "personality" than on any other field in psychology. With the volumes of books about "personality" one would think that the subject is fairly well understood. Unfortunately, this is not the case. We would all agree that everyone has "a personality", some distinctive way of responding, thinking and feeling. However, scientists disagree on how to differentiate people reliably on characteristics or traits that comprise the individual. The reason for the problem of classification by personality traits is that other terms like "character" or "temperament" become confused with "personality". The average person thinks largely about "character flaws" or "temperament" of a child or adult, not personality type. After centuries of research, scientists still disagree on typing or categorizing people on the basis of personality traits. Scientists have trouble differentiating between personality, character or temperament, yet many attempt to do so. To resolve the theoretical problems in this chapter is not possible. This introduction is only to suggest that disagreements on personality lead to problems in identifying disorders of personality. Nevertheless, the reader is encouraged to accept a few common definitions and descriptions, with the proviso that complex problems of personality and their amelioration have few simple answers.

What Is Personality?

Most scientists agree on a basic, general definition that "personality" or "character" traits are deeply engrained, internal and external patterns of adjustment to life. Maxmen (1986) draws the parallel between physical appearance and personality in that both can be adjusted to some degree, they remain essentially the same throughout one's life. Thus, personality represents a reasonably consistent and persistent way a person thinks, acts, feels, copes and reacts to life's demands. This personality is the sum total of what we are, a pattern set genetically, as well as shaped through life by one's environment. Some features of personality may be more adaptive than others, depending on the situations. When the personality traits become inflexible, maladaptive and impair work, home and social life, or cause personal distress, a personality disorder is said to exist. Personality traits that are common to all people are indeed rare! However, scientists do agree that traits such as introversion, extraversion, neuroticism, active vs. passive, dependent vs. independent, ambivalent vs. detached are useful ways on which to differentiate people. These traits are usually found in varying combinations and result in a consistent pattern of responding or adjusting to life.

Personality, Character and Temperament

We allude to these terms in the introduction of this chapter as being used interchangeably by most people. To illustrate the complexity of "personality", a brief digression is needed to differentiate these terms."Personality" has already been defined. "Character" has come to mean those personal qualities of the individual with respect to values and customs of society, the moral or social dimensions of personality. Thus, one can hear others talking about an "honest character" or a "reliable character", phrases suggesting values and social customs. On the other hand, "temperament" is usually seen as referring to a person's mood and energy-level. People frequently are heard to comment on one's "quick temper" or "impulsive temperament". "Temperament" has come to signify biologically-based dispositions, genetically determined ways to respond to stimulation in particular ways. Put them all together and you have "a personality", a global, integrated, holistic way of adjusting and reacting to one's world. Although scientists must differentiate these terms and do, for our purpose we may use these words interchangeably. Keep in mind that "temperament" seems to reflect more a given biological predisposition. "Character", the learned social/moral customs, and "personality" includes those qualities of the person that are both inherited and learned.

Can Personality Change?

Change is an inevitable process of living. Children change into adults, adults grow through changes in the life process. When it comes to personality traits such as dependency, aggression, introversion, extraversion or character types such as extroverted-thinker, introverted-intuitive, to name a few, people seem to have less confidence in the question of changing one's personality. To illustrate, here are some examples of people wishing to change some personality traits that they find maladaptive:

"I'm 29 years old...through the years I've found things about myself which I wasn't pleased with or which affected my relationships with others. I've really worked to change these things, to be a better person...I often feel frustrated and angry with different areas of my life that I have no control over. At work I am conscientious and thorough. I try always to do good work...It bothers me to see a lot of the staff start late...they don't seem to care about the work they do...I get frustrated when I have to correct or redo someone elses work because it's done sloppy...I know it's not my responsibility or my business how other people are working. I should only be concerned about myself. Still it bothers me...I would like to be easy going...and this I want for my whole life...I think I need to change from an "A" type to "B" type personality. Any hope?"

"...I was listening to your talk on stress and Type A personalities...many of the things you were speaking of I could apply to myself. The one problem I find most stressful is being out for dinner or with friends and trying to relax, I always feel that I should be doing something else or that I've forgotten something. My mind is racing; I can't seem to concentrate on what is being said - I come across sounding "spaced out" or stupid, and people probably think I have no interest...I never considered, until today, that my problems could be categorized and dealt with as a whole..."

"...You may think that my "problem" is silly or trivial, but to me it is of real concern...Some people are high-strung, however, I am the complete opposite...low strung, if there is such a thing. I never get excited, scared, worried, angry, frustrated, etc...I am nothing short of an ice cube. This may make some people jealous, but I would frankly prefer to be an emotional/demonstrative kind of person. Many people think I am boring and some even think that I am shy (which I am not) simply because I seldom, if ever, show any emotions. Over the years, I have often been put in charge over people (usually children)...Because I am so relaxed, calm, and easy-going, they get away with everything short of murder...things that they should not get away with...."

Can these people really change their personality traits to ones more suited to their environment? Can a conscientious, compulsive person become more relaxed and easy-going? Can one change from a Type "A" to a Type "B" personality? Can an excitable, anxious person become more intuitive and thoughtful? This question is central to this chapter, because if personality traits are products of genetics, a biochemical, biological-neurological predisposition, then change would indeed be believed to be difficult, if not impossible.

Scientists are divided on this issue. The doctrine of "personality stability" has been accepted for at least a century. In 1887, William James, the first president of the American Psychological Association, stated that by the age of 30 the character has "set like plastic" and will never soften again. More recent writings suggest that one's personality is set by early adolescence, if not sooner. Aggressive children become aggressive adults. Self-defeating adolescents become self-defeating adults. Cheerful children become cheerful adults. Does nothing really change? Personality theorists, furthermore, point to people who lived and acted as Hippies in the early 70's but who now are successful business people on Wall Street. Did they really change?

On the other hand, the counter-argument to the stability or instability of the personality is offered by parents who see a neat, organized, cheerful, successful student turn into an angry, resentful, arrogant runaway, throwing aside all family values! Other examples abound. Dr. Richard Alpert, a professor at Harvard, moved to India to follow his interest in the effects of drugs on perception and personality. He returned to the USA as Bala Ram Das, a long-bearded mystic with a flowing white robe. Did he really change?

There is a body of literature that suggests that since there seems to be little consistency in human behavior, change is inevitable. The question is what really changes? Gail Sheehy, in her book *The Seasons of a Man's Life*, described life as a process of self-examination and transition. She argues convincingly that people "transform" as they age. Sheehy's work was based on the highly respected work of Yale's Dr. Daniel Levinson. Prominent personality theorists such as Carl Jung, Erik Erikson and more recently Jerome Kagen support the idea that people re-shape their self as they grow older, moving from stage to stage, phase to phase.

These writers influenced by a deterministic, biological philosophy argue that the core traits such as introversion, extraversion, neuroticism, etc. do not change. What changes is the behavior, the outward response to a specific situation. Nervous system response to inner and outer stimuli remains essentially the same. The ease or difficulty of conditioning, the rate of speed of excitation or extinction of the nervous system remains essentially the same throughout life. Determinists argue, therefore, that neurotics, who are quickly excited, are likely to remain impulsive, anxious and continue complaining. They just complain about different problems as they grow older!

A more blended and optimistic view of change is offered by scientists who hold an Interactionist view. Interactional psychologists and psychiatrists hold that genetics and environment, nature and nurture influence each other. One changes the other and both are very important. Through processes of living, family and other life circumstances, the genetic code is slowly changed over many generations. The code, as passed on the grand-parents and parents to their offspring, alters with each generation. Not only does the code change, but also the traits represented in the code. Thus, pre-determination, although partly true, is not a complete answer. Social environment, family upbringing, experiences of life, repeated exposure to stimuli can change not only the code, but the functional, behavioral responses as well.

This interactional view is described in detail by Dr. Theodore Millon, whose writings have strongly influenced current psychologists and psychiatrists. Millon recognizes the powerful influence of genetics, but gives the individual credit for adapting to life as circumstances demand. Whereas it is true that some people have little adaptive flexibility, others do not. Those who do not accept opportunities for learning new and adaptive behaviours will suffer stress. Their inflexible and rigid stance will eventually cause impairment in work, home and family situations. These people who do not adapt or change their behaviours as demanded by the situation will suffer subjective distress. Although capable of coping from day to day, their life is full of turmoil, frustration, and unhappiness. Others who are more flexible, who adapt more easily, who change habitual ways of responding as the situation demands will have a reasonably happy, stress-free life. Yes, change is possible for everyone. Core personality traits alter over generations. The traits that you have been given remain with you, but your children may receive a slightly altered genetic code. Yet even while these core traits are relatively fixed in you, you can learn to change your habitual way of responding to inner as well as outer stimuli. You can learn to adjust and adapt to the circumstances in your pathway.

The fact is that life is change. We change through life cycles. Some people get stuck-in-a-rut, stuck in a phase of life. Habits are hard to break but they can be altered. If other people around you change as circumstance demands, and you do not, conflict is likely to result. We need to keep our life in balance with the demands of our age and the demands of our environment. Change is a relative concept. It is always change relative to something or someone else. You can change customs, values, beliefs. You can change goals. You can change a low self-confidence. You can hold a more realistic appraisal of self. The brain-mind is a remarkably flexible unit. The genetic code is there to provide us with the needed stability and all the necessary "programs" needed for evolutionary survival. However, that code can be influenced.

Personality, your personality, is simply your usual way of responding. Each person is different and will respond differently. It is when your personality traits cause significant impairment in social or occupational functioning that they constitute a personality disorder.

Personality Disorders

Since each person has a unique personality code and different circumstances in which to develop that code, each person is said to have an individual personality structure or style. Every day new evidence is found suggesting that people can be grouped according to their personality traits. Since there are so many ways of organizing the personality, this chapter will rely on the work of Dr. Theodore Millon, referred to earlier, as a way of describing personalities and personality disorders. Not all disorders of personality will be discussed. Some readers may wish to consult Millon's book, *Disorders of Personality* (1981). It is our intention only to describe the traits giving rise to a personality type, and when these traits remain inflexible and unadaptive, do they give rise to a possible "disorder". Nevertheless, readers may find themselves identifying with one or several of the descriptions of "disorders" that follow. Remember that everyone has "a personality", everyone is inflexible and maladaptive from time to time. It is believed that over 30 per cent of the population feel subjective distress significant enough to be labelled having a "personality disorder". It is also known that very few of these individuals, although suffering from a "personality disorder", actually seek treatment. The reason being that people see the problem merely as a quirk in their personality, a "bad gene", something to live with but not do anything about. It is our belief that when the problems keep you from an adaptive and happy life, help should be sought.

Many of the features characteristic of various personality disorders may be seen as part of another mental disorder, such as major depression. The diagnosis of personality disorder is made only when the problems are long-term and not limited only to such times when one may experience a discrete mental disorder of some other kind. By definition, personality disorders may begin in early childhood, but most are recognized in adult life. Individuals with personality disorders rarely require hospitalization unless theirs is a concomitant major mental disorder.

Some personality disorders have been studied more extensively than others, some are more severe than others. By and large, there is great variability in the detail with which the various personality disorders have been described. Typically the disorders fall into three major groups. The first group includes those personality disorders with people who are considered odd or eccentric. Included in this group are the paranoid, schizoid and schizotypal personality disorders. The second group are defined by those individuals who appear emotional, dramatic and erratic. Disorders in this group include the histrionic, the narcissistic, antisocial and borderline. The final group of personality disorders are found in those people who are anxious, fearful and neurotic. This group includes the avoidant, dependent, compulsive and passive-aggressive personality disorders.

This style of clustering the personality disorders is based on theory and severity of the problem. For example, mild disorders are thought to include the histrionic and dependent, whereas severe disorders include the paranoid and schizotypal. The latter two types have symptoms similar to the schizophrenic cluster. In most cases, very little if any information on the personality disorder types is found with respect to predisposing factors, prevalence, sex ratio and familial pattern. Although treatment implications will be mentioned, more research is needed to verify that any particular mode or form of therapy is more useful than others. What follows, then, is a brief discussion of a selected number of personality disorders. It is our hope that as you read each description you will begin to see a pattern of responding similar to your own life. The extent to which you identify with a particular disorder is dependent not just on your own unique personality pattern but the way you have been able to adjust to it. Thus, you may identify with the compulsive type, but find it very adaptive to your work and home. Many women may see themselves as dependent or histrionic, but feel no subjective distress over the matter. However, if your personality traits and resulting thoughts, feelings and behaviors interfere significantly with your life, you should consider consultation with a psychologist or psychiatrist. The descriptions of personality disorder types that follow are based on listener request, rather than on any theoretical classification or level of severity of the problem.

Passive-Aggressive Personality

Passive-aggressive refers to an indirect resistance to a demand for adequate performance. In passive-aggression one resists the demands of others especially in social situations and at work. The resistance is thought to be aggression in disguise and may be seen as stubbornness or ineffectuality. Often, people who are late for appointments or who do not return phone calls or letters, people who procrastinate or seem to forget are responding in a passive-aggressive way. Most of the time passive-aggression is expressed as resentment in non-assertive ways. There is a resistance to authority demands. In children passive-aggression is seen in behaviors such as resisting bedtime, not eating, temper tantrums, not doing homework, forgetting things, whining, name-calling, dawdling, messiness, not following directions, demanding freedom and teasing. It is a way of controlling others without assuming responsibility for their own anger or feelings. Now it is true that each one of us develops a way of dealing with life's challenges, a style of relating. Some people are overly dependent while others challenge and aggress. Some people are shy and avoid people while others are more concerned with appearance. The passive-aggressive way of expression suggests a concern about self-esteem, about ego. There is said to be plenty of anger inside. Passive-aggressive people can be very indecisive, erratic, oppositional. They are not predictable - you never know how they'll act or what they are thinking. They can be quiet, seemingly cooperative, go along with plans but when you count on them they just don't seem to show up. They are sensitive people who do not want to fight. Instead, they will try almost anything to control their world by withdrawing or by not doing things you think need to be done.

People all over this world have used the passive-aggressive style from time to time. The question is often asked, "How does this style come about? What creates it?" There are a number of answers to these questions. First of all, it is said that contradictory parental messages produce a style of personality that is called passive-aggressive. Children do not know which way to turn or which way to respond to a parent's contradictory message and hence they act out on some occasions and withdraw on other occasions. Secondly, people who are pessimistic in their outlook also develop this style. Pessimistic people harbour plenty of fear inside and hence they are never sure how to act. Consequently, they tend to withdraw on some occasions and act out their aggression in passive ways. Thirdly, people with lots of guilt inside also act in this fashion. The guilt itself is pro-

duced by not meeting the requirements and standards of others. To allay their own fear and guilt, these people tend to be hesitant in their approach to life and withdraw. When they do act, they act out strongly and aggressively. Fourthly, people with low self-esteem also tend to develop the passive-aggressive style. The low self-esteem creates the lack of confidence in how they should respond. Hence, the passive-aggressive style suits them since they can avoid doing a number of responsible behaviors so that others will not know whether they can or cannot accomplish the things that have been asked of them. Fifthly, people who have experienced many disappointments or who are disillusioned also tend to develop this style. These individuals cannot trust willingly or be open about their feelings. Their disappointments have led them to a path of withdrawal. However, since these disappointments can also lead to storing up feelings of resentment and anger, they can, on occasion, act aggressively.

There have been other reasons cited for the passive-aggressive style. People who despise themselves for being so dependent, people who react to things with anxiety, immature people or irrational people also develop this very same style. When it is used often, it can become a personality disorder and needs treatment.

The passive-aggressive style may be a very fruitful way to cope with life. We are aggressive as a nation and as a people. We stand up for ourselves, we fight, we push ourselves ahead of others and press for our rights. We love to see aggressive hockey and sales people are told to be passively aggressive in their approach. People love excited animated speakers and lively active people and animals. Thus we encourage independence and curiosity. We encourage aggressiveness and yet this aggressiveness has to be couched in some form of acceptability. It is at this time then that people withdraw into a more passive stance from time to time so as to get along with other individuals. Therefore, passive-aggression is deemed as an appropriate defense and style of living.

Psychologists argue that passive-aggression is a style used to control anger. If this anger is not controlled it leads to aggressive acts or to aggressive language such as sarcasm, lewd jokes, biting wit or jokes on people. When it is in a more passive form it is seen in criticism, self-blame, withdrawal, avoidance of responsibility and denigration of the self. However, these behaviors in themselves lead to emotional arousal which can lead to another outburst of aggression. Therefore, the passive-aggressive style is circular in its effect and hence it keeps on being acted out in a passive and then aggressive and then a passive followed by an aggressive stance.

If this style is troublesome to people, one could suggest that it may be important not to teach aggressive behavior or to model it. One should examine the personality and see if it's a trait that is inborn. In some cases it may be that one is born with a more aggressive style and hence one learns to become more passive slowly by not entering into an action too quickly, taking time to think. With children it is necessary to supervise them much more closely at home and not give them contradictory messages. Compliment others who are behaving in an appropriate and responsible way. Calming down activities such as use of relaxation would also be helpful. Planning for short term goals and fulfilling them would be effective in treating the passive side of the nature. Channelling the outlets of aggression in more acceptable ways would be a way of handling the aggressive side of the personality. Providing for periodic release through free time would also help. In all these cases it is important to recognize that passive aggression is a common style of interacting but may lead to more difficult problems in the home and marriage if it is not dealt with. Thus, it can be a personality state, a motivational state, a response to frustration or a socially learned role. In any case it is a stable trait over time and only careful attention to its style and ways to modify it will help in the long run.

Clutter and Conflict: The Compulsive

People who collect things to the point of clutter save unusual items, often indiscriminately. For example, they collect junk mail, supermarket receipts, newspapers, business memos, empty cans, clothes, old Christmas and Birthday cards, lumber scraps, fabric remnants, auto parts, shoes or plastic meat trays and other items. The people who collect such clutter are different from the real COLLECTORS. Collectors specialize in a class of objects. Collectors often go to garage sales, or auctions and purchase very selective items. They also fix, organize, display, catalogue and study about the objects they collect. Most people believe that the people who collect clutter are all older people who lived through the great depression of the 1930's and stockpile just in case a depression hits again. To some degree my parents were like this too. But research suggests that we have a new generation of collectors of clutter that were born long after the 1930's. Why do they do it and what does it mean?

Psychotherapists who have been working with clients who collect such clutter report that this can cause many relationship problems. One partner may feel annoyed and frustrated with the clutter, frustrated with the growing mess and frustrated with the individuals' unwillingness to clean it up. People who collect such clutter seem to be defensive and unwilling to change. Usually the spouse of the collector of clutter sees them as being intolerant.

There are many explanations offered as to why people collect odd items that clutter up the house, garage or attic. Sigmund Freud wrote about it many years ago and later one of his disciples by the name of Erich Fromm called it a "hoarding orientation". Freud and Fromm saw hoarding as a basic flaw in the character; the person seemed to be adjusting to a reasonably unproductive life. Thus, such a person was seen as stubborn, a miser, disorganized and sentimental.

The new theories, however, describe these people differently. The collectors of clutter hoard for reasons such as sentimental attachment, or the feeling that they might need it some day. They collect things because they feel that these objects might be valuable to them some day or that they are just too good to throw away. When such reasoning exists people then become very difficult to change, but often there are less logical reasons for collections. For example, some people collect because they find getting rid of things upsetting emo-

tionally. Throwing away anything causes them personal distress. Secondly, they find that these people simply cannot make decisions as to what to keep and since they are afraid to make mistakes they just collect everything. Some day they feel it might be worth something.

The literature does suggest that the collectors of clutter have a compulsive personality. A compulsive personality is one who avoids or postpones decisions because he's afraid of making mistakes. Compulsives find it difficult to express warm tender emotions. They cannot see the big picture and they are preoccupied with trivial details, often with rules, schedules or lists. They are obsessed with keeping schedules. The compulsive person is not aware of how his behavior affects others. On the positive side, the compulsive is very devoted to his work to the exclusion of pleasures and is very successful at his job. However, underlying that success is a fear of making mistakes.

The compulsives rarely compliment others or give gifts. They believe in rules and won't bend them easily. They resist the authority of others and are stubborn in conforming to them. They are unaware of how they affect or even hurt others. They may ask a spouse to do errands regardless of their plans. They often complain that they cannot express feelings. They are distressed with their indecisiveness and ineffectiveness. Often, a depressed mood is common among the compulsive. They are excessively conscientious, moralistic, scrupulous and judgemental of self and others. When they cannot control others, they become depressed, ruminate about it and finally become angry. They are very sensitive to criticism especially if it comes from someone in authority. Men are more commonly found with this personality. The condition does not incapacitate them but social and personal relationship problems are frequent.

Collection of clutter or hoarding does meet a need. It says that throwing away things is like being abandoned or feeling rejected. When you feel rejected you are lonely, sad or depressed, so keeping objects saves you these feelings. The objects represent a sense of security and acceptance. These people identify with the object; they say "this is me". They often see their belongings as a reflection of themselves. The attachment to these objects is similar to a child's attachment to his blanket, soother or doll. Discarding these objects would trigger fears and sadness as well as guilt. By keeping them he avoids these feelings but he also becomes indecisive in that act. So the objects pile up and eventually they begin to control their life and their relationships. Hence, a marriage may fall apart because of the conflict it created. Cleaning it up just infuriates the partner. Children are affected as well. Children are loath to invite their friends over because of the clutter.

Many psychologists and psychiatrists feel that a collection of clutter expresses an unconscious feeling of hostilities that are repressed and cannot be expressed in a socially acceptable way. Often these people have had moralistic fathers who were very controlling. Collectors also fear disapproval. They have been raised by perfectionistic and demanding parents where positive regard and rewards were few and far between. So these people protect what is theirs. Materialism is therefore often the root and reason for the collection. These people prize everything they get even if it is seen by others as junk. Thus, the collection of clutter is a way in which they overindulge themselves.

Since these individuals are very hard to change, very little can be said about what might be done. However, it is true that one needs to treat the anxiety attacks, the fatigue as well as the guilt. It is useful for these individuals to seek counselling or at least find a friend to discuss these issues. However, since they do not tend to seek or like therapy, it is up to the spouse to be able to discuss these issues with their partner and reach a compromise that might make the situation liveable for them. Aside from that, it would seem that one could go in and organize all that clutter to the satisfaction of both individuals. Setting aside a special place for things and making sure that the appearance is neat and tidy would be a useful step in the right direction. Perfectionism is very difficult to change but over time, with a constant warm and supportive environment, compulsives will find themselves in less difficult situations in the future.

Masochistic Personality Disorder

There is a thin line, some writers say, between masochism and sainthood. Masochism is turning anger against the self and is often seen in a passive aggressive type of person. Someone who is masochistic may have experienced a lot of failure, may procrastinate, show silly or provocative behavior in a self-demeaning form and may be engaged in self-destructive behavior. Often masochistic people take on the burden of others.

The reason that there may be a thin line between masochism and any other problem that may exist which is not masochism, is that masochism often can take the guise of dependency. People who were very dependent on others often do things that maintains that dependency. The question then asked is whether or not this dependency problem is related to a more serious condition of "masochism".

Before the diagnosis of Masochistic Personality Disorder is given, the individual must have met at least six of the following nine criteria:

1. Staying in an abusive relationship.
2. Choosing friends or situations that lead to disappointments even when other options are available.
3. Reject or render ineffective the attempts of others to help them.
4. Following positive events, responds with depression and guilt.
5. Invites rejection or anger and then turns around and feels defeated, hurt and humiliated.
6. Turns down opportunities for pleasure and doesn't acknowledge enjoying themselves.
7. Has abilities, but doesn't use them. Helps others but not themselves.
8. Is uninterested in people who treat them well.
9. Engages in excessive self-sacrifice that is unsolicited and even discouraged by the recipients.

Dr. Paula Caplan, at the University of Toronto, is dead set against this new found mental disorder being placed in *The Handbook of Mental Disorders - DSM4*. She isn't against labels or new diseases, as long as there is good scientific evidence for it. But this new disorder, she says, is really striking hard against women who traditionally and currently are in roles that are seen as subservient and dependent.

Women's liberation movements have gone even further. Even in the act of sex, they say, a woman is subjected to a sort of beating by the man's penis. Men and women say they love it, but the feminists argue that it speaks of masochism. Indirectly they are arguing both for and against the idea that women are basically masochistic.

Believers in early Freudian notions demanded women to be nurturing, patient, deferential, willing to delay gratification and put other peoples' needs ahead of their own. Women, psychoanalysts said, were fundamentally masochistic, seeking suffering and pain. Today this concept is no longer linked with women. Men can have this problem too. Caplan argues that just changing the name doesn't change its bias to women.

Masochistic people like to be taken care of and like others to take care of them. They often reject help and insist on doing things for others even when others don't ask for help. They magnify flaws in others so as to destroy a relationship. They often remain in a very destructive relationship. In our view, these people do have self-defeating behaviors. Masochistic tendencies can occur for personality reasons, for religious or culturally imposed reasons, or because one has learned to be helpless. Masochists like to have someone's attention, even if that attention is negative and destructive. Some say that low self-esteem is at the core here. These individuals get little respect other than by imposing, helping or hindering others. There is no desire to be hurt - it's their only way to respond. They accept their role as subservient and dependent servants because this seemingly works best for them. This is often seen in the case where an abused woman chooses to stay with a violent husband. She rightly and rationally fears for her life. It is true that the battery of women by men comes in cycles. Men will hit them one day and the next bring flowers. The woman knows that refusing such gifts may lead to more battery. However, accepting such gifts also reinforces the batterer in that his act is expiated and therefore holds no guilt over the act.

The masochistic personality disorder is indeed a difficult one to accept. It is a difficult problem. Some people do bring on their own problems quite unwittingly and some deliberately. There are people who do exhibit self-defeating behaviors but this does not necessarily mean that it is always masochism, that they seek pain and suffering or enjoy it. Nevertheless, we need to recognize that this situation does exist and needs to be treated.

It is important, therefore, that individuals seek therapy immediately to try and correct or ameliorate this situation. Often it is helpful for them to seek work outside the home, even if it is volunteer work. It is important that they think about what they want and what needs they want fulfilled; to set some goals and objectives with which they can be happy. It is important to recognize that one must never accept any form of abuse. One needs to know whether better options are available or whether one invites or brings on rejection deliberately. One needs to know whether one is turning down opportunities for pleasure and examine the reasons why. One needs to know why one would reject people who do treat them well. In any case, something has to be done. The situation has to be changed.

The Hyperactive Adult

This topic was prepared because of numerous requests not only on telephone but through letters suggesting that the problem of hyperactivity simply does not go away after these children grow up. As adults, they experience similar difficulties and problems. Research on hyperactivity with adults is now receiving much greater atttention but unfortunately the attention is addressed to the emotional and social problems, rather than the thinking, reasoning and success experiences. Hyperactivity, whatever its cause, creates risks for school failure for the young adults, adjustment problems such as abuse of drugs and alcohol in later life, psychiatric problems such as depression and work problems such as inability to stick to a job. Naturally, a hyperactive adult creates many difficulties within a marriage as well.

Today, three to five percent of the population of adults are diagnosed as hyperactive. The *Deficit Model* suggests that hyperactivity is a brain based problem, caused by damage to certain strategic locations in the brain. Most of the research has focused on this deficit model but very little backs up the evidence that adults who are hyperactive are indeed brain damaged. Nevertheless, they do possess deficits and although damage may not be there, there may be weaknesses within the brain system that accounts for the hyperactivity. The second explanation for hyperactivity is the *Delay Model*. This means that there is a delay in emotional and cognitive development resulting in general immaturity. These people often seek younger friendships and get along fine with younger people but don't get along with people of their own age. If the hyperactivity is due to a delay, then it should disappear in adulthood. Therefore, when adults are hyperactive it may not be because of the delay but really due to some other factor. As a result, a third explanation for hyperactivity in adults has been offered. This model suggests that there are differences in stable personality characteristics, traits or styles based on genetics. These differences in personality traits cause or create the hyperactivity. Individuals possess at least four basic temperaments: emotionality, activity, sociability and impulsivity. In the case where any one of these traits is exaggerated or not developed sufficiently a style of responding results in the typical signs and symptoms of hyperactivity. If one is at an extreme of the traits, the resulting behavior is usually maladaptive.

Hyperactivity is *not* a disease but rather a particular style or way of action. To be so labelled depends upon a specific situation and expectations by parents, peers and society. A high activity level on its own is also not a clinical problem but when it combines with impulsivity to its extreme, it can then become a problem. Under these circumstances you might find adults who become very explosive, who hit and kick, who are usually angry, who don't pay attention to you or who buy impulsively and therefore get into financial trouble.

If a highly impulsive person has a low activity level, his problems, and his behaviors are contained or controlled and less problems result. The hyperactive adults, therefore, may appear similar in many behaviors but different in others. We need to examine the specific signs. If the adult experiences most of these symptoms, they can be so labelled.

SIGNS:

1. May be very active, cannot sit still and cannot wait for others to finish speaking. Is very restless, often pacing.

2. Explosive. The individual is very impulsive, may blow up, become very angry at times and feel very sorry. This is called the "big mouth syndrome" with differences noted in mood and activity.

3. Distractible. Cannot focus on one thing and must move around or move to other topics very quickly, never finishing. The language is speeded up and he cannot hold eye contact. This individual often seeks stimulation.

4. Overfocused. This means that one cannot keep one thought or idea and must move on. Conversely, they hold one idea and thought and keep repeating it over and over again. Overfocussing can also be created by the use of stimulants (drugs). In addition, overfocussing can lead to not seeking any stimulation, being very intolerant, cannot work with noise of any kind, very sensitive to irrelevant noise when working on an assignment.

5. Tense and anxious. Hyperactive adults are often found to be insecure, nervous, always feeling stressed, unable to relax, always in the need of doing something.

6. Social problems. The above signs may cause social problems. If one is very explosive or argumentative and leave the room it may create difficulties. Hyperactives often won't go to movies, or the opera, ballet or symphony because of the nature of their temperament and because of the restlessness. All kinds of relationship difficulties arise out of these situations.

7. Work. Hyperactive adults switch jobs frequently. They often don't get along with co-workers or their boss. They are inattentive, make many mistakes or get confused and do the wrong thing. This could lead to getting fired.

8. A combination of most or all of these symptoms must be present for the label to be used.

Many of the signs and symptoms may not stem out of hyperactivity alone. There may be other personal problems or even medical disorders. Therefore, an accurate diagnosis needs to be made to gain a full understanding of the problem. Environmental pollutants such as lead have been found to be a cause. Smoking during pregnancy of three packages of cigarettes a day or more has also been implicated. Family stress, genetic transmission, fluorescent lights and allergies have also been found related to hyperactivity.

The problem of hyperactivity is knowing exactly what to do. These people seem to have more car accidents, drop out of school, switch jobs. Criminal offenses can result because of hyperactivity. Many hyperactives are found to have more speeding tickets. Females may turn to hysterics and males to social failure. A highly structured environment with specific routines is often found to be helpful. Identifying strengths and working on hobbies that meet those strengths is another possibility. Medication and diet have also found to be helpful, especially for loss of appetite, insomnia, weight loss and irritability. More free time and continuous reward and reinforcement of these individuals is necessary. And then individual therapy or perhaps family therapy may be needed in some cases. Change is slow and intervention must be consistent to produce any positive results.

The Type "T" and "A" Personality

The Type "T" Personality can be an artistic individual who is physically active and seeks a very high arousal level. He is a good socializer and likely to be male because of the pressure of increased levels of the hormone testosterone.These individuals show strong sex drives with little repression in sexual activity. They enjoy erotic

drives with little re-
pression in sexual ac-
tivity. They enjoy
erotic material. When
this individual be-
comes over aroused it
is quite possible to be-
come aggressive and
violent. The young
tend to be delinquent
and hyperactive. Tak-
en to its extreme these
people can be highly
unpredictable, very
intense in everything
they do, enjoying vari-
ety. As adults they en-
joy fighting and are
disobedient of the law.

There are people
who suffer from
chronic over-arousal
or under-arousal. When our biological system does not supply us
with enough arousal to get us going, to help us pay attention, to keep
us on-task, to stimulate our mind and body, certain predictable results can occur. There is some evidence that neurotics seek high
levels of arousal. Schizophrenics suffer from excessively low levels of
arousal while others have very high levels. In each case their illnesses take on different patterns depending on this arousal level. Normally, children who are hyperactive may have a biological system
that is under-aroused so they go about wildly stimulating their body
and brain. This results in the behaviors that often drive us crazy. On
the other hand, manic-depressives already have a high arousal system. Depressives have a system that tries to diminish the arousal in
the body-brain system and hence they are often inactive and very
passive to try to diminish that very high arousal level.

The Type "T" Personality traits overlap with the Type "A". Type
"A" individuals are very active, aggressive, yet successful in the work
that they do. Both types need arousal and seek it. High arousal
personalities find it difficult to be alone, to be in the dark, to enjoy
silence or even low light. Instead, they enjoy debate and argument,
noise and action and are constantly looking for thrills. Sometimes

these traits can lead to success as an artist, a risk taker in business or in marriage. Taken to its extreme, some Type "A"s and "T"s become very violent and delinquent, even criminal.

We all seek an optimal level of arousal. If the arousal is too high or low, we try to adjust it to some middle ground often by choosing to do things that either soothe us or stimulate us. Some people are born with unusually low arousability. They are not very responsive and they seek high levels of stimulation to get them going to optimal levels of daily functioning. Others are just the opposite, they choose to do things that slow them down, to calm their nervous system. Most people, though, are in the middle ground.

The negative side effects of this type of personality is that at the younger ages it can lead to delinquency and rejection of social and legal rules. These people tend to take unnecessary risks and pursue the unknown. If they come to the attention of the criminal justice system, they are often difficult to manage in prison, because they don't like to be boxed in.

Some Type "T" and "A" personalities do just fine but this often depends on the social circumstances and the opportunities that they have had to be creative, artistic, doing normal and socially acceptable things. It's often good to get them into dance, art, music or sport; things that keep them very active. Also, the home environment is very important because parents can help children learn to be creatively active in doing things that are positive without having to punish them too often or too much. An educational system that allows for high arousal and activity would also be beneficial. And lastly, the implications of this type of personality are clear for marriages. It seems better to have two high arousal types together than one that is low arousal and one that is high arousal. If they are matched in terms of their arousal level they can enjoy similar activities. Hence, their relationship tends to blend. The problems that are often encountered between men and women are related to differing interests, interests that pull them apart rather than bring them together. Thus, it is important to compromise on interests and activities. A very active schedule for the high arousal type is almost mandatory, as is a relaxed pace for the low arousal person. Arousal is a key to understanding personality and is involved in both Type "T" and Type "A". Another form of the Type "A" personality is discussed in the next section.

Type "A" and Hostility

Hostility comes from the Latin word "hostis" meaning enemy. Out of interest, there is another word from this root which is "hotel", a place for strangers to stay. I suspect in earlier times very often the strangers were unfriendly. In today's jargon we often talk about "ceasing hostilities" or "resuming hostilities" on a world level. Usually when we speak of hostilities we are talking about anger, resentment and irritability. On the personal level, a hostile person has the belief that "others are treacherous and if given the chance will readily do you in if it is to their advantage".

I'm not surprised that we're hostile in today's world. If one checks the daily news, one often hears about violence. Dr. John Mitchell, a psychologist in Edmonton, has done research to show that the fear of nuclear war poses a threat to today's adolescents. Some scientists believe that with a combination of early childhood experiences, plus years of exposure to competitive behavior, a person can develop a "free-floating hostility", which simply means a suspicious attitude which spills over to all areas of daily life.

What is a hostile person? Check the following characteristics:

—They notice with irritation the perceived faults of others.

—A hostile person is extremely demanding of self and is very critical of self as well as others.

—There are frequent arguments with a hostile person. Often discussions become debates or arguments.

—This person has an intense need to win at all games and sports. We would see self-recrimination and anger upon losing.

—A hostile person is extremely sensitive to criticism or uncomplimentary remarks.

—This person is tense and tight - ready to quarrel, sometimes even when smiling.

I recognize that all of us are like this at times; however, if these behaviors are habitual, we have a hostile person.

Now, an attempt to relate this to health or illness. Thoreson showed in his article that hostile people are Type "A" people. We know from other experiences that Type "A" behavior is a predictor of heart disease. Other predictors include smoking, blood pressure and cholesterol level. There is some research evidence showing that "hostility" can predict heart disease, premature death and increase stress. This is a potentially serious health problem. For the individual, it's worth asking the questions "To what extent am I a hostile person?", and "What might I do to reduce hostility?"

Surely it is wise for parents to admit dangers to children, while at the same time teaching through modelling and examples that there are positives as well as negatives to most situations. If free-floating hostility is counterproductive and even dangerous, then it behooves us to look at the positive side of life as well as the negative. Granted, we can find people who will abuse our trust, but expecting this behavior will not diminish it. All of us become angry but most people, like ourselves, will do their best on most occasions. Checking one's hostility level might be an excellent mental health tip. Type A's, although high on the hostility trait, have found productive ways to channel their energy. Rechannelling negative energy into positive activities is a skill mastered by Type "A" Personalities.

The Dependent Personality

A major problem in recognizing and treating personality disorders is that people who suffer a disorder function quite well on most days and rarely think they need help. The dependent person, in most instances, rarely thinks it's a problem to be or feel dependent on others, whereas the hyperactive, the Type A's, the hostile, the passive-aggressive, the masochistic run into more serious difficulties daily. Dramatic examples of seriously disordered war criminals who were never treated or seen as pathological have been found in the trials at Nuremberg. Hitler, for example, was found to have a paranoid personality disorder, Goering a narcissistic one, Himmler a schizoid personality disorder and von Ribbentrop a passive-dependent one. Closer to home, Trudeau has been described as self-centered, histrionic and narcissistic by some political writers and Nixon as possibly paranoid, although his mistrust and suspiciousness may have been well-founded and appropriate. Both men were very successful, bright men who gave of their time and talent to their country. Thus with the dependent type. Since the disorder is found more common in women, frequently in women who work in the home, the problem went unrecognized. Nevertheless, it

appeared in the latest version of *The Handbook of Mental Disorders - DSM III* and the *DSM III-R* edition as a distinct personality disorder.

The dependent personality is an indecisive staller. They let others do things, can't make up their mind and stall on major decisions. They become very stressed if something or someone depends on them. Dependent personalities are usually pleasant and very supportive. They listen well, and in argument, encourage, look interested and ask challenging questions. Since they rely heavily on others for approval and affection, they live by the desires and opinions of others. Over time, their self-image is weakened and they constantly deny their own thoughts and feelings as significant or worthy. In the end, they avoid asserting themselves, have difficulty saying "NO", and feel paralysed when alone. Unable to draw on their own strengths for satisfaction and comfort, they arrange their lives to ensure constant dependency and a continual flow of nurturance and reinforcement. At its extreme, dependent people feel and act inferior, marry a "strong" person who becomes ever more frustrated over the strong attachments and dependencies. Resulting arguments in the marriage cause stress and anxieties. Dependent personalities thus can become pessimistic, passive, self-doubt-ing and anxious, falling prey to other problems, physical and psychological. Thus it is not uncommon for the therapist who is treating a person for generalized anxiety, or phobias or psychosomatic disorders to discover an underlying substrate of the dependent personality.

Dependent personalities actively seek treatment unlike persons having other personality styles. Treatment provides them with attention, approval and guidance. An examination of their past indicates that dependent people were obedient children of dominant parents, so they spent most of their childhood looking for support, learning to be helpful, asking others to make decisions for them. Others were raised in homes where the parents gave them a "poor little me" feeling, so that they needed all the "warm fuzzies" they could get to satisfy their dependency. Erich Fromm traced the roots of dependency to religions who teach subservience and demand obedience to authority. Freud saw it as a problem of inadequate satisfaction of the oral stage resolution. These infants became unnecessarily attached to their mothers. Still others see the dependency problem as "delayed maturation", the immature child who doesn't want to "grow up". Whatever the cause, overdependent people can find a marriage that works. In today's moral and social climate of feminism, this dependency is seen as pathological. This alone has made many housewives unhappy because others said they should be. The goals of therapy should be to establish self-confidence; foster adequacy in the marriage situation; develop independent hobbies and activities; encourage decision-making and improve responsibility taking. Parents who want independent children must allow the children to make decisions and take responsibilities. A more open home, a less authoritative parenting style will develop greater independence. However, there is nothing wrong with encouraging the dependents' good social nature. Remember, however, that for the dependent, criticism is very devastating. Therefore, focus on the positive and do not denigrate the person, rather specify the behaviors you want to change. Dependent people have many strengths. If the therapist develops those, the progress to a positive self-esteem and self-reliance is made much easier.

No one has complete control of one's life. The dependent personality type seeks dependence on others and hence gives up control. To use therapy to "gain control of one's life", is, in our view, a debatable issue and likely not a workable one for the dependency problem, unless the person wishes more "control". The issue of "controlling one's life" is at once philosophical and practical. We are all dependent on each other, on laws and customs, on self-imposed demands. To help the dependent person be more "in control" needs to be carefully delineated and specified in relation to significant others in their environment. Nevertheless, areas in one's domestic and occupational life can be examined as to how the dependent can begin to make decisions, choose actions that give them a feeling of being "in control".

In many ways, people suffering from a dependent personality disorder are like teenagers, one foot in the world of childhood, the other in the world of adults. The dependency problem creates the "marginal man", ambivalent about giving up the pleasures of childhood for the adult world of rights and responsibilities. On the one hand the dependent need the others for support, nurturance and structure; on the other hand they feel frustrated by the lack of choices in their life. Just as the adolescent is kept from adult responsibilities, so too the dependent adult. As a parent is reluctant to allow the adolescent to "grow up", so too, is the significant other, the spouse, in the dependent's world reluctant to give up the attention, admiration and warmth given by the dependent. Therapy, therefore, must include "significant others" if the relationship is to change. Subordination, willingly imposed, must be replaced by reciprocal service. As the dependent gains self-confidence, choices of action are easier to make without fear of jeopardizing the relationship. This is especially usual for women in abusing relationships. A wife with this disorder (dependency) often tolerates a physically abusive husband for fear that he will leave her. Giving that woman self-confidence and alternative actions is a first and necessary step.

The Histrionic Personality

Formerly known as the "hysterical" personality, histrionic individuals are the prima donnas of the world stage. Although diagnosed far more commonly in women, men are "histrionic" as well, and it is often found in the effeminate and homosexual.

The history of this personality disorder is rather interesting. First described in the first century A.D. as the "disease of the womb" by Celsus, a Roman physician, hysteria was thought to originate from a mysterious secretion in the uterus, analogous to secretion of the semen in the male. Retention of semen was thought to have the same pernicious effect. By the mid nineteenth century French physicians called this theory utter nonsense, as it is! Late in the nineteenth century, Karl Jaspers, whose classic textbook became the authority, described the hysterical personality as one who is totally engrossed in living in his own drama. Not much is known about this disorder, although recent writings find histrionics presenting histories of alcoholic fathers; bad homes; less often married; more often divorced;

having first child very early; more extramarital affairs; lower work attainment; employment in cosmetics; dramatic and musical arts; more frequent hospitalization and more frequent surgical interventions. In contrast to dependent, histrionics take initiative in assuring attention and affection.

The histrionic personality has strengths, however. They are charming and hyperalert; they are the life of a party; they are social; they love fun; they love intensely; they are colorful and interesting. The magic of this pure charm quickly dissipates because of their intense need for attention. Quickly impressed, they fall in and out of relationships. The need for approval leads to excessive attention-getting behaviors. When others don't respond to their liking, the charm disintegrates into demands, self-indulgence and emotional outbursts. Love quickly turns to hate and self-confidence to demoralization. With colorful and finely-tuned dramatics, histrionics exaggerate their feelings. As a result, over 50 per cent of histrionics attempt suicide (compared to 16 per cent of those suffering depression with other personality structures).

Histrionics are intelligent and articulate, albeit used to further intense ego needs. They can entertain and discuss with apparent insight. However, thought processes quickly break down, turning to irrationality and leading to inevitable failure. Without the drive to sustain interest in work, relationships and self, histrionics quickly become bored with routine. Marriages break down, they lose their jobs and as a result may fall into brief but mild psychotic episodes. Fortunately, they can bounce back from this breakdown as quickly as they fell into it.

All of us have temper tantrums, may even throw dishes from time to time. Histrionics, however, can turn minor stresses into major catastrophes. Reaction to the trivial is routine and hence their constant search for reassurance. People like the histrionics for their imagination, charm, enthusiasm, romance and excitement but the initial attraction quickly fades. Even so, histrionics do attract others, especially compulsives because the two complement each other. The compulsive likes detail, the histrionic global ideas; the compulsive works on logic and information, the histrionic on hunches. The compulsive can be loving, the histrionic always exciting. As a couple, they complement each other, one meeting needs and interests the other admires. Unfortunately, frequent arguments, unrealistic demands, inability to communicate logically, deception and vanity, infidelity and lack of loyalty, manipulation and seductiveness form a capricious pattern. The marriage turns sour, with an inevitable separation and divorce.

Histrionics often use physical problems, pains and aches to fill their empty moments. Rarely fatigued, they live a fast life, bordering on the hyperactive. Massive repression leads to continuance of values and modes of typical adolescent behavior. This leads the histrionic, like the adolescent, to a vicious cycle perpetuating dependency behaviours while seeking structure and independence. Although it is probably rare that histrionics will succumb to a serious mental disorder, their roller coaster personality provides them as many ups as downs. As a consequence, histrionics rarely seek therapy, and when they do, rarely persevere in it. Nevertheless, help is possible and so is change. The histrionic needs a stable environment, one built on patience and love. Overdramatizations ought to be ignored and general support given during their "down" periods. Since drugs and behavior therapy have been found ineffectual, a more long-term process of insight therapy, both individual and group-based is preferred. In essence, the personality style needs to be reconstructed and this takes time. With aid from friends and family, histrionics can become more self-assured and stable. With time, the roller coaster ride ends, the restraint unbuckled, with two feet firmly planted on even, solid surface.

The Paranoid Personality Disorder

Very few negative and angry letters have been written to the co-hosts of 930 CJCA's "That's Living" program. With every public endeavor, however, criticisms and outright rage at the ideas expressed openly on-air will be the norm and should be expected. Some two years ago, angry letters, written from cut-out newspaper words so as to disguise authorship, were received by the co-hosts of "That's Living". The writer of these letters expressed a deep mistrust of us. Concerned with hidden negatives, the letter accused us of being

puppets of a Fascist regime, exposing values of subversion and brainwashing. We were seen as the direct arm of a liberal government, leading the people astray through a draconian radio empire. We were to blame for the permissiveness, sexual abuse, alcoholism rampant in our society. People like us should be locked up, if not permanently silenced. We sent the letters to the police. Threats and innuendos are to be taken seriously, even if untrue. Right or wrong, such accusations come from a highly disturbed mind. Our diagnosis, based on letters only, was tentatively set as paranoid personality disorder, if not a full-blown paranoid or paranoid schizophrenic.

The paranoid person has few friends and many enemies. He/she is suspicious, guarded and hostile, feeling persecuted and alone. Always unpleasant and blaming, they cannot form any close, intimate friendships. They distrust help because they fear being tricked. They are leery of shrinks because shrinks can "read people's minds and subvert their thinking". Emotionally, paranoid personalities are cold, rational, rigid and ego-centric. Drawn to interests in politics, science and history, paranoids look to improve their rigid thinking. Their intelligence is used to provide counter-argument, look for hidden meaning. They disdain the weak and feel threatened by the strong, the visible. Always vigilant, their hypersensitivity leads to mistrust and feelings of jealousy, bordering on the pathological. Being highly secretive, communication becomes difficult if not impossible. Even a simple "Hello" can evoke a thought of "I wonder what he meant by that?" Someone once joked that a paranoid personality is one who, on watching a football team gather in a huddle on the field, thinks they are talking about him. This disorder is usually diagnosed in men, and little information is available on familial patterns. Driven to maintain secrecy, paranoids build an intricate logic to justify their delusions. Given their abilities, paranoids who do become visible, seek leadership in esoteric religious, quasi-political groups or cults. However, most individuals with a paranoid personality disorder keep to themselves, aloof and alone, realizing it is prudent to keep ideas to themselves. Thus, they rarely come to clinical attention and rarely seek help. Since the problem is not complicated by full-blown symptoms usually found in the paranoid schizophrenic, nor with the highly systematized delusions of the paranoid psychotic disorder, paranoid personalities move from one concern to the other, criticizing whomever and whatever they can. When they cannot stand their own subjective distress, they will come for help, complaining of being "hard done by", lacking friends, suffering from anxiety attacks, muscular tightness and cold sweats.

Very little is known as to how they got this way. Some writers blame overindulgent parents who over-valued them as a child. Others say it is parental antagonism and open resentment of them as a child. Severe punishment is often found in their histories, where parents oscillated between strong affection one moment and irrational hostility the next. Freud saw paranoia as a psychosis of defense, slowly transforming over the years. Initial feelings of worth and love had been repressed and denied, giving way to the opposite feelings of hatred. This is further transformed into projection of that hatred on to others. Thus, they deny love and feel that others hate them, not that he hates them. Finally, in rationalizing other peoples, antagonism toward them, they develop thoughts of persecution and delusions of jealousy.

Being straightforward, professional and rational is probably the best way to relate to a paranoid personality. When you are wrong, admit it, apologize and move on to other issues. Allow room for respect, but avoid intimacy. Discussions should be careful and objective. Since they view others as weak, it is important to show inner stability and consistency. Most importantly, help the paranoid learn to relax. This often takes months of therapy to establish. Always allow an "out" for him, since therapy can easily be terminated if the paranoid does not see trust in a relationship. Remember, paranoids can nurture themselves until their wounds are healed. They are capable people. Nevertheless, they need a boost to their ego. Seek to reinforce the positive, the social, the conforming attitudes. Living with a paranoid personality is not easy. Often the spouse gets drawn into his delusions and paranoid thinking, since this is the only way to survive.

Prognosis for the paranoid personality disorder is not good. Fortunately they do survive, with some help from drugs that relieve their anxiety and sufficient strength on our part. With patience and love, paranoids can be helped.

Summary

There are many good scientific books written about personality disorders, although popular paperbacks on the subject are rare. We have sampled only a few of the major personality disorders in this chapter. A complete coverage would require an entire book. For the trained reader, sections on the hyperactive adult and the hostile, as well as the section on Type A and T, will be recognized as character trait conditions and not personality disorders per se. Nevertheless, these sections were included because of frequent requests on these issues. Omitted in this chapter were disorders of personality related to narcissism, avoidance, schizoid, schizotypal, anti-social and borderline conditions. Four of these categories (Narcissism, Avoidant, Borderline, Schizotypal) are newly found personality disorder patterns. The anti-social category, frequently referred to as the "psychopath" was not included because of overlap with the Histrionic pattern, although not entirely. Schizotypal personality disorder is the forerunner of schizophrenia and is more fully discussed elsewhere in this book.

Personality theories are many and varied. Disorders of personality overlap one with another. For the most part, this chapter has sampled disorders from the mild conditions (dependent, histrionic) to the moderate (compulsive, passive/aggressive) and the severe (paranoid). The descriptions provided are based on recent scientific writings but they do not tell all. The reader is encouraged to consult other sources as provided in the bibliography. Remember that each one of us runs into personality problems from time to time. It is important to repeat that when personality traits are inflexible, maladaptive and cause significant disruption emotionally, mentally and socially is a problem, really a problem. Most of the time, people with "personality disorders" do not come to our attention, and even if they do, it is rarely a clear or clean picture of one "type" over another. Empirical research does little to support the view that syndromes (clusters of personality traits) can be clearly separated.

Central to our views as presented in this book is a recognition that normality and pathology are relative concepts. What works at one time doesn't work at another time. Behaviors and styles adaptive in one setting, fail in another. Pathology results from the same forces that foster normal functioning. When a person shows an ability to cope with their world in a flexible manner and when his perceptions and behaviors lead to personal satisfaction, then a person is said to have a healthy personality, regardless of some quirks and quarks.

The key to understanding personality disorders are the phrases "enduring characteristic ways of responding" and "significant subjective distress". There is a consistency to our life based on personality, character and temperament. Although we modulate our behaviour from occasion to occasion, a certain pattern is evident. When that pattern continually runs into trouble, subjective distress is the result, affecting not just your life, but others as well. It is at this point that patients come to the attention of the doctors. A typical example, taken from a letter written to the co-host of "That's Living" illustrates this point well:

> "...when you spoke (on That's Living) on the topic "Personality Disorders" you described my husband and daughter, I'm very concerned about both, their lives and mine. Life has been one continuous crises for them...my husband is never happy or satisfied about anything, his self-esteem is low, always; he has never read a book or watched a complete TV program. He says terrible things to everyone (me included)...my concern is that now, maybe there's hope that our life could be better...this problem feels very serious to me to the point that I feel like 104 years old..."

When people learn more about themselves and when they search honestly for answers, subjective distress can be turned into subjective relief from that distress. The old adage "you can't make a silk purse out of a sow's ear" can be replaced with "you're never too old to learn". Although personality traits are deeply engrained, your style of responding, your behaviors can change. As you change, the whole vista in front of you changes, the night sky is filled with stars, invisible by day.

CHAPTER 9

Alzheimer's Disease

ALZHEIMER'S DISEASE

I am writing this section under the name "Alzheimer's Disease" because it is the commonest cause of Dementia and it is the most popular term that is used in magazines, television and radio. The problems that patients experience from the different types of "Dementia" are frequently identical to that of the Alzheimer's patients. Many of the other causes of "Dementia" can only be distinguished from Alzheimer's Disease by special tests.

You may ask "How could I recognize a person who has "Alzheimer's Disease"? To understand the nature of Alzheimer's Disease, we must be aware that Alzheimer's Disease may be very mild or very severe in nature. I will therefore talk about Alzheimer's Disease in terms of "Early Phase", "Middle Phase" and "Late Phase".

People suffering from Alzheimer's Disease have disturbances in orientation (inability to know what day and year it is and where they are at a given moment), memory, intellectual functions, reasoning and judgement. It is not possible to describe an individual who suffers from Alzheimer's Disease at any given moment since the person may appear quite normal at one moment but severely confused at another. Also, the disease tends to be slowly progressive. This means that the person slowly becomes more disturbed over a period of weeks or months. Many individuals may develop the initial symptoms of Alzheimer's Disease very rapidly and then stabilize. A person may have periods of confusion or difficulty remembering the names of family and friends but does not worsen over the next few years. Other Alzheimer's patients may deteriorate rapidly and die within a few months.

Patients who are diagnosed with a mild degree of Alzheimer's Disease are able to understand the nature of their disorder and are extremely interested in knowing what to expect in the future. Unfortunately, there is no test which can tell us which patients will remain relatively well and which will deteriorate rapidly. Patients and their families experience anxiety and stress because the future is predictable.

▎ The Early Phase

It is difficult to diagnose Alzheimer's Disease in its early phase. Some patients develop physical symptoms such as shortness of breath, pain in the chest, and stomach pains. In medicine, we say that these individuals "somatize". That is, they complain of a physical symptom such as chest pain for which there is no physical disease or cause.

Patients in their early phases often complain of psychological symptoms such as irritability, depression, and loss of interest.

In the early phases, the patient and family may notice a loss of vigor, an inability to be enthusiastic about work or family, a tendency to become preoccupied with oneself, excessive suspiciousness or compulsiveness and a tendency to have a reduced interest with their habits and grooming. The person may complain about loss of memory but this loss is minimal and difficult to evaluate.

Patients will often complain that they have to struggle with tasks that were previously easy. There is a tendency for the mind to wander from topic to topic. That is, the person may begin talking about one item such as shopping and immediately go to another unrelated item such as the weather. Patients often recognize these limitations in memory and start using lists and other methods of reminders.

Most patients are not diagnosed in this early phase. Even the most experienced psychologists and psychiatrists have a difficult time establishing the onset of the disease. As you can see, many of the symptoms in the early phases are very vague.

To summarize, we can say that patients in the early phases of Alzheimer's Disease often complain of physical symptoms for which there is no disease and psychological symptoms such as irritability, mild memory impairment, and difficulties completing tasks that were previously easy to do.

▎ The Middle Phase

Friends, relatives and professionals easily recognize the symptoms of an individual who is suffering from the middle phase of Alzheimer's Disease. The patient usually shows major difficulties with memory. I would like to throw in a term at this point because you will be noticing it in your readings — Benign Senescent Forget-fulness. This term refers to normal aging wherein we have difficulty with recall. That is, we will often forget the name of a person or place but if somebody gave us the name then we would immediately recognize it. As an example, a person may have difficulty recalling the name of a city in Hawaii but if another person says Honolulu, immediately the person would recognize this as the city they wanted to talk about. The memory disorder of "Benign Senescent Forgetfulness" is a normal aging process. This is different from a person who has Alzheimer's Disease where there is "Defective Registration of Memory". This means that a person cannot recall events of their everyday life. I will give you a short interchange that occurred in my office with Mrs. M., an eighty year old patient who was accompanied by her daughter.

Doctor: "Do you ever have problems with your memory Mrs. M.?"

Mrs. M.: "No, never. I have an excellent memory."

Doctor: "Does your daughter ever call you by telephone Mrs. M.?"

Mrs. M.: "No, never. I wonder what's wrong with kids nowadays. They aren't interested in their parents anymore."

Daughter: "Mother, I just called you this morning and twice yes-terday."

Mrs. M.: "You didn't."

Mrs. M. has a problem with "registration" and "recent memory". Mrs. M. was not able to learn new information and commit it to memory.

Patients like Mrs. M., frequently have good memory for "Remote Events". Patients in this phase will be able to recall details of their past. They can remember people that they work with, and places they travelled to, etc. Here is an example of good "Remote Memory":

Doctor: "Mrs. M., can you tell me what your job was when you worked?"

Mrs. M.: "Of course I could. I worked for the government. My job was to get requests from different government offices for repair work. I would then send people to do repair work in buildings from Edmonton to the Northwest Territories."

Doctor: "Who was your boss?"

Mrs. M.:   "I was there for many years and I had different bosses."

I asked many more questions about Mrs. M.'s, past and she responded quickly and appropriately. Mrs. M.'s daughter was able to tell me that everything her mother said was correct.

Patients in this phase of Alzheimer's disease begin having problems with "orientation".

Doctor: "Can you tell me where you are at this moment?"

Patient: "Of course I could."

Doctor: "What is the name of this building?"

Patient: "Who really cares about the name of this building. I know where I am."

Doctor: "Please try and cooperate with me. It is very important for me to get an answer to my question. Let me try it again. What is the name of this building?"

Patient: "I don't know, there is no sign."

Doctor: "This is the "Edmonton General Hospital". Please tell me the name of this building?"

Patient: "I don't know and I don't care."

Doctor: "I'm going to try this again. This is the Edmonton General Hospital. Please say Edmonton General Hospital."

Patient: "Edmonton General Hospital."

Doctor: "That's good. I would now like to talk to you about some other things such as where you live, and where you work. Before I do this, tell me the name of this place? What is the name of this place?"

Patient: "I don't know and don't care to know."

Doctor: "I told you this is the Edmonton General Hospital."

Patient: "Okay."

Patients are not able to orient themselves to the place that they are at. You may have heard about patients leaving their home and not being able to find their way back again. This is a common problem in some senior citizens residences and nursing homes. There is a constant fear that patients will lose their way and be unable to return to their residence. This is particularly disturbing during the winter months when patients may die from exposure. This reminds me of Mrs. Mac who wandered away from the nursing home late in the evening and was found frozen to death next morning in an alley two blocks from the home.

Patients frequently come to the attention of physicians when they become lost. The following is a discussion that I had with a hospitalized patient and his neighbor.

Doctor: "Thank you for coming to the hospital to talk to me about Mr. B."

Neighbor: "That's okay. I'd like to help."

Doctor: "Why did you bring Mr. B. to the hospital yesterday?"

Neighbor: "I've been worried about Mr. B. for a while. He is really a perfect gentleman. He has been my neighbor for 15 years. I really like him a lot. However, I have been getting worried about him for the last six months. Six months ago, I awakened in the middle of the night because of some noise outside my door. Mr. B. was standing at my door in his shorts. It was snowing outside. I brought him to the house and gave him some clothes. He seemed to be okay so I took him to his home. This happened a few times since then. About ten o'clock last night, I noticed Mr. B. walking around in the nude. I thought this was terrible. I went to him and he was not able to talk to me. He seemed very scared. I called Social Services and they brought him to the emergency department."

Doctor: "Thank you very much for helping. Have you been in his house recently."

Neighbor: "He is a very private man and I don't usually go to his house."

Doctor: "Were you ever in his house?"

Neighbor: "I was in his house about a year ago. He gave me some coffee and cookies. He always kept his house perfectly clean."

Doctor: "Have you seen his house in the last two or three months?"

Neighbor: "Yes. It is a mess. It stinks. There are dishes all over the place. There are bags all over the place."

This interchange gives you a clear picture of what these unfortunate individuals go through. They often deteriorate to a severe degree before they come to medical attention. This example also high-lights the fact that there is an impairment of all intellectual func-tions. That is, a person is unable to develop a plan. They are unable to purchase food, prepare food, clean the house, carry out the garbage and accomplish other activities of daily living.

When talking to a person with Alzheimer's Disease, you may often notice that they keep repeating themselves. This is called "Perseveration"

Doctor: "How are you today Mr. B.?"

Mr. B.:   "Really great."

Doctor: "Who brought your clothes for you to the hospital?"

Mr. B.:   "Somebody is stealing my clothes."

Doctor: "Were they stealing your clothes in the hospital or at your home?"

Mr. B.:   "Somebody is stealing my clothes."

Doctor: "I would like to talk to you about your lunch today."

Mr. B.:   "Somebody is stealing my clothes."

Doctor: "I know that you told me that someone is stealing your clothes but I would like to talk to you about your lunch. I'd like to know what you ate for lunch."

Mr. B.:   "Somebody is stealing my clothes."

Another problem with orientation includes the difficulty to under-stand time.

Doctor: "Can you tell me what year it is?"

Mr. J.:   "It is 1934."

Doctor: "No, it is 1988."

Mr. J.:   "Oh, I didn't look at my calendar today."

Doctor: "What month is it?"

Mr. J.:   "It looks like January."

Doctor: "No, it is June. Look at the green grass and the trees."

Mr. J.:   "Oh, okay."

Doctor: "What year is it?"

Mr. J.: "1934."

Patients lose the ability to calculate. Medical students are taught to ask patients to subtract 7 from 100 in a serial manner. Patients will make many mistakes. Patients will have difficulty counting money. They are not able to give the appropriate amount of money for a purchase. Patients will often give a twenty dollar bill for a one dollar purchase and not expect any change.

The Late Phase

In the late phase of Alzheimer's Disease many other problems develop. Memory is severely affected. The patient may not recognize any members of his family. The person may not know how many children or grandchildren he/she has.

Doctor: "Good afternoon, Mr. C."

Mr. C.: "(There is a pause and no response.)"

Doctor: "I would like to thank the three of you for coming for a family meeting. I would like to talk to you about the severity of your father's Alzheimer's Disease."

1st Daughter: "Oh, Dad has always been quiet. He doesn't like to talk too much. I don't think he has the disease too severely."

Doctor: "I know that this may be a difficult interview. I know that I am diagnosing your father with a much more severe case of Alzheimer's than you think he has."

2nd Daughter: "I talked to Dad yesterday and he seemed pretty good to me."

Doctor: "Mr. C., tell me who is sitting beside you?"

Mr. C.: "I don't know her name."

1st Daughter: "Sure Dad, you know my name. My name is ___."

Doctor: "Let me interfere for a second. Please don't tell him your name. I want to demonstrate something to you. Mr. C., did you ever see this person before?"

Mr. C.: "No, I don't think so. Maybe I did many years ago."

1st Daughter: (Begins to cry)

2nd Daughter: "Dad, you remember me?"

Mr. C.:   (There is a long pause, he looks intensely at the daughter. He does not respond).

Doctor: "I think it is very difficult for you to believe that your father is profoundly affected by Alzheimer's Disease. It's true. He does not recognize you as his daughters. I know when you talk to him he seems to respond. However, he doesn't know what you are talking about. He doesn't know that you are his daughter. We have to discuss plans for your father's care because of the severity of his illness."

This example demonstrates how greatly affected a person may become with this disorder. There is probably nothing more destructive to family and friends experiencing a living person who has no ability to use their brain.

Orientation for time and place are totally lost and the person is then permanently lost in whatever setting he may be. If an individual is in a nursing home, he may not be able to find his room. Speech is reduced. Phrases are stated repetitively. The following is an excerpt from an interview that I had with Mr. D. and his wife.

Doctor: "Good afternoon Mr. D."

Mr. D.:   (Smiles to doctor)

Wife: "I shouldn't really talk right now but I want to say something. In the last six months my husband has hardly spoken. He was a civil servant in a high position. He was a wonderful speaker. He could make people laugh or move them to tears. I don't know what's going on. My family doctor told me that he has Alzheimer's Disease. I think he has something else."

Doctor: "Thank you Mrs. D. for telling me that. I want to ask Mr. D. a few questions. What is your name?"

Mr. D.:   "Jim"

Doctor: "Mr. D., do you go to a bank?"

Mr. D.:   "Yes"

Wife: "No. He hasn't gone for two or three years."

Doctor: "Mr. D., do you ever worry about your money?"

Mr. D.: "The stock market. The stock market (Mr. D. shows severe agitation and upsetness because he is not able to communicate)."

Doctor: "Tell me about the stock market."

Mr. D.: "The stock market. The stock market."

Doctor: "I see what you mean Mrs. D. He can't explain himself. He can't use words well. He repeats himself."

Doctor: "Mr. D., I would like you to raise your right hand."

Mr. D.: (Mr. D. smiles and raises his right hand.)

Doctor: "Mr. D., I would like you to stand up."

Mr. D.: (Mr. D. stands up.)

Doctor: "Mrs. D., I guess you were able to have your husband at home and take care of him because he could follow simple orders."

Mrs. D.: "He seems to understand what I tell him. I have to be very simple. I tell him when he ought to go to the bathroom. And he does."

This is an example of how an individual, in this case Mr. D., can understand words and respond to simple directions but has no ability to use words. This can become very frustrating to the patient. The patient may react with crying or hostility. The patient often becomes very frustrated by this inability to communicate and frequently gets angry at the person closest to him. In more severe cases, the patient will not be able to understand even simple words.

The person loses the ability to manipulate objects. They are no longer able to dress themselves, button their clothes, or use spoons or forks to feed themselves. At this late stage, they must be fed. Frequently, patients may maintain good strength and mobility. This becomes a serious problem because the person will wander away from their residence such as their home or their nursing home. If a nurse or family member should try to return them to the home, they may become very oppositional and aggressive. Here is an example of a family meeting with Mr. A., his wife and the nurse.

Doctor: "Mrs. A., thank you for coming to discuss some problems we are having in the hospital with your husband."

Mrs. A.: "I hope that we could solve them easily."

Doctor: "Unfortunately, there is no easy solution to your husband's problem. I would like to tell you beforehand that we are going to be talking about something very serious today."

Mrs. A.: "I'll be ready to help in any way I could."

Doctor: "I would like the nurse to tell you our problem and we would like to give you a solution to the problem."

Nurse: "Mr. A. is a very strong man. He can walk very well. In fact, he could run. He is always trying to leave the ward. It is winter and very cold outside. We are very worried that he will walk away from our ward when we are not watching him. He may injure himself or die from exposure. When we try to bring him back to the ward he fights with us. One of our nurses was sent home yesterday because he punched her in the face. A number of nurses were hurt. We now have orders that we can only bring Mr. A. back to the ward if several of us go to get him. He is taking so much time that we have no time left for the other patients. He does not know where he is. He does not know what he is doing here. He cannot communicate with us. We have tried to medicate him but he gets side effects from the medications. One of the medications gave him low blood pressure. He had to have constant nursing care for 48 hours because he was always getting out of bed and tending to fall. We were afraid that he would fall and injure himself. I know that I am talking too much right now. I know this is very hard for you to hear. However, the problem is serious. We did have a meeting and we have all come to the conclusion that he will have to go into a locked geriatric ward in a psychiatric hospital."

Mrs. A.: "This is very hard on me. I understand what you mean. Yes, I think that's best."

This example demonstrates the fact that patients may have very severe deficits in some areas but maintain great strengths in other areas. In this case, we have an individual who has severe deficits in orientation and memory. His abilities are his strength and his agility.

In the late phases, the Alzheimer patient suffers from disturbances in appetite, weight loss, and sleep. What does all this mean? Let's take the example of Mrs. Z. She was living quite independently one year ago. She needed some assistance until six months ago when she was hospitalized. One of her major problems was loss of appetite. The patient had no desire to eat. Discussions were held with the dietitian and family to identify her preferences. Special foods were brought to her but to no avail. The family then decided to bring home-cooked food to the hospital. She simply did not want to eat. The family would sit for endless hours with Mrs. Z. and encourage her to take even a single bite of food. A spoonful of food would be placed in her mouth but the food would not be swallowed. The patient may remain alive for many months in this state. This is a very difficult time for family and staff. There is a sense of helplessness. This is a time when the staff and family have to maintain open communication and be supportive to each other. It is very easy for staff to blame each other. It is even easier for family to blame the staff for not doing something. It is important to have the family involved in staff meetings so that they understand the severity of the problem.

Patients with Alzheimer's Disease sleep very irregularly. They may catnap in a sitting position for a few minutes and then begin wandering about the hospital. They walk about the unit throughout the night. These patients frequently awaken other patients.

There is probably nothing more embarrassing to staff and family than the problems of incontinence. Patients do not understand how to use the bathroom. They frequently soil themselves. They urinate on the floor. The feces then irritate the buttocks. The patient must be changed frequently. It seems that the patient is always smelly.

As the disease progresses, the person eventually becomes totally bedridden. They are unable to move, speak, or swallow. The patient then dies from an infection or cardiac arrest.

I would like to re-emphasize that there is no "typical patient" with Alzheimer's disease. That is, some patients deteriorate and die in a matter of six months. Other patients remain in a "middle phase" for many years. Some patients remain kind and pleasant. Other patients become aggressive. Some patients sit quietly. Others are very agitated and wander about the ward frequently looking for an escape.

Diagnosis

When a patient is in the late phases of Alzheimer's disease, it is easy to make the diagnosis. However, we do have problems with diagnosis in the early and middle phases. It is often difficult to decide whether a person is experiencing problems related to "normal aging" or due to an early phase of Alzheimer's disease. There is no way of examining or testing a person to decide whether they are going to become more ill and progress to Alzheimer's disease or whether they are simply in a normal aging state. The only method we have at the present time is simply to wait and re-examine. If the individual worsens, the diagnosis is Alzheimer's Disease.

There are other disorders that could mimic Alzheimer's Disease. The following paragraphs will discuss some of those disorders.

Another problem with diagnosis is "DELIRIUM". The patient who is delirious may sometimes be diagnosed as suffering from Alzheimer's Disease. The patient may present with the same problems of memory impairment, speech impairment of Alzheimer's Disease. However, delirium refers to the fact that the brain is affected by conditions such as pneumonia, urinary infection, vitamin deficiency, drug reaction or other factors. In other words, if the patient is treated for the disorder, for example, a urinary tract infection, then the patient will revert back to a normal state.

Elderly patients may develop a "DEPRESSION" but appear to have Alzheimer's Disease. Mr. K. was admitted to hospital because he spent his whole day in bed for the last six months, refused to shave, lost his appetite and lost sixty pounds. He appeared to have Alzheimer's Disease. Patients such as Mr. K. may be wrongly diagnosed and placed in a nursing home. Instead, Mr. K. was hospitalized and treated with anti-depressant drugs and electro-therapy. Two months after his discharge from hospital he was driving his car, visiting with friends, shopping, banking, and babysitting his grandchildren.

Elderly patients may become extremely "DEPENDENT". These patients do not have Alzheimer's Disease. They have a great need to be dependent on other family members. To this extent, these patients often claim to have many physical illnesses, telephone family members frequently, and cry when left alone. They seem to be helpless. These individuals may appear to have many characteristics of Alzheimer's Disease. The main disorder is that they want to maintain their relationship to their family and therefore "act" in a manner that would cause people to be sympathetic to them. They act helpless. These people are sometimes called "pseudodemented".

Causes

All my patients and their family ask me "what causes Alzheimer's Disease?". The simple answer to this question is "no one knows the cause of Alzheimer's Disease".

It appears that Alzheimer's Disease may be a genetic disorder. In other words, it is an inherited disease. It may be that Alzheimer's Disease is due to a viral disease. There are many other theories. Let me state it again. We Don't Know What Causes Alzheimer's Disease.

Patient Management

I would like to emphasize that there is no treatment which can stop the progress of this disease. Families frequently refuse to accept the diagnosis of Alzheimer's Disease and frequently demand more tests, further consultation and treatments for the person they love. As cruel as it may sound, I will say it again "there is no cure for Alzheimer's Disease".

There are many things that we know about Alzheimer's Disease. The following paragraphs will outline some of the things that should be considered when caring for a person with Alzheimer's Disease.

All medical and physical problems should be treated to the greatest degree. The person with Alzheimer's Disease has a brain that is very sensitive to many things. If a person has a urinary infection (infection of the bladder) this may cause their Alzheimer's Disease to appear more severe. Let me give you an example. Mr. J. is a 75 year old man who was brought to my office because he was now awakening throughout the night, was confused and unable to find his way to the bathroom. He was examined and it was noted that he had bacteria and white blood cells in his urine. He was treated with antibiotics and the nighttime awakening and confusion disappeared. This does not mean that the Alzheimer's Disease stopped. It just means that the brain is very sensitive and the patient deteriorates more with each untreated disorder. I can give you many other examples of this problem but I think that you understand what I mean. Quite simply, let's make sure that the person is not suffering from any medical disorder because this could make this condition appear more severe.

All attempts should be made to encourage a good diet and an adequate exercise program. Patients with Alzheimer's Disease will often do better over a longer period of time if they eat a well balanced meal and exercise regularly. Mr. J. is a 73 year old man who was hospitalized after being found wandering in the streets in the middle of the night by his neighbor. We were able to get a good history about his diet from the neighborhood grocer. Apparently this patient did not like to cook for himself. For many years he ate nothing but oatmeal. Tests revealed he suffered from a vitamin deficiency. With vitamins and a well balanced diet, he improved dramatically over the next five weeks. He was not able to return to his home and live independently but he was much healthier and was able to live in a seniors' lodge.

Because people with Alzheimer's Disease are usually elderly, they may have visual or hearing deficiencies. Patients who have Alzheimer's Disease appeared to be much more disturbed if they cannot see or hear adequately. It is very important that the patient's eyes and ears be checked and that glasses and hearing aids are ordered when necessary.

Patients with Alzheimer's Disease do best in quiet and familiar surroundings. Families should be educated about this particular requirement. Families often feel that they should encourage the person with Alzheimer's Disease to visit others, to go shopping, to go to concerts, etc. This will often cause more stress and the patient could deteriorate. It is important to offer a simple environment. Whenever a major change is experienced, such as a move from home to hospital, confusion increases. It may then take two weeks for the confusion to disappear. When a person is moved from their home to an apartment or hospital, it is best to take along some cherished objects. This helps to orient them and give them some comfort. If Alzheimer's Disease is incapacitating, vacations and travel should be discouraged.

Please remember that Alzheimer's Disease can be mild, moderate or severe. It is very difficult to write about this disorder and make suggestions for all patients. I think it is important for you to think of the various things that I'm telling you but to use this information intelligently. For example, patients with mild or moderate degrees of Alzheimer's may be able to travel successfully. It may be best to discuss these types of life style considerations with your family doctor.

Medications may be important for patients with Alzheimer's Disease but must be used with great care. Usually much lower dosages must be used. Elderly patients with Alzheimer's Disease experience medication side effects more frequently than younger individuals. The elderly person frequently has other diseases and therefore is taking different types of drugs. Drugs are very powerful and can interact negatively with each other. It is essential for the patient to bring all medications to each office visit. In this manner, the patient could be assured that the physician will know all the drugs and dosages that are presently being used and will take special care in ordering new medications for other disorders.

Some patients with Alzheimer's Disease experience a great deal of anxiety and therefore anti-anxiety drugs are of assistance. Other patients may suffer from depression and may require antidepressant medications. Some patients become elated, hyperactive, suspicious or assaultive. These patients will need tranquilizers to settle their agitated behavior. For insomnia, night sedatives may be used. Please refer to the chapters which describe these drugs.

Help professionals assist persons with Alzheimer's Disease by being supportive to them. Patients with this disorder need much encouragement and emotional support. Professionals and family should encourage the patient to reduce their stress level and to move away from demanding situations. Patients should be encouraged to become involved in hobbies, social activities and household activities that are easily handled.

In the early and middle phases, the spouse frequently assists the patient with Alzheimer's Disease. However, the spouse may need education and support. The spouse or other relative may be spending a great deal of time with the person suffering from Alzheimer's Disease and need relief help. Let me give you an example. Mr. B., a 75 year old male, was brought to my office by his wife because she was concerned about her husband's inability to sleep. The following is part of my discussion that I had with Mrs. B.

Doctor: "Can you tell me what you are concerned about?"

Mrs. B.: "My husband frequently awakens at night and wanders about. I would like to know if you can give him something to assist him with his sleep."

Doctor: "This must be quite difficult on you Mrs. B. It is my experience that the person caring for an individual with Alzheimer's Disease is frequently very anxious and awakens each time that the patient awakens."

Mrs. B.: "Yes, this is true"

Doctor: "You look quite exhausted. How are you feeling?"

Mrs. B.: "I feel terrible. I don't think I have slept one proper night in two years. I have never had a break from my husband in two years. I have not gone for a vacation. Sometimes I wonder how long I could continue."

Doctor: "I am sorry that you are so exhausted. Did you know that you can get assistance for your husband so that you can get a break for yourself?"

Mrs. B.: "No."

Doctor: "I think several things could be done. Did you ever think of hiring someone during the day time so that you can get some rest during the day or take a break from your husband and go shopping?"

Mrs. B.:   "No, I didn't."

Doctor: "Many nursing homes have so-called "Vacation Beds" so that you can have your husband at a nursing home for a number of weeks. This can give you a chance to rest, go for a trip, or take care of special errands."

Mrs. B.:   "I think I need some help now. Please tell me how this can be done."

I think that this short discussion will give you an idea of the stresses experienced by family members and the resources that could be mobilized. These resources could be reached through community nurses, social services, and the physician's office. It is not uncommon for family members to sacrifice their own health and sense of well-being to attend the needs of the Alzheimer's patient.

Patients and their families should ask their physician for other kinds of community services. Some services may provide meals to the home so that the patient and spouse do not have to do their own shopping or cooking. Nurses may come to the home on a regular basis to help with a variety of activities such as bathing, foot care, mouth care and other medical attention. Nurses may also organize medications in special medication boxes called dosettes. The person with Alzheimer's Disease may not be able to take medications appropriately from a regular pill bottle but may be able to take them in an orderly manner from this special type of medication dispenser.

A patient may continue to live at home but may require some activities outside the home. Many cities have special bus systems that transport patients to a variety of recreational activities or day hospital programs.

A patient in the early or middle phases of Alzheimer's Disease may not be able to live at home but could live in a seniors' residence. In the seniors' residence, the person may live in a single or shared room. All the meals are provided. There is usually a person on duty on a 24 hour basis. However, patients must be able to take care of their own general hygiene, bathroom activities and clothing.

As the Alzheimer's Disease progresses, the patient may not be able to remain in a seniors' residence and would then require assistance in a nursing home. Nursing homes are moderate to large size institutions that provide a number of services to their patients. Services include housekeeping, laundry, meals, dispensing of medications, occupational and recreational therapy and special nursing procedures. Patients in a nursing home generally require less than 1.5

hours of nursing care per 24 hours. This figure may be different in different cities.

If a patient requires more than 1.5 hours of nursing care per 24 hour period, they then require the services of an auxiliary hospital. An auxiliary hospital provides essentially all the services of a general hospital. However, physicians examine the patients less frequently than in an active treatment hospital. Diagnostic procedures are more limited in the auxiliary hospital.

Legal Problems

In the early phases of Alzheimer's Disease, the patient is able to make his own decisions on items such as medical care, contracts and finances. However, eventually the individual can no longer take care of these important aspects of living. Every province and state has an act which governs the rights of patients with brain impairment. This act has various names in different provinces and states. It is often called the "Dependent Adults Act". This is an act which helps protect those adults who cannot protect themselves.

In the "Dependent Adults Act", there is provision for a guardian and trustee. A guardian is an individual who has the ability to make decisions on the patient's behalf for activities of daily living. The guardian is given the responsibility of taking the patient to a physician, signing consent forms for examination and treatment, etc. The trustee has the responsibility and right to control the individual's finances and contractual arrangements. The patient then no longer has the right to enter into contracts or to make monetary decisions. The patient is usually not allowed to use a credit card, write a cheque, or draw cash from the bank. The trustee must do these transactions for the patient.

It is a very serious act to take away an individual's rights as I have described. This is done by a family member, friend or professional such as a social worker, who makes an application through a lawyer. The lawyer must apply to the courts to assign the guardian and/or trustee. The judge rules whether the person comes under the provisions of the Dependent Adults Act, and who the guardian or trustee shall be. The guardian and trustee may be a friend or relative or a publicly appointed individual. At times, there may be serious conflict among competing members of the family as to who should become the guardian and/or trustee. This may then involve fairly lengthy court procedures.

Ethical Aspects

The Hippocratic oath instructs us to prevent suffering and provide treatment. With the advances of modern medicine, an individual can be treated and kept alive for many years. This has produced a number of problems for the patient, his family, professionals and society. Ethical questions include: "When do you stop treatment?" and "If a new disorder develops, should treatment be withheld?"

Let us look at the first question. Let us look at the case of Mrs. Z who has lost her appetite completely and is weakened. As you recall, I stated that staff and family placed food into the patient's mouth but she would not swallow the food. Should we stop trying to feed the patient and let her die? If we stop trying to feed her, then we are really withholding treatment. That is, when a member of the medical staff is feeding the patient, the patient is receiving treatment. When no one is feeding the patient, treatment is being withheld. Should we stick tubes into the patient to keep her alive? This is a serious ethical problem.

Let us take the second ethical question. If a new disorder develops, should treatment be withheld? I would like you to imagine a person who is suffering from an advanced phase of Alzheimer's Disease. The patient is now unable to dress himself, eat independently, and go to the bathroom. The patient is unable to control his bladder and bowels. The patient is constantly wet or soiled from urine and feces. This patient now develops a severe pneumonia. If the pneumonia is left untreated, the patient will quickly die. If the patient is treated with modern medical approaches, the patient will not die. The patient may live for months and possibly years. Let us now ask the question in a very specific manner. The question is: "Should the patient be immediately treated in an intensive manner with intravenous fluids, oxygen, and powerful antibiotics?" or "Should the patient be left to die?" In other words, should treatment be withheld?

I don't have the answers to these questions. I know the arguments FOR TREATMENT and AGAINST TREATMENT. What do you think should be the answers to the two questions?

Extent of Alzheimer's Disease

Alzheimer's Disease occurs in the elderly. Two percent of adults 65 to 70 years of age suffer from Alzheimers. Twenty percent of those over the age of 80 suffer from Alzheimers. These figures relate to the "moderate to severe" forms of Alzheimers. Two to three times as many patients in these age groups suffer from the mild form of Alzheimers.

In 1900, only 4% of the population was over the age of 65. In 1970, 20% of the population in the United States was over the age of 65. It is believed that in the year 2030, 50% of the population will be over the age of 65. Although these figures relate to the United States, they are comparable to those in Canada and other industrialized nations.

By knowing the population of the country, you can now calculate the number of individuals who will be suffering from Alzheimer's Disease.

It is obvious that Alzheimer's Disease is a very common disease. We do not know the cause of Alzheimer's Disease. We do not have a cure. We must assist those less fortunate than ourselves.

CHAPTER 10

Habit Control

HABIT CONTROL

Whenever one of the hosts of "That's Living" does a program on habit control, many listeners expect us to start talking about smoking. Other adults with problems in other areas, such as compulsive gambling or drinking, believe that we will be preparing cookbook recipes to solve these problems. Well, stopping smoking has been a feature of "That's Living" since the inception of the program, so that topic will not be avoided. Nevertheless it is important to recognize that habit control is as necessary for young children as it is for adults, and many of the developmental questions frequently bothering parents, have to do with habit and habit development.

Developmental Habits

These are habits that occur naturally at a particular stage of development. The problem comes when the habit continues at an age level when it is not appropriate. There are thousands of examples. The one that most frequently appears on "That's Living" is poor bladder control. This is absolutely natural when the child is one year of age. In later years, it becomes a problem labelled as enuresis. Control of the bowels is particularly difficult for a one or two year old, but a school child needs medical attention when he/she cannot control this function; encopresis is the label given. Other habits include thumb sucking, stuttering, nail biting and temper tantrums. All of these habits develop as a child explores his or her environment. They become inappropriate at a later stage of development.

It should be noted in this section that with the possible exception of fears and phobias, the most common question asked of our psychologist/psychiatrist hosts has to do with sleep problems. Therefore, it should at least be noted that sleep habits can be a major family problem for children and adults.

So, an entire range of problems can be developed which stultify normal growth and development if allowed to continue. Yet most of us would have great difficulty even proceeding through everyday routines, without the use of habit formation. For example, most of us start walking up a flight of stairs with the same foot. It seems unlikely that every time we started a flight of stairs we would debate and make a conscious decision as to which foot would "lead off". In the morning, putting on shoes and socks, we usually start with the right or left foot. We don't make a decision about "should I put on the left shoe first?" or "this morning will it be the right shoe?" Bathroom activities in the morning including shaving for the men, brushing of teeth, etc., are all done without conscious decision making processes becoming involved. Habits are useful, they are time savers, they help us; it is only when the habit is inappropriate to the developmental stage of the person that the professional needs to become involved, or the parents need to take some action. Well then, what is a habit?

A habit can be an "acquired activity that has become fixed and consistent as a result of repeated performances". This definition was put in quotation marks, because the language does not sound at all like the language used by this author. The definition though has been used and repeated so many times, the original source has been forgotten. As a side-line to this discussion, it should be noted that not all people even agree that habits exist. For example, existential philosophers don't believe in habits at all. These people think that all things have meaning each time they occur. Most of us would not agree with this, nor would we want to start debating with ourselves as to which hand we use to squeeze the toothpaste.

Now each habit that has been discussed as an example could be handled separately. Entire books with scientific documentation have been written about bedwetting, often with professionals giving contradictory advice. Parents though can take comfort from the fact that there seems to be some principles that can assist in breaking or reframing habits so children can once again take control of their own behavior.

Lets look at some strategies for handling developmental habits.

Toilet Training

What on earth does a professional man not in the field of medicine know about toilet training? Not very much according to his own family. The first day toilet training was an issue for discussion with this particular radio host, he arrived home to be greeted with the comment "the only thing you ever did around here to assist in toilet training was disappear". Sad, but true.

Yet psychological principles do apply, and toilet training can be where a parent attempts to establish a habit, hopefully that will last for the rest of an individual's life. The habit has more ramifications than producing urine and stools in a toilet rather than in one's diapers. Commonsense rules of hygiene are taught by parents at the same time children learn the value of basic principles such as flushing and washing hands. Well, if we wish to cement a habit,

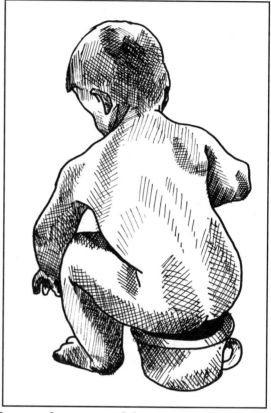

the rules are fairly simple. We reward success and do not punish failure. The reason we do not punish failure is because the attention gained by this negative action can be as reinforcing as praise for success. The famous psychologist B.F. Skinner, utilizing the process of operant conditioning, showed us that if you wait for an action to appear naturally, then provide positive reinforcement, that action will occur again. So mother may have been right by sitting a child on a potty, and waiting for something to happen. Wise parents begin to realize when a child is producing symptoms of being about ready to perform, and a dash to the potty can result in a positive experience for all. The child of course, will regress on occasion, and as little fuss as possible should be made about these incidents. Most readers will already know that when a new baby, or for that matter even a new puppy or kitten arrives in the family, a well trained child may revert back to behavior more appropriate to an earlier stage of development. Unfortunately lack of toilet training becomes the very best example of this regression phenomenon.

Some advice for parents would include the suggestion that when things are not working well and when you become thoroughly frustrated, this is a good time to back off from the training period for a week or two until you can approach it with more confidence. Many years ago Freud was wise enough to discover that children can utilize lack of control in this area to in fact gain attention and exert control over their parents. As a matter of fact Freud made the supposition that difficulties with early toilet training often led to difficulties later in life. So parents, keep your sense of humor, be consistent, reward success, pay as little attention to failure as possible. Once proper toilet training habits are developed and cemented, they do last a lifetime.

Nail Biting

Many listeners have brought to our attention this common and apparently serious problem. This one though is one where we really do have answers. The hosts of "That's Living" are proud to say that with nail biting we have received 100% positive comments when people have tried strictly behavioral methods as discussed on the program. Let's then talk about the problem.

When one thinks of nail biting, one thinks of small children. However, most of us know of at least one adult in our acquaintantship who is very concerned, perhaps overly concerned, about nail biting. People hate to have their fingernails bitten "to the quick" with the resulting hangnails, red inflammation, etc.. Yet it seems to be a habit that is difficult to break, and particularly under stress or tension, it occurs over and over again.

To break this habit it is necessary to bring the procedure into consciousness, take control of it, and then be alert and aware should the habit re-occur. The simplest possible strategy is one where psychologists have more than a modicum of success.

Okay parents; let's suggest to the child with a nail biting problem that he or she first make a fist, put hands in front of eyes to take a good look at what fingernails look like when they have been chewed and bitten. After having a good look at the nails, encourage youngsters to stop biting the fingernail of the little finger. That is the first and only suggestion one needs to make. After approximately one week, if the child takes the admonition seriously, fingernails on the little finger begin to look very different from the rest of the hand. Surprisingly, this is often all that needs to be done. When children or adults brings into consciousness how easy it is to improve the situation, they take control of their own habits.

It doesn't work this easily every time. The author has personally worked with clients where it was necessary to do the same thing one finger at a time. The psychology behind the treatment is that by making the suggestion that you stop biting one finger, you put the person back in control of the habit. Once the person is in control, he or she now knows when a particular finger is bitten. When a person is aware, he or she not only stops biting the little finger, the other nails receive less attention. It really does work!

Thumb Sucking

It was a surprise to this psychologist that there are as many children who bite and suck their thumbs, as evidenced by the phone calls we receive. I think parents must take rather dramatic action by saying "stop" or "no". Lectures don't particularly help. We need to take swift and sure action before another child gets hurt. I don't really know why children bite, but suspect it is a part of developmental phases at approximately age two and age four. The problem is compounded by the fact that once bitten, a person's reaction is so violent that the reinforcement encourages, not discourages the child to try the same behavior again. It must stop. Say "no" or "stop" in a loud voice. Take the child out of the situation. Do not discuss it with him other than to indicate this must not happen again.

Back to thumb sucking. One doesn't need much imagination to recognize that thumb sucking is a very normal developmental childhood phase. The child sucks and is rewarded even as an infant. He or she will suck to eat. Later the mouth and hand are used almost exclusively as the child explores the environment. The thumb, or often the two fingers next to the thumb, are used by the child when he or she no longer has a bottle or a pacifier. In fact, while the use of pacifiers is somewhat controversial, research studies generally have shown that the child who uses a pacifier seldom sucks thumbs or fingers. The desire to suck is natural. The habit of thumb sucking does not appear to be serious at first; it becomes very difficult to control when it continues, when children cannot sleep unless they are sucking, when they are embarrassed by this behavior in school.

Well the first bit of advice would be that lectures don't help. If this behavior is habitual, then discussing it in the abstract will not likely make any behavior change. Also, there is a danger by bringing the behavior directly to the attention of the child; if there is an attention getting component, the behavior then is likely to continue.

My suggestion would be that we encourage and reward the child when he or she is not engaging in this behavior. Let the child know

how attractive she looks or how alert he appears when they are in
fact sitting, standing, or lying down without fingers in the mouth.
When the child is thumb sucking I would suggest that a parent
gently but firmly remove the thumb from the mouth, at the same
time giving the child a smile or a word of encouragement. Do not at
that time talk a lot about crooked teeth, or misshapen fingers, or
whatever. Threats about putting material like red pepper on the
finger, do not appear to be very useful.

It will be admitted that there are aids and devices which can be
purchased to cover fingers so they cannot be sucked. This may in fact
be necessary in some isolated instances. An early strategy though is
to reward the child when the behavior is not occurring. When it
occurs, even in sleep, parents should remove the fingers always in a
spirit of friendliness and encouragement. Good luck with this one!

Acquired Habits

Well now, we come to the kind of habits of most concern to adults
in their personal lives. Usually people begin to smoke, or drink
alcohol or gamble, through conscious choice. It is later that these
activities become habitual and in some cases addictive. Stopping the
habit for many people is much more difficult than starting and some
individuals spend most of their lifetime fighting the dangers of tobacco or alcohol, or other addicting substances. Yet not all acquired
habits fall into the adult domain. Sometimes speech patterns of
children can become sloppy, as words are pronounced incorrectly, or
shortened to make speech easier. Before embarking upon a treatise
about smoking, let's look at one of the problems most families face
with young children. This is the problem of "bedtime blues".

Bedtime Confusion

A protracted battle at bedtime is a habit that is acquired, rather
than developed. However, many parents begin to wish that bedtime
would never happen, because of the fights, tantrums, arguments and
frustration associated with this time of day. It is easy to see why
these episodes develop. In the first instance, some children are actually afraid of the dark and of going to bed, and will use any possible
way they can to avoid being left alone in their beds. Other children
learn that by pouting or being disagreeable, often mother or dad will
read a story, allow them to stay up a little later, or reward this
behavior in some other fashion. This of course means that the behavior is likely to be reinforced and continue.

This problem won't be solved "overnight". Many children do have nightmares and difficulties with sleep patterns that can't be overcome easily. One useful suggestion though, is to use the child's bedroom for other activities during the day in addition to sleeping. It is important that the child should not view the bedroom as a place where he or she is sent for punishment and sleep. The two concepts then will become synonymous and the battle begins. Use the bedroom for fun activities like play and story time and story telling. The child then will not fear nearly so much to go to that room alone.

Other suggestions would include structure without rigidity. It almost sounds like I'm contradicting myself, but hopefully this explanation will make sense. If a child has a structure and understands that bedtime occurs at a particular time of day, this will help form habits which encourage tiredness when bedtime approaches. On the other hand, bedtime should not be seen by the child as a punishment. If something is happening which is exciting for family members, it should be the parent who suggests maybe we can delay the bedtime for a little while until this is concluded. If we always have child versus parent in these arguments, they continue longer than if we have child and the parent working together to reach a reasonable compromise; the child receives enough sleep, but is also "in on the action" at home.

When reading stories at bedtime, parents often make the mistake of reading exciting new material and the child stays awake to hear the story. An alternate method is to tell the same story over and over with lots of repetition, so the voice of the parent promotes through an almost rhythmic sing-song quality, relaxation and then sleep. Some years ago an Alberta psychologist, Keith Floyd, wrote a book, *Sandman's Land* which really makes no sense, but possesses a rhythm and structure conducive to relaxation (Floyd, 1986). This book encourages sleep if read aloud to adults as well as children.

In summary, remember children are individuals. The same bedtime will not suit every family member. Be consistent yet somewhat flexible, and make the bedroom a fun place. After a child is asleep it is often a good idea to chat a bit with the sleeping child telling him or her what a great person you have for a youngster. Trust me, they hear.

Stopping Smoking

The authors of this book have been involved in stop smoking campaigns for a decade. In 1985 when the program "That's Living" was presented with a Gold Ribbon Award for Broadcasting in Canada, it was to a large extent on the basis of a very successful stop smoking program that was held both on the program and through a mass rally in Edmonton, Alberta. Later some of the findings of our participants in that program were tabulated and became a master's thesis written by Elaine Morrison from the University of Alberta.

When it comes time to discuss such a well known topic, it is difficult to maintain a conversational style. This author is tempted to go to the literature and talk about all of the things that have been written about smoking, all of the research that has been done and there has been a great deal. Let's make two points at the start of this section.

(1) Cigarette smoking is dangerous to the health of the smoker as well as to the health of others in proximity to the smoker.

(2) The problem of smoking may well be the most serious national and international health concern in the second half of the twentieth century. Smokers are becoming an "embattled breed" as more and more efforts are made by the majority of the people to keep a smoke-free atmosphere.

Smoking is also a very emotional issue. Smokers feel, as a minority group, that they are being attacked for something out of control. Non-smokers and particularly reformed smokers are bitter in their attacks on smoking, and many citizens are finding themselves forced to work in smoke-free atmospheres including office buildings, restaurants, lounges, hospitals, schools, government buildings. The problem is a serious one.

Some listeners have written us almost in desperation advising that this habit cannot be broken, hoping for some miracle which will take away the urge to smoke. Letters such as the following are common to the hosts of "That's Living":

> "...I have been smoking for about 22 years and although I have seriously tried on several occasions to stop completely, trying various approaches, I have only succeeded in eventually increasing the amount I smoke. I am presently smoking one and one half packages daily, I'm 40 years old and my only health concern at this time is high cholesterol levels which have been recognized by my general practitioner. I am controlling this through diet. I feel very encouraged with the success of (others) with (their) ability to stop smoking ... I am at my wits end to think of any other ways I might be able to quit smoking; I have attended the "Five Day Smoking Program" acupuncture, snacking on fresh fruits and veggies, and nicotine gum prescribed by my physician ... any suggestions ... would be appreciated."

This man or woman is in real trouble and probably the chances of successfully quitting smoking are minimal. The type of person who visits specialists, experts, stop smoking clinics, is hoping someone or something can solve a problem which clearly belongs to the addicted smoker. In fact, some of our listeners argue about whether smoking is an addiction, a habit, or both. Perhaps it doesn't matter. What matters is that the individual must decide he or she wants to and needs to stop smoking. This must take precedence in the person's life style. There will be difficulties, but it can be done. The answer written to the letter above included the suggestion that the person stop looking for someone to affect a cure. The first step in breaking this habit is to take responsibility for it.

Now let's be more optimistic. The following letter contains a suggestion which worked for the writer. Could it be that this would work for the rest of us? Let's see.

> "... I smoked for years - but that was years ago - probably thirty, so you can tell I'm no spring chicken. But I found a trick to help myself that I've never ever heard mentioned ... When you really want to sit down and treat yourself to a cigarette - do it - but your cigarette is a length of hollow spaghetti. This gives you a "break". You can inhale as deeply as you like - let the pretend smoke curl up your nostrils. Enjoy the usual sensations. Smoke time is over - then go about all your other usual activities until your next smoke break. You'd probably look a little foolish at a card party, but it works at home ..."

Success stories are what we need, and this is a positive letter. One of the unfortunate things about success stories, though, is that often they cannot be transferred intact to another person. The authors of this book have worked with clients and patients and have assisted people to stop smoking through groups, through the use of Bantron or Nicorettes, through the use of relaxation and hypnosis, through the use of individual therapy, through a "cold turkey" approach, etc. There is no universal cure and what works for one individual may not for another, yet people can and do stop smoking and we're pleased to have assisted some individuals do just that. It should be noted that radio and TV counselling has become an acceptable way to assist people to work on habit control. Large projects have been successfully completed in Finland and California where television and radio stations cooperated in mass media stop smoking programs. Like all stop smoking programs, many people were helped, others were not.

To stop smoking, it is wise to first consider some of the biases you need to drop before you will be successful. In the first instance many people believe that habit control is simply willpower. Reformed smokers are perhaps the most active proponents of this myth, you simply need more self control, more willpower and you will be able to stop. The unfortunate part of this belief is that people see it as a sign of weakness to ask for help and most people, really - most people, cannot stop smoking "cold turkey" simply by quitting. We need assistance. Asking for help is a realistic first step. If a person has a positive self-image, this will help. If you believe you can be a non-smoker, if you can see yourself and visualize yourself as a non-smoker, then assistance through groups or individual help from professionals will be even more useful. The one phrase to avoid when attempting to beat any habit like smoking is "I'm trying". This implies defeat. The advice given by many professionals is don't try - succeed. In practical terms this simply means that it is better to successfully stop smoking between 2:00 and 5:00 p.m. every day for a week than it is to stop for 24 hours and then return to the former state. The trick for successful complete abstinence is to first set realistic goals, then meet them. Finally, it is hard to see your friends, spouse, parents, etc. as saboteurs, but this is another real danger when a person alters his or her life style. Smokers will attempt to keep others around them smoking as well. They are not being vicious. Through a process of rationalization they are maintaining the status quo in their world. The responsibility for quitting smoking belongs to the smoker. Any advice such as "just this once" or "only until you get over this problem" is bad advice. Sometimes when we fail at an important task it helps to blame, but it is better to succeed.

Well, now that you feel good about yourself and you have decided to succeed, seek help. There are many places where one can receive assistance. A group movement has developed. Many private companies are involved. One of the best known group approaches to stopping smoking has been developed by the Christian Science Church. The idea of groups is to provide instant feedback to people, so that collectively people can look for success rather than failure. Much of our educational system is also based on groups; so often in a group situation we learn easier and more efficiently. Group counselling is a helpful way to assist people to stop smoking. The results are better than simple individual effort, but still leave much to be desired.

Because smoking is both an addiction and a habit, our medical practitioners have assisted through developing "nicotine substitutes" (Nicorettes®) which can be obtained by patients through their medical doctor. The idea of this strategy is that to make withdrawal easier one habit is substituted for another; that is, one can chew gum, receive nicotine, and then withdraw from gum chewing. The results are effective with some people, but not everybody. It is well known that the psychological trauma of withdrawal is often more difficult than the physiological problem. People use smoking for many different activities, some of which are not known to the smoker until some time after initial withdrawal. It is for this reason that some people have had good luck in stopping on holidays. When returning to work the pressure to smoke returns.

Other techniques commonly used by psychologists include visualization, relaxation, or hypnosis. With this technique, individuals are taught to think positively, to visualize themselves as non-smokers, to think less about problems and more about the benefits that will accrue following successful cessation of this habit. Again, mixed results, although the authors have had some excellent success with this particular strategy.

In summary, it is not easy to stop smoking. Most professionals would agree that if an individual can cut down smoking fifty percent on his or her own hook, this is a useful first step. It stands to reason that if a person can control fifty percent of a habit, that person will be convinced already that a professional or group can assist with the remaining fifty percent. Positive thinking does help. If at first you are not able to simply quit, be proud of the efforts you make and the small successes you do achieve. By all means, seek professional assistance.

CHAPTER 11

Addictions

ADDICTIONS

Alcoholism and Physical Illness

Alcoholism has become such a negative term that it is probably good that the American Psychiatric Association is recommending that we use the word "alcohol abuse" or "alcohol dependence". In my practice, I frequently talk to patients and their families about the problems that develop in relationship to alcohol. I will often use the term "alcohol related problems". All these terms relate to the same problem, namely, alcohol use and its consequences.

Social drinking is extremely common. The question then arises, "When does the use of alcohol become alcohol abuse"?

A person is said to be suffering from alcoholism or alcohol abuse if the following problems develop: (1) a preoccupation with alcohol use - the person tends to drink alcohol every day. There is a preoccupation as to when to get the "next drink". There are attempts to "go on the wagon" (not drink for a few days). Instead, there is a constant return to alcohol use every day. (2) Binges - remaining intoxicated for at least two days, (3) Blackouts - during a blackout, an individual may appear quite normal and reasonable. The person may be talking to others and acting fairly appropriately. However, next morning there is no recollection of what happened or what was said the night before. (4) Drinking in spite of physical disorders which are caused by alcohol use such as liver damage. In other words, the person has been told that he now has liver damage but is unable to stop drinking. (5) Difficulties at work - Alcohol use to the degree that work is missed. If an individual is drunk at work, many errors will be made which could be dangerous to the drunk person or others. An individual who is drunk at work may argue and cause difficulties for other

co-workers. There may be difficulties with reflexes, coordination and judgement leading to accidents on the job. (6) Difficulties in personal and social relationships - the person who is drunk frequently argues with his children or wife. The person may be very irritable. There is a disregard for the needs of others. Conflicts in the family may lead to arguments, fighting, separation and divorce.

In the medical and popular literature, you will find the term "alcohol dependency". "Alcohol dependence" is exactly the same as "alcohol abuse" except for two features which are labelled "tolerance" and "withdrawal". Tolerance means there is a need to drink more to get the same effect. It's more difficult to get "high". Withdrawal means that symptoms such as nausea, vomiting, nightmares, "shakiness", and tiredness occur when drinking is stopped. Think of your own experience when you were at a party and drank too much. Next morning you have a headache, feel tired, and experience shakiness. In the usual person, this is fairly mild. These symptoms disappear when alcohol is used again. You have heard the statement, "I feel better after a beer in the morning". However, individuals who have been drinking large amounts for a long time, develop a very severe withdrawal. The withdrawal can be so severe that hospitalization is needed. This individual is extremely sick and could die if immediate medical care is not provided. In the most severe state, this is referred to as delirium tremens (the D.T.'s).

I have just told you how to diagnose yourself or someone else who is suffering from alcohol abuse or alcoholism. Let's put this into a different form to provide a more vivid picture. Let me carry you through the evaluation and treatment of one of my patients. Let's start with a telephone call that I received from Tom's wife, Jean, on Christmas Eve.

Doctor: "Hi Jean. It's a long time since I've heard from you. How are things going?"

Jean: "Terrible doctor, you've got to help us immediately. Tom isn't well at all. I'm upset. The whole family is upset. The children are crying and Tom just had an argument with our oldest daughter."

Family disturbed

Doctor: "I'm sorry to hear this. Tom has been hospitalized on two previous occasions. It sounds as though he will have to be hospitalized again. Bring him to emergency and I'll meet you there."

Alcoholism tends to recur

Jean: "I can't. He's really angry. He threatened me and the kids. He said if I called anybody, he would shoot me. He's totally drunk. He's been drinking for three days. He hasn't had a bite to eat. He staggers and falls."

Hostility and Binge Drinking

Doctor: "Take it easy, take it easy. I will get more history from you when we meet at emergency. The main thing is to get him there. I know some of your family. It's Christmas Eve and I'm sure that there are family members around to help you."

Disturbing special occasions

Jean: "Yes, we were to go for Christmas Eve dinner to my brother's place. Everybody will be there."

Doctor: "Okay, you phone your brother and ask him to come along with one other person. The three of you should be able to bring him to the hospital. I know that he will be angry. But if all three of you hold your ground he will come. Tell him that I'll meet you there."

Need for others to help

Pretend that you are with me in the emergency department. We are sitting in a room with Tom, Jean, Jean's brother and Jean's brother-in-law."

Tom: "Look Doc, I'm perfectly healthy. I'm standing. I'm talking. I'm making sense. Nobody can hospitalize me against my will. I have my rights. There is no problem. I don't know what everybody is complaining about. I was a bit tired so I wanted to get some good sleep and I stayed in bed for a while. What's wrong with that."

Denial and Lack of Judgement

Doctor: "You don't look good to me. Your face is all red and blotchy. I notice some big red marks on your chest which tell me that you have been drinking quite a lot."

Jean: "Please stay, Tom. The kids are crying. You're threatening suicide. I'm petrified. I'm fearful of you. You were on the phone for two hours yesterday. Today you were arguing with me and saying that you weren't on the phone at all yesterday. You were having blackouts."

Suicidal behavior is common
Alcoholic "blackout"

Tom: "Forget it. I'm healthy as a horse.

Brother: "Look Tom. I hate to say it but this is becoming silly. Everybody is at our home waiting to start the Christmas Eve dinner and we're arguing here at emergency. Come in for a while and let the doctor do some tests on you. You have to "dry up". You haven't been at work for a week. People are covering up for you but everyone is getting tired of this cover up."

Work difficulties

Doctor: "Look Tom, I can't force you to stay in hospital nor can anyone else. You are denying that you have a problem. You are acting as though you are normal and everyone else is acting silly and you are blaming them. You have been in hospital before and you know the routine. I will call the internist to help me out with you because you have had the shakes in the past. I am afraid that you will get the D.T.'s. I want some other physical things checked up also."

Withdrawal is frequent

Hospitalization to detoxify

Tom: "Okay, okay."

This is Christmas Day and you are in the hospital with me in Tom's room. Jean has come to the hospital to visit Tom and to ask about his progress."

Jean: "How are things, doctor?"

Doctor: "Not too good. We have some blood tests back and a number of tests are abnormal. The liver tests are abnormally high. This means that he has a lot of damage to his liver. Another blood test shows that the pancreas has been affected by the alcohol and this is a very dangerous situation. We call it pancreatitis. We don't know how abnormal the pancreas is but Tom could become frightfully ill if we don't treat him immediately. We did some vitamin studies and it shows that he is lacking B12 and Folic Acid. Tom must not have been eating properly for a long time. As you can see, we have the intravenous going because he has so much nausea and vomiting. He can't keep fluids down."

Alcoholic Hepatitis
Pancreatitis
Vitamin Deficiency
Gastritis
Dehydration

Tom: "I guess it's a good thing I came to hospital. I really feel terrible. I feel shaky all over. I didn't have a wink of sleep. When I did go to sleep, I had these violent nightmares. I was scared out of my wits. What can you do?"

Withdrawal

Doctor: "We will give you some tranquilizers to settle you down. We will also give you something to assist you to sleep. You're having quite severe withdrawal symptoms. You had one convulsion in the past and I'm afraid that you may have another convulsion if we don't give you some anti-convulsant medication."

Tom: "Do anything you have to. I can't stand this. Don't let me suffer any more."

Jean: "What shall I tell the family? They are so upset and worried."

Doctor: "I think it's best to talk simply and truthfully. Tell them that Tom will be in hospital for at least a week. Tell them that all of his problems are related to his excessive alcohol use. Tell them to carry on with their lives. They have many things to do with their holiday. I don't want the family to stop functioning. If you would like, I can have a family meeting with the children to discuss this. If they are having trouble functioning after our discussion then they should consider going to Alateen. I would encourage you to go to Al-Anon."

Jean: "I don't know where to start. It seems everything is wrong.
Our financial situation is terrible. I don't know where Tom spends
all the money."

Loss of income and excessive spending

Doctor: "It's Christmas Day. I don't think that we can solve everything right now. The most important thing is that Tom is in
hospital and we are treating him. The next most important thing
is that the family pull together and get some enjoyment out of
Christmas. When Tom is better, we will have a family meeting."

Family encouraged to continue usual activities

Imagine that you are now in a family interview with Tom, Jean,
their daughters, 18 and 16 years of age, and son, 12 years of age."

Doctor: "Kids, I invited you and your mother to have a meeting
with Dad to discuss alcoholism."

Support Group

Jean: "I got the kids to go to a couple of Alateen meetings. They
felt really good about it. I went to an Al-Anon meeting. I should
have gone years ago. Probably the most important thing we covered last week at the meeting was that I and the children should
carry on with our lives as best we could."

Doctor: "I'm glad you made the decision to seek assistance. Being
with other people who have similar problems helps give us support
and new ideas. If one member of the family has an alcohol related
problem, it often affects all other members of the family. Tom, you
have attended A.A. on an irregular basis. You have now had
experience with the large groups as well as private "closed" home
groups. How are things going?"

Tom: "Well, I guess I fell off the wagon. I was doing really good for
a while. I developed a good friend (sponsor) and we really helped
each other. I will have to try again. I admit that I tend to think of
the A.A. meetings as being silly. It's this kind of thinking that got
me into trouble again. If I didn't have this depression, I wouldn't
drink."

Rationalization - excuses for the drinking

Doctor: "We know that some individuals who drink excessively
eventually develop a depressed mood and become suicidal. We

have also seen individuals who have a depression and cannot tolerate the depressive feelings so they begin drinking alcohol. You seem to do so well when you're not drinking alcohol. This makes me believe that the alcohol is causing your depression."

Tom: "No way. Everything is fine until I get depressed. Then I start drinking."

Doctor: "This may be so. But I wouldn't blame the depression. There are many people who are depressed but do not use alcohol. What's more, in your case the depression worsens with alcohol use."

Alcohol related depression

Tom: "I think I've learned my lesson."

Insight

Let's analyze Tom's problem. The children asked many questions and got direct and truthful answers. There was a great deal of emotion in the meeting. The children felt embarrassed. The oldest daughter was extremely angry and said that she did not want to stay at home any longer. Jean was talking about how she was controlled by Tom and continued to buy him liquor because he threatened her.

Tom developed many physical illnesses from the alcohol. He had an inflamation of the stomach which is called gastritis. This caused him nausea and pain. The blood tests showed that the liver was being destroyed and this is called "alcoholic hepatitis". This can lead to a disorder called cirrhosis. He developed an inflammation of his pancreas. The blood tests revealed that he had a vitamin deficiency due to poor nutrition. His blood findings revealed that he was anemic. In his first two days in hospital, he felt very shaky from withdrawal. In the past he had a convulsion. Tom complained about a tingling and numb sensation in his legs. This is called alcoholic neuropathy. There are many other physical disorders that occur from excessive alcohol use.

Psychological Dependency

Let's look at what happens to him psychologically. It is clear that he had a "blackout". This refers to a state where an individual appears to be normal (walks, talks, and has conversations) but next day cannot remember where he was or what he said. Remember how Tom acted when he was brought to hospital? He said "I'm perfectly healthy". This is a frequent finding in alcoholics and it is called denial. It simply means that the person does not believe that he has a problem and certainly not an alcohol related problem. Remember how he said that he worked a lot and was tired. This is a common psychological experience. The person is rationalizing. This means that the person gives excuses for feelings of tiredness and inability to work. The true reason for tiredness is alcohol abuse. This rationalization can be of absurd proportions. One of my patients told me that he suffered a head and knee injury because "the damn city didn't fix the cracks in the sidewalk". The correct reason for this injury was drunkenness. It seems that the alcoholic would like to blame anyone and anything for whatever goes wrong in his or her life. Remember how Tom was hospitalized on two previous occasions and did not go to work. He often felt tired, exhausted, and unable to motivate himself to go to work.

When Jean called Christmas Eve, she indicated that Tom threatened her. He also threatened suicide. At a certain point the alcoholic becomes so irrational that he may become hostile, argumentative, physically abusive and homicidal. Many alcoholics attempt suicide.

Let's look at some of the effects on the alcoholic's family. The oldest daughter could not tolerate the situation, was having difficulties concentrating at school, and was threatening to leave home. She was 18 years of age and was in her first year at university. She did not have the finances to live independently. The second daughter simply kept away from the house. She spent long periods of time with her friends at their home. She rarely stayed at home. This caused a great deal of anguish to Jean because she wanted to be near her daughter. There is a high rate of family conflict, separation and divorce in the family where one member is an alcoholic.

There are many social, economic and vocational difficulties. Tom missed a great deal of work. He was covered by a health plan for some of his time away from work. However, on other occasions, he was not paid because of absenteeism. Tom is an intelligent individual who would be able to do well financially but his family was almost bankrupt at this point. Invitations stopped coming because of Tom's behavior at parties. Nobody wanted him because he would disrupt the social event with arguments or unusual behaviors such as "making a pass at some other woman".

The next question that we may ask is "how much alcohol is too much?" "How large a problem is alcohol?"

In the United States, it is estimated that three gallons of pure alcohol are consumed by every individual over the age of 14 in a one year period. This is equal to 320 twelve ounce cans of beer, two and a half bottles of table wine and ten and a half bottles of distilled spirits in one year.

It is estimated that 20% of Canadian men and 8% of Canadian women are heavy drinkers. It is estimated that there are 500,000 alcoholics in Canada and 5 million alcoholics in the United States. There is some evidence that alcoholism may be decreasing at this time. I hope that's true!

It is estimated that of all the fatal motor vehicle accidents that occur in North America, half of these are due to excessive alcohol use. There are 55,000 highway deaths in the United States each year. It is therefore estimated that approximately 25,000 of these deaths occurred because someone was drinking. It is estimated that half of the police activities in any major city are due to an alcohol-related offense.

What causes a person to become an alcoholic? We don't know! There are many theories as to the cause of alcoholism. We don't know what causes alcoholism. From Tom's case, you will gain knowledge about the treatment of alcoholism.

Alcoholism is a large problem. If you notice that some of the things I am talking about in this chapter occur to you, please, please go to your family doctor, a psychologist, a psychiatrist, or A.A. and get help before it's too late. The financial and human costs are so extreme with alcoholism. If only one person stopped drinking because of this chapter, I will feel satisfied!

Heroin and Other Street Drugs

There are a number of drugs which are called opioids (narcotics). Drugs in this group include heroin, opium, morphine, demerol, codeine and methadone.

A person is said to be abusing opioids if the individual is unable to stop the use of the drug, is intoxicated throughout the day, experiences overdoses, has difficult social relationships (becomes involved in fights, loses friends, and experiences separation or divorce), has frequent absences from work, loss of job, and legal difficulties (arrest for possession or sale of the substance or theft).

It is very difficult to know how many addicts there are at any given time. Addicts tend to move from one city to another. Addicts frequently change their names because of their difficulties with the law. There are probably half a million opioid addicts in North America. An opioid addict develops physical dependence. Every time the addict stops the drug, withdrawal symptoms develop. Excessive sweating,

rapid heart rate, shakiness, nausea, vomiting and diarrhea and extreme anxiety develop.

Heroin is often "cut" (mixed with other white powders such as sugar). An addict never knows whether he is getting pure heroin or a mixture. This frequently leads to overdose and death. Why is this so? The reason for this is that the addict may be getting a poor quality of heroin and therefore knows that he should use "four caps" per day. The next time the addict buys some heroin, it may be pure. Four caps of pure heroin are equal to about 20 caps of "cut" heroin. When the addict takes these four caps, his body cannot tolerate this high dose and the addict may die.

It is not known why a person becomes addicted. It is believed that there is a great drive to get the "rush" or "flash" when the drug is taken. This is experienced as a very pleasurable experience and the person therefore wants to repeat it. Addicts also say that they "feel good" and sedated. They feel they can forget the problems they have. Research shows that if a person takes heroin on five occasions, that person will almost certainly become addicted. Once a person begins taking the drug, the person needs higher and higher dosages to get the same "rush". This is called "tolerance". After a few hours, the addict may begin experiencing "withdrawal symptoms". It seems that the addict continues using the drug not so much for the "rush", but rather to prevent withdrawal symptoms.

The addict develops many medical problems. The addict often develops severe constipation and sleep disturbance. The addict may develop many abnormalities of the brain and nervous system. There is evidence that the intellect deteriorates. The addict has a personality change. Frequently the addict will become hostile when looking for drugs. The person who has not been in difficulty with the law, finds himself in difficulty with the law on many occasions because of theft. Addicts develop many infections because they use "dirty needles". These dirty needles can put bacteria into the blood stream and infections develop in the lungs, kidneys, heart and brain. These dirty needles transmit hepatitis and AIDS. It is estimated that opioid addicts have a 20-fold higher death rate than the non-addicts.

Non-Narcotic Drug Dependence

Marijuana

Marijuana has been used for thousands of years as a medicine and an intoxicant. Marijuana comes from the hemp plant. The active ingredient in Marijuana is tetrahydrocannabinol. Marijuana produces a number of physical effects including rapid heart rate, redness in the eyes, dry mouth, and increased appetite. The psychological effects of marijuana are euphoria (a sense of well being), sensation that time is slowed, apathy (a sense of being extremely relaxed and unconcerned)

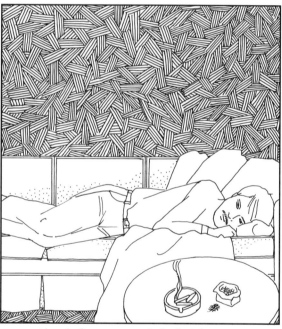

and a feeling of heightened perception (colors appear to be brigher, music sounds more beautiful).

Marijuana can be bought as a sticky resin or as finely chopped leaves (looks like dry parsley). Marijuana can be eaten in cookies or smoked in a pipe or a cigarette (toke). Marijuana does not seem to produce tolerance (there is no need to have a higher dose to produce the same effect). There are few withdrawal symptoms (there are no physical symptoms such as excessive craving for the drug, or physical symptoms when the drug is stopped).

There is no evidence that the marijuana smoker becomes aggressive. In fact, the opposite seems to happen. That is, the marijuana smoker becomes very passive and apathetic. There is a belief that marijuana improves sexual desire and power. There is no evidence to show that this is true. Marijuana use can produce an anxiety attack. This usually occurs in the individual who is using marijuana for the first time. No treatment is necessary. Simple reassurance is adequate. Marijuana probably does not lead to a psychosis. The most serious effect of excessive marijuana use is the production of the "amotivational state". With long-standing use of marijuana, the individual may feel weakness, tiredness, lack of drive, lack of motivation and be unable to function in a student and work role. Probably the most serious physical problem with excessive marijuana use is its effects on the lungs. The smoke of marijuana contains many of the tars that occur in tobacco smoke. Individuals develop long lasting disease of the lungs and may develop lung cancer.

Psychostimulants

The drugs in this category are Dexedrine, Methedrine, Benzedrine and Ritalin.

The physical experience that these drugs produce includes rapid heart rate, enlargement of the pupils, increased blood pressure, excessive sweating, chills, nausea and vomiting.

Psychological symptoms include restlessness, elation (feeling high, excited, and very happy), grandiose feelings (a belief that one possesses special abilities, creative powers, or strength) talkativeness and a high awareness of the environment. The individual may become aggressive. In this psychological state, an individual may have a great deal of difficulty concentrating at work and may be distracted. Because of this over-talkativeness, sense of excitement, an sense of power, the person may be very difficult to deal with in social settings such as meetings, luncheons, dinner or parties.

Amphetamines are very addictive and the abuser often develops a great craving for the drug. The addict becomes preoccupied with getting the drug. When an amphetamine abuser stops the drug, the individual feel a "let down" or "crash". During this time, the person feels tired, weak, depressed and suicidal. One of the most severe problems with this drug is that it produces a paranoid state. The individual becomes very anxious and believes others are watching him or plotting against him.

Cocaine

Cocaine is obtained from the coca shrub that is found in Bolivia and Peru. Natives chew the leaves of this shrub to produce stimulant effects. Cocaine is gaining in prestige and popularity. Cocaine is often bought as a powder. It is frequently "cut". Cocaine is snorted, (inhaled through the nose), injected by needle or freebased. Freebasing refers to the fact that pure cocaine is obtained and then smoked from a pipe or in a cigarette. Physical symptoms of cocaine include rapid heart rate, enlargement of the pupil, elevated blood pressure, sweating, chills, nausea and vomiting. Psychological symptoms include irritability, restlessness, a sense of extreme excitement, a belief in oneself as having special powers, excessive talkativeness and a heightened sensitivity of the environment. The person has a sense of increased energy and physical aggression. Weight loss and insomnia (inability to sleep) develop. This drug leads to a severe "craving" for more drug. Too high a dosage will lead to a very rapid heart rate, high blood pressure, convulsions, and death.

Barbiturates

There are several barbiturates that are available on the market including Amytal, Nembutal, Seconal and Phenobarbital. Barbiturates are used as anti-anxiety drugs, sleeping medications, anticonvulsants and anaesthesia. Because these drugs are made in large quantities, the black market is met by diverting shipments from manufacturers or robbing drug warehouses. Addicts frequently go from physican to physician and complain about anxiety or inability to sleep (Doctor shopping). In my teaching at the medical school, I tell my students that barbiturates should never be ordered for anxiety or insomnia. There are better drugs for these two disorders.

Physical symptoms of these drugs include slurred speech, incoordination and unsteady gait, and impairment in attention and memory.

Psychological symptoms include changeability of mood (the person may be relaxed one moment and cry the next moment), irritability, talkativeness, sexual acting-out, or aggressiveness. Individuals who use this drug often have difficulty with their families, social relationships and occupations. Because they are often sedated (drowsy), they cannot think clearly. The most common intoxication leading to car accidents, next to alcohol, is barbiturate abuse.

Barbiturate abusers state that they enjoy the pleasant warm and drowsy feelings the drug produces. Many of the effects of the barbiturates are similar to those of alcohol intoxication.

Next to aspirin, barbiturates are the commonest cause of death in children from overdose. Barbiturates are one of the most commonly used drugs in a suicidal overdose. Individuals who take an overdose often take a combination of alcohol and barbiturates. Intoxication leading to car accidents, overdose by children and suicidal overdose by adolescents and adults are very serious medical and psychological concerns.

Barbiturates are deadly drugs!

When a person tries to stop their use of barbiturates, withdrawal symptoms of insomnia, restlessness, nausea, and excessive sweating develop. Confusion and death may occur during withdrawal.

Methaqualone (Quaalude)

Methaqualone is a non-barbiturate drug that is used for anxiety and insomnia. This drug should never be ordered.

Its effects are similar to that of barbiturates and alcohol.

Benzodiazepines

Common Benzodiazepine are Valium, Serax, Ativan, Librium and Dalmane. There are approximately 25 drugs in this group. These drugs are prescribed for anxiety and insomnia. They are also used as muscle relaxants and anaesthetics.

When these drugs were introduced to the market in the 1960's, it appeared that they would not produce addiction. This has not been the case. Both physicians and patients are recognizing the severe addictive qualities of these drugs. Physicians are recognizing the problems with these drugs and are prescribing them less often.

An individual using a relatively small dosage of this medication for sleep, often has a difficult time stopping the drug. When an individual tries to stop the drug, "rebound insomnia" and "rebound dreaming" occurs. When sleep does occur, it is a very light sleep full of vivid dreams. Sometimes it is difficult for the person to decide whether they are awake and thinking or asleep and dreaming.

Individuals who have been on benzodiazapines for a long time, develop a withdrawal reaction including anxiety, depression, intolerance to bright lights and noises, nausea, sweating and muscle twitching. There is rarely a craving for the drug.

Solvents

Volatile solvents that are abused include gasoline, varnish remover, lighter fluid, airplane glue, rubber cement, cleaning fluid and aerosols (especially spray paints). The active ingredients in these solvents are Toluene, Acetone and Benzene.

These substances are easily obtained and cheap. They are usually used by the very young (ages 6-16) and the poor. The individual usually inhales from a tube, a plastic bag, or a rag. Intoxication lasts for about 15 minutes.

Individuals who abuse this drug say that they develop a sense of excitement, dizziness and a sense of power. They usually have slurred speech and cannot walk straight. They often have memory impairments. Severe side effects include damage to the liver and kidneys. Death can occur with overdosage.

Psychedelics (hallucinogenic drugs)

The best known drugs in this category are LSD (lysergic acid diethylamide), Mescaline, Psilocybin and MDA. The effect of the drug depends on the amount of drug taken, the personality of the individual, the setting in which the drug is taken and the expectation. An individual who tends to be aggressive, may become more aggressive. If an individual expects to see bright colors, then they will do so. If individuals are in a pleasant setting, they may have pleasant feelings. If the same individual is in an aggressive setting, hostility may develop.

Individuals who take hallucinogenic drugs often feel that they can see better, colors appear more vivid, textures are richer, and outlines seem clearer. The individual experiences a profound emotion when listening to music. Smells and tastes tend to be heightened. Individuals using the hallucinogenic drugs often feel that their emotions are highly intensified. When they have a positive emotional experience, such as love or a good feeling for another person, this seems to be the "best experience they've ever had in their life". Often there are feelings that one has suddenly stumbled onto some great insight about the universe or philosophy or religion.

The "bad trip" refers to the person who has developed a severe anxiety state after taking the drug. The person becomes frightened, cries, screams and may become violent. "Flashbacks" refer to the sudden experience that the person is taking the drug but, in fact, none has been taken for weeks or months.

Hallucinogens may cause the development of a schizophrenic disorder in individuals who are predisposed to schizophrenia.

Summary

There are many drugs that are potentially addictive. These drugs can cause psychological dependence (a psychological desire for the drug), physical dependence (and a need for more drugs to produce the same effect), withdrawal and intoxication. The drugs could lead to medical, educational, work, financial, psychological, marital, family and social difficulties.

ARE YOU ABUSING ALCOHOL OR DRUGS?
ANSWER TRUTHFULLY.
IF YOU ARE, GET HELP!!!

Caffeine Dependence

The American Psychiatric Association now has considered caffeine a drug that can produce intoxication, dependence and withdrawal. I will talk about each of these different states that occur from caffeine.

Caffeine is common in so many products and is found in beverages such as coffee, tea, cocoa and cola drinks. There are many over the counter prescriptions that contain caffeine and I would encourage you to read the ingredients any time you buy a drug from your local drugstore. Many stimulants and appetite suppressants have caffeine as their main ingredient.

I know that many of you reading this chapter will think that there is no disorder with caffeine. Our children, young people and elderly people drink caffeine. Caffeine is all over the place. How could it be a problem? I am intrigued by how long it took our medical associations to identify caffeine as a very powerful drug that produces many problems. I feel quite confident about writing my comments on caffeine to you, as caffeine is very toxic to me. That means that even small amounts of caffeine produce all sorts of symptoms including rapid heart beat, headache and tiredness (the tiredness usually occurs 2 to hours after I have taken caffeine.)

What does caffeine do? Caffeine affects many parts of our body. In small doses we can have decreased drowsiness, clear thoughts, ability to continue working mentally and physically, and a sense of increased muscle power. It is these effects that we often want. How often have you heard yourself or someone say "I just got up. I can't think. I just have to have my morning coffee"? In fact, many individuals just use coffee in the morning to give them this increased mental alertness. Caffeine is found in drinks that give us a great deal of pleasure because of the smell, taste, warmth or cold qualities of the beverage, color of the beverage and other factors. For example, when we take a cup of coffee, we don't think of drinking it simply for caffeine. How often have we heard it said "Ah, what a nice aroma". We don't frequently think of taking a drink of cola and saying "Ah, wonderful, what a nice glass of caffeine". Our taking the drinks usually has nothing to do with the caffeine and has everything to do with the appearance of the drink and the setting. For example, when you or I sit in a restaurant with a really good friend, hear a large number of individuals happy in that setting, listen to nice music, and even possibly look at the pretty eyes and nice smile of the waitress, we lift our tall frosted glass with a nice dark cola filled with ice cubes and a lemon wedge on the glass and say "Wow, what a nice evening, what a wonderful thing it is to spend some time together". In this situation, we don't say "I can't stand your company and this dump of a place but I needed someone to go with me to have some caffeine".

Let me try this again. Caffeine produces certain mental actions such as increased alertness, is found in a drink which is tasty and is taken in any setting that we often enjoy. It is these three factors that cause us to drink caffeine.

Let's talk about caffeine intoxification. When an individual is sensitive to caffeine as I am, or takes excessive amounts of caffeine, then the person experiences restlessness, irritability, nervousness, shakiness of the hands, and a general increased twitching of the body. These twitching activities of the muscles could be very small or could be very large and frequent to the point that a person is blinking the eyes, making facial expressions (grimacing) coughing, moving the arms and legs a great deal or in fact, having total inability to sit still. Headaches are extemely common. Inability to sleep is very severe and these individuals usually take some sort of sedative such as alcohol or minor tranquilizer to fall asleep. Individuals frequently complain of ringing in the ears, light headedness, difficulties with their vision. The person often has to pee a lot. Heart symptoms such as thumping of the heart, or increased heart rate are common. Abdominal symptoms such as nausea, vomiting, diarrhea, and pain are common. About 2 hours after having this intoxication, individuals frequently feel very weak and tired and therefore frequently try and take some more caffeine to feel a little better.

With caffeine use, individuals often say such things as "I'm more upset, I'm more irritable, I can't seem to settle down, I really get angry, I seem to be so tense". These symptoms are common symptoms of anxiety. I'm quite sure that a large number of people are diagnosed as having anxiety disorders when they really are only having caffeine intoxication problems. These people will often be put on minor tranquilizers. It is very well known that individuals with anxiety have increased anxiety symptoms when they use caffeine products.

There are many individuals who go to their physicians with a wide variety of physical disorders because of the effects of caffeine. I know a neurologist who will not even try and treat headaches unless the person is able to quit his use of caffeine. Caffeine can stimulate the about of acid in the stomach and produce symptoms of gastritis which include a hollow feeling in the stomach, sense of nausea and pain. I often wonder how many people will have no need for sleep medication if they should stop their caffeine use.

Withdrawal symptoms develop after as little as three hours from the last drink. During the withdrawal the person feels increased anxiety, headaches, tiredness, weakness, nervousness and a sense of inability to work, vague feelings of depression and yawning.

❙ Tobacco Dependence

I am really pleased with the American Psychiatric Association position of placing tobacco dependence and tobacco withdrawal as a major mental disorder.

Tobacco is first used by a person because of social factors. A child wants to be like the parent. An adolescent wants to be like his friend. I know a person who is violently anti-smoking. However, at the age of 35 she re-entered the university to complete a master's degree and sat around in groups where many others smoked. Her friends finally told her to try a cigarette. These "friends" have now made this person simply into a tobacco addict (drug addict).

Once a person has used nicotine, he or she must continue using it otherwise they would have withdrawal symptoms. It is this fact that probably makes tobacco and nicotine such an addictive drug. Even after two hours without a cigarette, the individual begins to have withdrawal side effects such as irritability, restlessness and stomach discomfort, headaches, difficulty concentrating, difficulty with memory, and anxiety. The smoker never says "I am having a number of withdrawal symptoms such as tension, anxiety and irritability and therefore I have to take a cigarette". This need for more nicotine happens on a very automatic basis. In fact, the smoker usually rationalizes his withdrawal symptoms by saying "I've just got to sit down. I've got to have a cigarette and relax". Every cigarette smoker will tell you that they feel better, think better, concentrate better, and feel less tension when they have a cigarette. Every cigarette smoker will say that the cigarette is a "relaxer". Nothing could be further from the truth. The only reason that the cigarette smokers feels better when smoking is that they increase their blood concentration of nicotine and remove the withdrawal of symptoms.

I would like to restate the above paragraph. Nicotine does not cause increased relaxation in individuals. Nicotine gives a "sense of relaxation" in the smoker because the smoking takes away the withdrawal symptoms that start developing 1 to 2 hours after the last cigarette was used. The tobacco companies really found a money maker in this cigarette. Isn't is wonderful to sell something that causes uncomfortable feelings when you don't take the product any more? Let's imagine what a great seller milk could become. Let's put something in milk that will lead to addiction. As soon as a person has had a few glasses of milk over a number of days they are addicted. This means that if they try and stop drinking milk, they will get a variety of symptoms such as irritibility, stomach pain, shakiness, angry feeling and difficulties with concentration. As soon as they have a glass of milk all these symptoms will disappear. The person will then say that they feel better and will automatically say "Boy, is this milk relaxing". There is such a thing as nicotine poisoning. When a person is extremely sensitive to nicotine or has too much nicotine, then the person will often have a headache, nausea, sense of dizziness, cold sweat and a sense of passing out. The person will have difficulty concentrating, feel the heart pounding, and the pulse will be rapid and weak. Try it sometimes, buy yourself a nice cigar (I'm talking to non-cigar smokers) and then smoke the whole thing. You don't even have to inhale. Just suck it in, hold it in your mouth, blow it out again and see if you don't get sick as a dog.

I have a friend who is a great cigar smoker. We love to have a few games of golf in the summer first thing in the morning. We light up a cigar (I am a non smoker) on the first hole. I get really stimulated by the second hole when the cigar is one quarter done. If I'm stupid enough to smoke for the next few holes and finish off the cigar I will be nauseated, dizzy and feel as if I'm about to pass out. Unfortunately, I didn't learn from just the first experience and I had a few of these experiences through the years.

I am absolutely pleased that our government has shown leadership in recognizing the severe problems of addiction from nicotine and the severe health problems from the tar in the tobacco products. Tobacco products cannot be advertised on radio and television. It was very common for actors in old movies and commercials to hold a cigarette. I would suggest that you and I turn off the television every time we see a program or a movie where the actors smoke. Let's get smart. It is wonderful to see the tremendous decrease in smoking in our population. Approximately 20 years ago, more that 60% of the adult population smoked on a regular basis. Today, less than 30% of the adult population smokes. I am pleased with the leadership shown by the medical profession in that only 10% of physicians smoke. Let's keep it up. Let's use common sense, education, and government programs to stamp out tobacco and tobacco products.

CHAPTER 12

Education is Everyone's Business

EDUCATION IS EVERYONE'S BUSINESS

Introduction

"...our home is in a complete panic. Our six year old may fail grade one. It's really not fair. We've worked with him every night, what more can we do? I just want what's right for him, but he's devastated. We'll fight this; I won't have his self image destroyed."

Yes, this was a real letter, and we did answer it. As many readers will guess, our answer had to do with pressure. Normally four year olds and six year olds and eight year olds do not put intense pressure on themselves. Parents and teachers can create pressure though, and if the pressure is intense enough, then children's self-images can be destroyed. The issue for this grade one student is not so much whether he passes or fails, it is that he retains confidence in himself, so that he believes he will learn to read and learn to do arithmetic. If the question in this little boy's mind is only "Will I pass or fail?" our emphasis is wrong. Parental involvement in the educational process is very necessary. Surely it is important that we have a stake in our child's future and we should help him or her all we can. Yet, regularized homework at grade one is quite sad. As the developing child learns to crawl before she can walk, young children must learn to interact in groups and play before they can be subjected to intense pressure, study skills, etc..

It is not surprising on "That's Living" the authors have dealt with educational problems since the inception of the radio program. Dr. Blashko has specialized in assisting children to plan educational programs and was involved in educational film making. The other two authors of this book are both educational psychologists, with experiences in public as well as adult education.

This chapter contains a potpourri of topics that have been covered on the radio; hopefully the information will provide some strategies in helping children maximize potential; surely that is one of the goals of any educational system.

▌ Psychological Rights of the Child

Perhaps it is wise when discussing educational matters to start with children. One of the major features of North American society in the last half of the twentieth century has been the rediscovery of adult learning, but when most of us think of education we think of a child, and of schooling. Let's start then with some discussion about the psychological rights of children.

Need for Definition

According to a report of the Canadian Council on Children and Youth there are seven million children in Canada now who have almost no legal rights; absolutely no psychological rights, and poorly defined educational rights. Over one-and-a-half million children live in poverty. In 1978, nearly 80,000 were found to be in need of protection, and consequently are growing up outside the realm of normal family life, as wards or foster children. The physical fitness of our children declines after they enter school, so that the average 12 year old Canadian child is compared in fitness to the average 35 year old Swede. Our education system - one of the costliest and most advanced in the world - is producing some graduates who cannot read and many who cannot find a job. Native children have a disproportionately high mortality rate. Children in Canada are born unequal to each other as individuals. They lack rights in a society that prides itself on the rights and freedoms of the individual. Nevertheless, children and their rights are not even mentioned in human-rights legislation.

The difficulties of this situation is that the children themselves cannot change this situation. It's up to the adult population. Now I'm sure that no adult (parents, teachers, to be more specific) gets up in the morning planning to make a child's life miserable. No teacher says, "Today I'll yell, nag and humiliate my children whenever possible." On the contrary, teachers, (and everyone else, for that matter), get up in the morning and say to themselves, "Today I will resolve to have a perfect day, an enjoyable day, a happy day - no arguing, no yelling, no nagging, no fighting - a wonderful day!" Yet in spite of our good intentions, the unwarranted wars break out and we start saying and doing things we really don't mean. The children invariably end up the losers in the power struggle.

At times today, it appears that the child in Canada is merely tolerated in society - that he or she is a hardship for young parents, a pawn between divorcing parents, a defenceless victim in a bitter custody battle, a salary cheque to a multitude of social workers, tenure to school teachers, a profitable market for the manufacturer of consumer goods, a captive audience for the television industry, a ready subject for the psychologist. In our fast-paced, live-it-up, marry-and-divorce world, an interesting lifestyle comes first - children come last.

If the comments just raised seem to overstate the concerns, then it is only to stress a point, a need for urgency. Rights of children are an important matter. Psychological rights of our children need to be defined.

The International Year of the Child - 1979 (IYC) was designed by the General Assembly of the United Nations as a time when the world community should centre its attention on the child and "reaffirm its concern for the present condition and the future of its children". One of the major purposes of the year was to "provide an opportunity to emphasize the intellectual, psychological, and social development of children in addition to their physical welfare".

IYC came about 20 years after the 1959 unanimous adoption by the United Nation's General Assembly of the broad-based Declaration of the Rights of the Child (Declaration of the Rights of the Child, 1973). It encourages all countries of the world to determine whether or not its most valuable resources, its children, are receiving the basic services which they need to enable them to grow and to participate fully in the development of the society in which they live.

Whereas the earlier Declaration did contain some provisions for the psychological rights of the child, it placed more emphasis on the physical and nutritional needs which are so basic to all further development. Although the entire rights movement has come a long way since 1959, because of the difficulties in precisely defining them, there still exists a need to carefully define the Psychological Rights of the Child. Few would question that there are a variety of psychological factors which surround the child, for good or for bad, which affect his or her cognitive, emotional, and social development.

Such a Declaration would be most useful if it covered the entire psychological domain of development in sufficient detail to enable all countries to evaluate the effectiveness of present programs attempting to provide for these needs and rights. It should be stated with sufficient flexibility, however, so that the need could be provided for with a great deal of adaptability within the context of different cultures and levels of economic development. It should also provide practical goals for the future development of improved levels of services for children as all the countries of the world attempt to improve the psychological climate in which their children and youth will grow.

Initiating the Process for Definition

Because of their high level of training in the behavioral sciences and their intense work with children with all kinds of unmet psychological and academic needs, psychologists are in a unique position to provide leadership for defining the Psychological Rights of the Child. Psychologists feel strongly about the need for planning and implementing advocacy programs which provide for and protect these rights and have initiated a campaign which invites the active participation of other professionals, as well as the general public, to produce the strongest Declaration of these rights possible. Because of the need for a universal statement of these rights and because not all educational systems enjoy the advantages of having applied psychological services for their school-aged population, the International School Psychology Committee has provided the leadership for an international process designed to ultimately implement a strong rights-advocacy program all over the world.

Because it tends to be difficult to ask people to consider these rights in the abstract, the first phase of the campaign was to formulate a tentative Declaration. This was done to illustrate the problems which one encounters in this process and to provide something for people around the world to react to and improve upon. There were four factors used the selection of items for inclusion in the tentative statement:

1. An attempt was made to provide rights-statements which covered the entire domain of psychological, intellectual development. Although there is obvious overlap with physical and other developmental factors, only those factors which most closely defined the psychological rights of the child were considered.

2. Insofar as possible, the rights are stated in positive terms rather than as an absence of sickness or harm. Earlier efforts to describe mental health had frequently resulted in a list of the absence of mental aberration or mental dysfunction. A right should be a more positive factor which can be programmed into the growth and development of both the normal and the atypical child.

3. The conceptual model utilized envisioned age-appropriate dimensions for every level of development rather than a specific development task at a given age level.

4. The rights were also chosen and worded as simply, yet precisely as possible, in order to provide positive guidelines against which various countries could evaluate their existing programs. The more the rights-statement met the above criteria, the more use they would be for different cultures to identify new programs that were needed to provide for these rights for all their children.

The Tentative Declaration of
The Psychological Rights of the Child

Right I: PERSONAL IDENTITY. The right to have a name, a feeling of identity, to be wanted, and to have a feeling of personal worth regardless of sex or identification with any religious, political, or ethnic group.

Right II: EMOTIONAL SUPPORT FROM ADULTS. The right to both physical and psychological care and support from his or her parents and/or other adults in the culture, especially during the dependent stages of infancy with childhood.

Right III: PARTICIPATE IN AND LEARN FROM PLAY AND FANTASY. The right to the time and opportunity to participate in and learn from other structured and nonstructured activities.

Right IV: FREEDOM FROM FEAR OF PHYSICAL HARM OR ABUSE. The right to be protected from all forms of neglect, cruelty, physical hurt, or exploitation and/or the danger of man-made events such as riots or war.

Right V: ENCOURAGEMENT. The right to encouragement from adults and peers to use his or her abilities, to explore new activities, to risk, and to accept, when necessary, the effects of adversity, defeat, and disappointment.

Right VI: SATISFYING RELATIONSHIPS WITH OTHERS. The right to the opportunity to develop and foster positive, satisfying relationships with other children and adults.

Right VII: GROWING AWARENESS OF STRENGTHS. The right to be aware of individual differences, to overcome one's weaknesses, and, at the same time, to become aware of, to be proud of, and to make use of one's strengths in facing the responsibilities of life.

Right VIII: MAKE AGE-APPROPRIATE DECISIONS. The right to an opportunity to make appropriate decisions about what he or she can and cannot do, including the right to be thought of as wrong or different by others, in order to assist him or her to become a mature adult.

Right IX: APPROPRIATE EDUCATION. The right to obtain the facts necessary to function within their culture and to develop their cognitive potential in an appropriate educational program which helps them move toward taking a productive place in the culture and, when desirable or necessary, to move freely from one culture to another.

Right X: SPECIALIZED SERVICES. The right to specialized physical, educational, and psychological services to meet the child's unique needs in as normal and non-stigmatizing a setting as possible.

These rights cannot and should not be defined just by professionals. Because of the importance of an individual's psychological adjustment to help him or her adapt to the society of which they are a part, the public in general and parents in particular must be actively involved in identifying these rights and in implementing programs. These are the people who are in the homes, the churches, and the other institutions in the society which all have a major effect on the psychological climate in which the child is brought up. The expectations of these people serve as "silent tugs of anticipation" on the developing child. To fulfil the intent of the International Year of the Child, the discussion process must also reach out and involve people from as wide a range of cultures as possible.

Both the process of formulating a statement of the psychological rights of the child and the final Declaration should have positive effects in increasing educational, social, physical and psychological services to all children.

"Normal" Learning Problems

Readers will note that in this book there is a special chapter on learning disabilities. It seemed fair when discussing education to make sure that there is ample opportunity to discuss normal learning problems. None of us can learn all material, all skills, all strategies in an effective manner. In his work with the psychological testing centre, at the University of Alberta, Faculty of Education Clinic, Dr. Henry Janzen developed strategies for diagnosing, remediating and intervening to assist children. These strategies have been taught to many school psychologists in training, but they have also proved to be of real assistance to both classroom teachers and parents who are working with their children in a variety of settings.

What Is Normal?

Parents, teachers and counselors are often so close to children that they fail to recognize the complexities and interrelated patterns of their growing, learning, and personality patterns. Parents who have raised more than one child usually have a small sample, but at least *some* basis on which to judge relative "normalcy" of behavior. Teachers and counselors, although given training in developmental psychology, without any practical experience can have tremendous difficulties in judging "normal" student behaviors and learning patterns.

Although teachers, counselors and parents can have an excellent track-record for detecting unusual behaviors in children, the meaning attached to those "unusual behaviors" is usually not clear. Whereas some individuals view "normality" as meaning "no gross pathology" (normality as health), others see it in the light of an ideal functioning (normality as ideal); whereas some counsellors view "normalcy" as the average, normal, expected behavior (normality as average), others view it as the normative expectations of a given society, or group within that society (normality as socially acceptable behaviors).

In the light of strictly medical classifications of behaviors, there was actually very little room for the demonstration of "normal" behavior patterns. Today, we seem to be re-thinking such a nomological description.

Informal Diagnosis

What informal diagnosis and early detection need to achieve is for our children to receive not only maximum attention from teacher and counselor, but just and fair judgement of their potential. In adulthood the pressures of renewed and persistent learning are past. Learning has slowed down to a pace suitable for ourselves. In childhood we always seem to want to quicken the pace and push the child to early readiness or to achievement just beyond the neighbor's kid. You see, our own self-image and pride are very much tied up in our children. In light of this, we cannot be upset about minor deviations even if they do point to potential or present learning disabilities.

In many cases, detailed evaluation of the present functioning of the child can provide one with sufficient information so that a specific

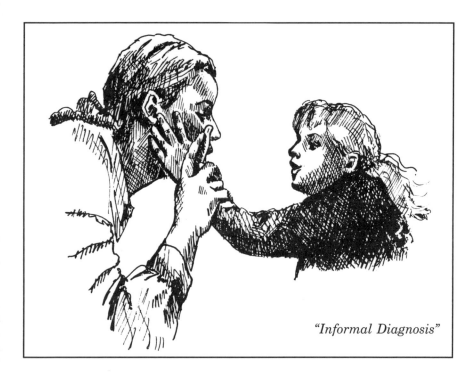

"*Informal Diagnosis*"

program can be planned without too much concern for etiology. The following are the basic signs and symptoms to watch for in recognizing problems in the two main learning modalities.

Indicators of Visual Problems
1. Losing place while reading.
2. Avoiding close work.
3. Consistent reliance upon marker or pointing at words.
4. Poor sitting position or posture while reading.
5. Holding reading material closer than regarded normal.
6. Frowning, blinking, scowling, etc.
7. Excessive head movement while reading or viewing distant objects.
8. Excessive rubbing of eyes.
9. Thrusting head forward while reading or focusing on objects.
10. Tension during close work.

Indicators of Auditory Problems
1. Frequent ear ache.

2. Faulty pronunciation and speech.
3. Tending to turn head and favour one ear.
4. Breathing through mouth.
5. Complaints of head noises or dizziness.
6. Unnatural pitch of voice.
7. Inattention or poor scholastic achievement.
8. Frequent rubbing of ear.
9. Blank expression when directions are given.
10. Frequent questions of "What?" asked.

Summary

A concept that we must accept and foster is the attitude that normalcy is only relevant when you tell me when and where and what the students, background, experiences, and growth patterns are. For anyone to assume that all children of a given age must achieve a certain standard, belies the evidence that shows such a great range of development and abilities at any given age. Children with learning disabilities are "normal" children. The disabilities they show are signs that their strengths have yet to be developed. The ideas presented in this chapter suggest that we look compassionately and humanistically at the students we meet. Proper diagnosis, unwillingness to label, use of one or several remedial techniques are a beginning of a new teaching-learning relationship. The student who has trouble learning and eventually drops out is not the product of a system which failed to provide him information. Our failures are almost never failures of information. Rather, they are human problems; breakdowns of personal meaning. For the teacher, counselor or parent, actions speak much louder than words. It has been said that:

> *No printed word, no spoken plea*
> *Can teach young minds what men should be*
> *Not all the books on all the shelves*
> *But what the teachers are themselves.*

The Problem of Slow Learners

Oh! That it could be otherwise. Yet it's not. Some children do not outgrow problems that start in early grades. Pressure from teachers, parents and administrators seems to focus the problem, but not solve it. There are strategies for working with slow learners, these people can be assisted, but recognition of the problem can aid rather than resolve the dilemma.

"...My concern is my son...He is 28 years old. He was very
sick as a child with convulsions which I believe left him as
a very slow learner. He was a very unhappy child during
his elementary years at school. Repeated grades and still
was unable to understand. He then went into special education in High School and he was a changed boy. He finished high school three credits short of his high school
diploma...His big setback is that he does not understand
or comprehend what he reads...he works very hard. He
lives at home. He is very quiet and has trouble expressing
himself. He is a non-drinker and a non-smoker... Would
there be a program for the disabled persons where they
can be trained and later find a suitable career for them?
Can comprehension be learned?"

That letter was answered and local resources in the Edmonton
area were named for the parent. Perhaps a more complete answer
would have dealt with the question of slow learners as they progress
through our educational system. It is our hope that the writer of that
letter reads this chapter which may provide the kinds of detail that
really are needed.

The problem of slow learners presents one of the most critical
unsolved problems for administrators, teachers, psychologists and
social agencies. Nationwide, the slow learners constitute the most
disregarded and neglected group in the educational system. Programs and provisions for the mentally handicapped, who comprise
two to three percent of the population, are being encouraged. In
many schools the gifted are finally beginning to receive attention,
which is resulting in noticeable improvement in educational provisions for children with superior intelligence. Unfortunately, the slow
learners who compose fifteen to twenty percent of the population,
have not received such consideration, and few schools are making
distinct, individual provisions for them. However, educators are
slowly awakening to the fact that offering the same educational
opportunity for all does not necessarily give everyone an equal opportunity to become educated. Offering a curriculum designed for the
"average" child often produces only frustration and degradation for
the slow learner.

The problem of slow learners has always been with us and will
continue. Any positive action which has been made has been hampered by a lack of definition and a lack of universally accepted terminology. In fact, the present use of terms seems to have confused

rather than clarified the situation. To various people the expression "slow learner" has meant several things. The emotionally disturbed, the mentally handicapped, behavioral deviates, remedial problems, children uninterested in school, and the actual slow learner have all been referred to as slow learners. Although these children are all slow in their academic progress, more exact, descriptive terms can be applied to them. To some people the term slow learner refers to specific groups with restricted degrees of mental retardation. To others the expression merely signifies a descriptive term. Many principals and teachers, when talking with parents, use the term slow learner when referring to observable degrees of mental retardation to soften the shock of the diagnosis. Obviously, the expression "slow learner" seems more socially acceptable than terms such as "mentally deficient" or "weak-minded". When authorities use the term slow learner, they refer to groups of children with varying degrees of intellectual ability. To others slow learners are a group of retarded children who only have a potential learning ability of Grade II to Grade V. Some schools believe slow learners pertain to children of any level of mental retardation, while others use the term to imply the educable group requiring special placement. This lack of commonly accepted terminology and the inability to clarify the terms have been one of the primary factors which has caused educators to fail to arrive at an acceptable, permanent solution.

The typical slow learner, whose I.Q. ranges from 75 to 90, is identified by a psychological assessment of the quantity, amount, or rate of intellectual development, although I.Q. should not be the sole predictor of the slow learner. The slow learner not only has a "slower" rate of learning, but also is qualitatively different. He or she comprehends and remembers less; is less perceptive of relations and contrasts than the "normal" pupil. The slow learner is not the child with an average, get-by performance. School work is not easy for them. Achievement is uniformly low. Because of the innumerable, consistent failures and frustrating situations they encounter (discipline, lack of interest, inability to adjust socially), they may become adjustment problems for teachers and principals.

General Characteristics

The slow learners have been victims of misinstruction and misconceptions regarding their characteristics. Basically, the slow learners are children with similar physical, intellectual, educational, and emotional characteristics to other children. These students have the same fundamental needs of food, air, clothing, shelter; the psychological needs to feel secure, to manipulate, to satisfy their curiosity, to achieve, to be independent; and the social needs to be loved, to be accepted, to be recognized as being of worth, and to have companionship, as those of the normal or the gifted students. Since their appearance and responses are almost identical to those of children in general, it is impossible to differentiate them by simple inspection or by a physical examination. As a result, the unwary teacher or the casual observer are unable to detect deviations and problems.

Physically, the slow learners as a group are apt to be somewhat inferior in size and in motor coordination. However, among them one finds some who are tall, short, fat, thin, poorly or well coordinated, so that individually, they range from one end of a physical and motor development scale to the other with the majority clustered near the centre in the same way as the general population is distributed. A population misconception about slow learners is that they are the "big but dumb" football or basketball player type, who are unable to do the academic work, and who pass because of sympathetic teachers and pressures of school administrators who desire winning teams at any expense. This concept is a fallacy.

Psychologically, the "slow learners" learn at a slower rate than the average. Since their mental age always languishes behind their chronological age, they are mentally immature. In the first grade they are too immature to learn the complicated task of reading; their failure causes them to feel inadequate among their able peers. Seemingly, these children have a shorter attention span and a poorer memory than the average except when the material is meaningful, interesting, and designed for their level. Since they do not have the intellectual curiosity, nor the ability to question the nature of things, nor good abstract reasoning, slow learners find it difficult to generalize, to see relationships, to draw conclusions, and to make deductions except when material is concrete and firsthand. Poor ability to follow instructions, difficulty in transferring learning, poor work habits, and poor attendance hinder the achievement of slow learners in the academic area. Because of limited abstract ability, these students have difficulty foreseeing future events, awaiting the results of their actions, critically evaluating their work, developing their potential creative abilities, and adjusting to the world around them. Emotionally, slow learners are comparable to normal children except that slow learning students have a greater desire to be accepted and reassured because of their insecurity and lack of psychosocial stimulation in their homes. Thus, the general intellectual slowness displayed by slow learners is evident in all phases of mental development. With their development, lower level of learning ability, lower intellectual level, and restricted psychosocial stimulation, they require a unique curriculum which takes these factors into consideration. However, the most important factor to remember is that the slow learner is a person very much like the rest of humanity. He or she is *not* a type or category but has more or less the characteristics common to other pupils in school - the same basic needs, the same ways of learning, and similar variability of abilities.

Diagnosis

No pupil should be considered as slow learner without the benefit of many tests, medical and psychological. Diagnostic information, containing a description of the child's characteristics, is essential, if a program of maximum educational value is to be designed for them. This information must be obtained from *several sources*. First, the child should be examined by a psychologist before entering school or should be evaluated by a previous teacher who will report any indication of slow learning. Achievement tests should disclose below-average competence. Final identification should be attempted through an individual comprehensive examination administered by a school psychologist. The analysis, combined with data attained from school records, home visits, and reports of teachers and principals will serve to distinguish the true slow learner, with limitations, and abilities.

Creativity and Giftedness

"...My child is bored, just plain bored stiff. She started out like gangbusters in kindergarden and grade 1, seemed to enjoy school in grade 2, still gets good marks, but in grade 4 now she just seems uninterested in school, greatly interested in everthing else. What on earth do I do?"

Well, another actual letter. This one also denotes a common problem. One factor that many of us do not recognize is that is is quite easy for a gifted child to act average or even slow in school, while it is impossible for an average or a slow learning student to act gifted. If our schools do not pay sufficient attention though to our creative and gifted students, we may be shortchanging the future of our country, as these could well be our leaders, politically, in the arts, in business. Even though most of the problems that come to us on radio are about children with academic problems in school, there is need to discuss problems of the gifted student and to find out what we mean by creativity.

Well, another actual letter. This one also denotes a common problem. One factor that many of us do not recognize is that is is quite easy for a gifted child to act average or even slow in school, while it is impossible for an average or a slow learning student to act gifted. If our schools do not pay sufficient attention though to our creative and gifted students, we may be shortchanging the future of our country, as these could well be our leaders, politically, in the arts, in business. Even though most of the problems that come to us on radio are about children with academic problems in school, there is need to discuss problems of the gifted student and to find out what we mean by creativity.

This is a topic that has been receiving a good deal of attention in psychological literature. Perhaps there is no other area where so much misinformation seems to exist. Many of the ideas expressed now are taken from the work of an American psychologist, with roots in the province of Alberta. Dr. Maurice Freehill, now retired, wrote extensively in the area of giftedness and has many ideas about creativity, particularly in children, that are of real assistance not only to teachers and psychologists, but also to parents. In a way dealing with strategies for encouraging creativity seems to be a denial of some of the strategies brought forward on other issues. This is natural, because it seems in today's society creativity is not encouraged. In our world there is an emphasis on sameness, on problem solving, perhaps on a return to basic values. Creativity in people is difficult to predict; if we are to study creativity we have to look at people who have been creative. Isn't this an exciting concept for developing theories about personality and about people? The psychologist, Gordon Allport found it strange that many of our theories about personal development were "based on the antics of captive and desperate rats". What a much more exciting way for a social scientist to proceed, with real people who have made outstanding contributions.

Psychologists have found through considerable research that when we are testing children it is easiest to predict negatively. Our tests can ascribe limits, but we have greater difficulty attempting to predict whether or not bright people will live up to their potential. Many people never seem to accomplish those things that are within their capabilities.

In this section let's try to "shoot down" some of the myths that surround the concept of creativity.

MYTH #1: "A chosen few of us are born creative".

This just isn't true. The development of creative ability is a natural process, common to all of us. Often, for a variety of reasons the creative potential of an individual will never surface. There are basically three kinds of creativity.

1) The expression of the creator's inner state.

This category would include the giants of literature or artistic expression such as writers, composers, sculptors, and painters.

2) The creator works to meet defined goals.

This is where a creator will use his or her ingenuity to meet the needs of others. He or she may come up with a novel product, but often this type of creativity requires social skills as well and more than one person. People who fit easily into this category would include engineers, inventors, scientists, or physicists.

3) The architect or builder.

This person produces a very personal product, which also has utility, or meets the need of others.

John Updike was once quoted as saying, "any activity becomes creative when the doer cares about doing it right, or better." The purpose of this section was to show that creativity can exist across professions, in many different kinds of environments and work states. Also people with lesser abilities in some areas can be creative in others.

MYTH #2. "Creative thinking is a lazy, hazy process."

This conjures up the image, doesn't it, of someone under an apple tree like Sir Isaac Newton? Perhaps some of us think of creative people operating in bursts of energy and a novel or an artistic work is created through sudden urges. This just isn't so. As Mark Twain once commented, creativity is "1% inspiration, 99% perspiration".

Well let's look at psychologists again, and what research has to offer. Is creativity related to intelligence or to an intelligence quotient? Well, there is no guarantee, but there's more chance for a bright person to be creative. When one has more potential, we also have more potential for creative behavior. The truly creative person knows when to be disciplined and when to allow his or her mind to wander. Salvador Dali summed up this point by suggesting "no masterpiece was ever created by a lazy artist".

MYTH #3. "Creative people are basically unhappy".

Well there's lots of anecdotal evidence for such a statement. We know that Van Gogh and Judy Garland and Oscar Levant, were desperately troubled people, while outstandingly creative in their own field. Yet research studies show us that when one studies creative people we may find them more anxious or under more pressure, but basically they surface as healthier than the general population. One basic fact seems to emerge that cuts across areas; creative people are always independent thinkers and rarely conformists. It is difficult to chart new areas if we stick only to old paths.

Summary

The message for parents and teachers is that while remediation is often necessary for children, it is also necessary to encourage them in areas of strength. When we discover talents, let's make sure they are developed, not every child will emerge as a ballet dancer or hockey player, but all of them will be better people if they have allowed their talents to develop on the stage or on the rink.

Special efforts must be made in our educational system to provide challanges for gifted and talented people to keep them from becoming bored, like the ten year old girl referred to earlier. Gifted children in classrooms do not necessarily need more of the same kind of work, they often need less, as they grasp concepts quicker, but they do need challenges. Very often the very best kind of remedial education for all students is found by working through strengths, so gifted and creative children must not be hampered and held back but be allowed to utilize their talents. Often identifying children with special talents is as much a part of the work of the school psychologist, as identifying those with special needs.

The Psychologist as a Problem Solver
Psychological Testing

"...Well we followed your advice and the advice of the school principal and had our child tested. What good had that done? I did receive a psychological report from the

psychologist, but it doesn't make any sense to me. I would simply like to know our child's I.Q. Why won't anybody give me that number?"

The above statement is written as a direct quotation but it is actually a paraphrase from a caller during one of our radio shows. The question though, is a common one. There appears to be still some mysticism about psychological testing, some people believe that miricles will occur if we have more information, others are afraid of what the tests might reveal. In this next section an attempt will be made to describe psychological testing very simply and briefly. There really isn't very much magic.

All readers will be familiar with teacher type tests or achievement tests. These tests, as we all know, can be essay or objective and ask questions that usually measure recall of material that has been studied or learned. Actually, tests used by psychologists are not very different. When we talk of an aptitude test, we are trying to gauge the individual's potential for learning new material and we make this estimate from what an individual already knows. Some achievement and aptitude tests are administered by psychologists individually and in groups and can be administered to children or adults across provinces or countries. The advantages of these kind of instruments is that they have been standardized on a large population so that we can compare the results from one child to another, from one school system to another, from one district or region to another. Probably the most common types of test that will be interpreted to parents are intelligence, interest and personality tests. Each of these has been treated separately in this section.

What about giving you a number for a child's I.Q? Probably the authors would agree with the psychologist who did not reveal the score. There is no magic about a number. Sometimes an IQ score should be written in disappearing ink, so it will not follow a child for an entire school year. Any psychological test result is an estimate. It stands to reason that an individual test administered under controlled conditions will be a better estimate than a guess, but it is nevertheless just an estimate. When a child has been given an individual assessment it is always in everyone's best interest to sit down and discuss the results in detail, rather than utilize global results like an IQ number to summarize the entire interaction. When a psychologist tests a child or adult he or she is looking not only for weaknesses, but also for stengths. A profile of a picture of an individual will emerge from the test results and it is that picture that must be transmitted to others to make the results most meaningful.

There are many other kinds of specialized aptitude tests. Often, for various reasons, a child may be given a neuropsychological test battery, and much valuable information can result from such an assessment. Now, some particular types of psychological testing.

Psychological Testing - The I.Q.

It might have been better simply to discuss intelligence testing, but is seemed important to use the term I.Q., because certainly this concept, the concept of an intelligence quotient, has been badly misunderstood over the years.

Often I.Q. tests are blamed when we don't like the results. That is why it is important that we understand the basic concepts behind the tests. Intelligence tests are still widely utilized, particularly when we are attemping to identify children in need of some form of special educational programming. One of the groups of exceptional children making wide use of I.Q. tests would be "the gifted".

What do we mean then by intelligence quotient? Two concepts are involved, chronological age - that one is easy, and mental age which is a little more difficult. Let's think of mental age as simply the age where a child is performing on particular kinds of tasks. The I.Q. then is simply MA/CA x 100 =_____. For example, if we have a four year old child who is handling tasks usually accomplished by five year olds, we substitute in the formula in the fashion: 5/4 x 100 = 125

I.Q. tests have been with us for over eighty years. The first really useful I.Q. test was developed by Alfred Binet in France in 1905. Binet made his test of tasks that were age related. He first studied what skills were in fact developed in this fashion. He then looked at the age level where most children could perform the skill, and utilized it in his test. The latest revision of the Stanford Binet Intelligence Test was in 1986. It is still widely used and is a very good predictor, particularly of academic achievement. In fact, the Stanford Binet, when administered to children in grade 1, can help psychologists to predict grades in later years.

The other most common individual intelligence test was developed by and American, David Wechsler. His most common tests are the Wechsler Intelligence Scale for Children - Revised and the Wechsler Adult Intelligence Scale - Revised. Prototypes of these tests were first developed following World War II and the psychologist can learn much more information about a child after administering these tests, than can ever be related by a number. The Wechsler Tests show how a child performs, verbally, as well as non-verbally. These tests can predict school success, but they also provice an estimate of ability not so closely related to background and verbal skills.

The I.Q. is not a formula anymore. Test makers have compared the results to a norming group, and the mean or average is in fact now set at 100. Approximately two thirds of us will have an I.Q. score between 85 and 115, which means that scores above 115 or below 85 are somewhat unusual.

It should be stressed that intelligence tests provide much more information than simply scores. Sometimes, as reported earlier, psychologists believe that the actual scores should be restricted information, they're useful when administered, but not so useful in later years. The scores also cannot be interpreted by themselves; it depends on which test, who administered it, etc. So when we hear somebody talk about his or her I.Q. as 127, this by itself is meaningless.

A few suggestions about I.Q. scores. When a child is tested, often parents are better with a report, than with actual scores. It is often very important to look for strengths on these tests rather than weaknesses. Remember, the I.Q. can be a good predictor, but it unfortunately predicts negatively better than positively. Properly administered intelligence tests can tell us a good deal about our real limits.

Psychological Testing: Interest Inventories

Interest inventories are known to junior and senior high school students, who take interest tests as part of courses and guidance on: careers and career information. Recently, however, interest tests have been available to adults and many people are taking these inventories with a view to either mid-life career change, or even just for information and possible avocational experience. In times of economic recession interest tests became very valuable, as people search for recreational, social, and educational outlets different from the work environment.

There are basically two kind of interest inventories. One such inventory was produced by Dr. Carl Safran from Calgary, Alberta and the Kuder Tests have been well known to generations of Canadian students. With these tests you simply choose most and least liked areas, educational experiences, and occupations, etc. Scoring of these tests sorts out areas of interest. As well as sorting out areas of interest, test makers usually provide examples of occupations and interests that are common to these areas. For example, you would expect medical doctors to be high in social and scientific areas, while farmers could be expected to have high scores in agricultural and mechanical activities.

A more empirical test was developed in Stanford University by Edward Strong in the 1930's. The current version of this test, Strong-Campbell Interest Inventory, provides 325 questions where you mark "like","dislike", or "indifferent". The feature of this inventory is that you can match your profile and compare yourself to people successful in many different kinds of occupational areas. The test predicts very well, and follows fifty years of research. Basically, with those occupations where you have a low score, you can be quite confident you will not be happy in that occupation, even if you meet all of the academic prerequisites. On the other hand, high scores will likely predict people staying in a profession, if they have been successful in preparational training programs. There is also more information provided by this test on things like introversion, extroversion, a persons' comfort level with academic learning and etc.

Two kind of people then need to think seriously about interest testing. The obvious group includes those people making a first foray into the work world. Another group would include others thinking of changing occupations, or currently unemployed. Some people take interest inventories simply for their own information and self knowledge.

Students can obtain interest testing from counselors in all secondary schools and post-education institutions. Adults might wish to phone the nearest Alberta Career Centre or the Alberta Career Centre Hotline for further information. Other provinces have similar opportunities - information can usually be obtained from provincial departments involved with career planning or post-secondary education.

Psychological Testing: Personality

Personality testing is probably the most difficult and the least accurate area of psychological testing. It is also the most important. Individual personality tests are rarely administered in school settings. Psychologists use these inventories more often as part of a team in a mental health or hospital setting. It is, of course, impossible to ever fully describe another individual's personality, so personality testing is an art as well as a science.

Personality testing is almost always needed when a patient is in a psychiatric ward of a hospital. Very often personality changes can occur as the result of other factors such as illness, accidents, loss of loved one's etc. Elsewhere in the book personality disorders are discussed. Personality testing by psychologists is one strategy for diagnosing depression, anxiety, hysteria, manic episodes, psychoses, neuroses, etc. In many instances medical practitioners will ask psychologists to assist with diagnostic statements and personality tests can help these professionals to find the closest diagnostic category, as treatment strategies are often quite different, depending upon the diagnosed problem. Perhaps more commonly, personality tests are used to help professionals point out tendencies toward shyness, or outgoing behavior for normal people. In other instances, needs can be uncovered as a person plans life goals. All of us have different requirements and needs for such factors as achievement, love and affection, or control.

Objective personality tests usually ask for "yes" or "no", or perhaps "true" or "false" responses. The individual can then be compared on the basis of this test to a norming group within the population. You can then be identified as being more like group A than group B on a set of variables.

Many people have heard about psychologists asking individuals to tell stories about pictures or ink blots. These "projective tests" can reveal much more about a person's personality, but at the same time are much more difficult to score and interpret. Adults undergoing personality and/or interest testing often find out useful information about themselves which can be utilized to assist in decision making.

Maximizing Potential - Assisting The Learner

"...I read for pleasure, relaxation and for the purpose of learning. To read for pleasure and relaxation is great, it can be something in which I can totally lose myself in, take a mini-vacation. Not remembering all the detail of material like this is fine. On the other hand when I am reading for information and to learn, and gain new knowledge, I find I must read, re-read and re-read. It is true I have always been a handsome learner, but I am extremely frustrated at this inability to grasp. My comprehension is good, and I do not get in over my head with terminology. One of the things I do is to write out and summarize what I have read, but this is not always practical."

That letter, of course, was answered. In answering it, our research lead to an earlier paper written by one of the authors actually for teachers. The title was "Teaching for Retention". While the article is summarized here, it seemed to us that the suggestions are as useful for parents as teachers. All of us can focus better, study better, and function better if we are organized. By discussing teaching for retention and improving study habits it is hoped that the listener that wrote us the letter can be helped and also others can see the problem in a broader perspective.

Teaching for Retention

The following are suggestions made from research facts to help you organize for more effective instruction. The premise of every classroom teacher should be that "what is worth teaching, is also worth remembering!" Teachers, tutors and parents face the problems

of forgetting as much as students. You can use the following suggestions to aid your own memory and also to assist the students in remembering what you presented.

Ways to Improve Memory

1. All factual material will be retained longer if it is meaningful. Since facts are more difficult to relate to existing ideational systems in the brain than abstract items, we need to stress meaning of facts so that the student can correlate the fact with another important concept.

   eg. Teach the facts as associated concepts.

   eg. Use vocabulary exercises as larger categories i.e. group words into categories for better retention.

2. Retention of rote-learning material is very brief. If you use rote learning, use association to tie new facts to existing material. This is known as an anchoring technique. It reduces forgetting. eg. Teaching from old to new ideas anchors the new idea to an existing, familiar one.

3. Subject-Matter Organization.
   a) Subject-matter must be logically organized and logically presented.
   b) Misconceptions should be corrected promptly.
   c) Teach "meaning" by relating to other subject-area relevance or by attaching new learning to the old.
   d) Frequent review.
   e) Pace your teaching to the average or lower student. Better that all understand, rather than just the bright ones.
   f) Use exams, not for judgement, but to help students in recalling previously learned material. Getting students to recall information increases its strength in memory. That is, it increases the probability of recalling it again in the future.
   g) Interference Theory has taught us that when you have two very similar concepts to teach, teach them at different times. eg. Never teach the letters m and n, or b and d on the same day.

4. Conditions of Practice to increase memory.
   a) Practice consolidates new and old material by anchoring it to other concepts in the cortex. Therefore, frequency of practice is a fundamental rule. Drill is still important, but use variations in drill techniques. Frequent practice need not necessarily be rote.

b) Overlearning is always stressed by psychologists. The famous "learning curve" clearly illustrated that as you increase practice and overlearn, you make consistent increments in the learning curve. If you use the rule of frequency and overlearning, then the use of techniques like feedback and knowledge of results are not as necessary.

c) As a rule, it is better to have distributed practice than massed practice (cramming). Distributed practice is suggested in particular for:
   i)   younger students
   ii) for the less stable
   iii) for longer tasks
   iv) for more difficult tasks, therefore, the older you are, the brighter, the shorter the task and the less difficult, cramming as a technique can be useful.

5. Practice Rules
   a) Provide for overt responses. This may include mental responses as well. Emitted responses, however, can be reinforced.
   b) Have students construct rather than select answers during practice. Construction brings back what is in the students' memory bank.
   c) When practice is guided, lead the students in a graded difficulty hierarchy of questions.
   d) If there is meaning in a total unit or lesson, use the "whole" method, instead of the "part" method. If the unit is very large, break it into logical units for the student. The more mature the student, the better the "whole" technique.
   e) Where possible, have the condition of practice resemble the condition under which the knowledge or skill will eventually be used.

6. The Affective Dimension
   a) Where attitudes are positive retention, association, and meaningfulness is greater.
   b) Negative feelings and attitudes inhibit learning.
   c) Anxiety-producing situations lead to repressions or hostility and enhance forgetting. Therefore, reduce anxiety before beginning any teaching.

Remember:

Remembering is a Process
Memory is the Product
Forgetting is the decay of memory

Developing Study Habits

Probably one of the most frequent causes of disagreement between parents and children has to do with studying and study habits. This is unfortunate, because parents can be instrumental in helping children develop study habits that will serve them in good stead for the rest of their lives.

Let's remember that "all learning is personal and emotional". If we wish a child to learn something, the child must take some personal involvement for this learning. Children learn in many ways - modelling or imitation, through their eyes, ears, touch, smell - in fact all of their senses. They will work for reinforcement or rewards, and the wise parent knows that the best reward is intrinsic motivation, that is, the child learns for the love of learning, in order to acquire knowledge. Most students, though, work best for short term goals, for example pass an examination.

There is a danger of overemphasizing home study. If the child's work is constantly checked, and must be produced on a daily basis, the child could learn to believe that the real action is at home. Therefore, the child may fool around at school. More importantly though, is the fact that if the child were to do no home study, if there was no homework, then parents would be really kept out of the education of their children. It is extremely important that we be part of this development.

Here are some study guidelines based on research, which should make this a successful enterprise.

Study Guidelines

1. Rewards should be for effort and progress, never time.
   What we are saying is that what is accomplished is the most important. The idea of a certain amount of time that must be spent studying every night is not a wise idea, as this could lead to the concept that study is punishment. Students should never have the

feeling that they deserve marks on the basis of time spent in study, rather it is what is accomplished that is important.

2. Study Timetables

There is an excellent device to motivate children. The trick in building a study timetable is to make it easy and flexible. Make sure the child has lots of breaks for exercise, fun and TV. It is better to have a child working when they are at a study table, than putting in time. Make the timetable easy and then add one simple rule. "You must work when you are sitting at the desk at your study space".

3. Take fear of study and panic seriously

There really is such a thing as examination phobia. At the university level we see it in graduate students, and students in all faculties. But we also see it in grade 2 students. The suggestion here would be not to motivate through fear. Your best students are frightened already and trying hard to do their best.

4. Assist when asked

This is the ideal way of helping children, which is to help out when help is requested. Remember, don't do your students' work for them. Help out when you can, and when helping look for strengths as well as weakness. In particular notice improvements.

5. Be future oriented

Many students can change their study habits, or as is often indicated "can turn over a new leaf". Baron de Montesquieu in the early 1700's indicated "you have to study a great deal to know a little". The best strategy is to help them to accomplish something. Once they are in the habit of going to a study setting, accomplishing something, and then feeling good about it, studying can really be a rewarding experience. Punishment and rewards can be worked out for both effort and accomplishment.

Summary

Education is everyone's business. Increased professionalism in education, however, has shifted the responsibility squarely on the teachers. Perhaps this is only right. Nevertheless, research consistently has shown that increased parental concern and involvement in their child's education has led to improved student performance. Parents need to know about learning problems, slow learners, giftedness, creativity, assessment techniques, memory and study habits so as to be better able to assist their children. In addition, as educators and professionals in the helping professions, the co-hosts on "That's Living" have an implicit agenda of promoting children's rights. This chapter has been written for parents as much as teachers. The more parents learn about the education process and specialized knowledge, the better able they are to not only assist their children, but also effect change in the educational system. Parents need to meet with the educators informed and concerned. The issues in this chapter are relevant and contemporary, written to help all of us, since "education is everyone's business".

CHAPTER 13

Psychiatric Hospitalization

PSYCHIATRIC HOSPITALIZATION

Negative attitudes about psychiatric hospitalization are based on many historical facts. Until recent times, mental illness was frequently thought to be caused by some sort of "demonic (devil) possession". That is, individuals who were mentally ill were considered to be possessed by the devil and should be considered dangerous. Throughout history and in many societies, the mentally ill individual was frequently ridiculed, isolated, tortured and even killed. Treatment included bloodletting, enemas, emetics, flogging and long term institutionalization.

I think everybody knows the term "bedlam". This word originated from the name of a British mental hospital; Hospital of St Mary of Bethlehem (in London). Individuals who were mentally retarded, mentally ill, crippled, poor or "undesirable" were placed into a large setting with no privacy. These individuals had little care and poor hygiene. The "mess" in which they lived came to be known as "bedlam". This term is still used when there is chaos. The implication is that this chaos is related to some sort of mental disorder.

The Asylum

Everyone knows the term asylum. This term is associated with the word "insane" to form the two words "insane asylum". There is probably nothing more derogatory that one can tell another than that they "ought to be in an insane asylum". This term is often used with a modern twist of language where people say "the nuthouse". It is still very common for patients who require hospitalization to fear hospitalization because they will be "labelled" that they were in a "nuthouse". Patients frequently comment that they are afraid to go into a psychiatric unit because they would lose their job, be ridiculed by their community and be disowned by their family.

Many individuals firmly believe that psychiatric care is similar to that which they read in the book or saw in the movie "One Flew Over The Cuckoo's Nest". Unfortunately, it is a historical fact that treatment of the psychiatrically ill was inhumane and tragic. Hospitalized patients were deprived of their liberties and stripped of their dignity. In my training in Bellevue Hospital in New York City, I studied and worked in a setting that was far from ideal. It was not infrequent for the head nurse in the emergency department to tell a patient "Why the hell are you here?" The nurse may then go on to berate the patient and tell the patient "You should smarten up. You're acting so stupid. Go sit down over there".

This type of attitude was not unique to this one nurse or just this nursing staff. This attitude was seen in physicians, psychologists and social workers on a regular basis. For example, one of the residents (a doctor training to be a psychiatrist) simply tolerated the hospital so that he could become a psychoanalyst. He did not want to study in a psychiatric hospital. He just wanted to become a psychoanalyst. His attitude towards the severely ill patients was terrible. I remember an occasion when he told the patient "If you want to kill yourself, go ahead. Here's a rope". He then pulled out a rope from the desk and threw it at the patient.

Psychiatric hospitals were grossly underfunded. The hospitals were poorly maintained and the staff poorly educated. This has changed significantly in the last 20 years with the introduction of a universal health care system in Canada and the introduction of private medical insurances, Medicare and Medicaid in the United States.

▌Improvements in Care

As research dramatically increased our knowledge about mental illness in the last few years, the treatment approach changed. As the treatment approach changed, facilities and programs changed. These improvements produced an attitude change in society.

Let me give you two examples of what I mean by "research" leading to improvements. In the mid 1950's, the drug Largactil (called Thorazine in the United States) caused a very great change in the care of the severely mentally ill. Patients who were previously psychotic and manifested their disorder with aggression and hostility could now be treated and their symptoms controlled. Prior to this time, this individual would remain in a mental hospital for many years and was frequently isolated from other patients and staff. This individual would be feared by patients, staff and family. With the introduction of Largactil, the patient improved to the point that discharge was possible.

A second drug that was discovered in mid 1950's was the antidepressant Elavil. Depressed individuals who were totally unable to function in respect of their studies, job, or families, suddenly improved after only short periods of time. With the introduction of drug therapy, mental illness could now be treated successfully.

Since the 1950's, there has been a dramatic reduction in the number of psychiatric beds even though the general population has increased in both Canada and the United States. There are probably only one-third the number of psychiatric beds presently that there were in the 1950's. Further, during the 1950's, approximately 60% of all psychiatric patients were treated in the large mental hospitals. Presently, only about 10% of all patients are treated in the large mental hospitals. Ninety percent of all patients are presently treated in psychiatric units of general hospitals. Care is given primarily in an out-patient setting or through partial hospitalization rather than total hospitalization.

Short-term Treatment

Hospitalization has become directed towards "short term treatment", meaning, less than 30 days. Of all patients hospitalized, less than 10% will require some sort of extended in-patient care. There is also a growing recognition that a large number of emotional illnesses are caused by physical disease. It is estimated that 10-15% of patients diagnosed at emergency departments as psychiatric conditions are really suffering some major medical disorder such as hypothyroidism or head trauma.

Many of the new directions in psychiatric treatment have a positive implication. However, there is one feature of treatment that has a negative consequence. A small percentage of individuals who have become psychiatrically ill seem never to recover adequately and are unable to care for themselves in society. Many of these patients have a diagnosis of schizophrenia. These individuals are hospitalized, given anti-psychotic drugs, and protected within the hospital setting. Within the hospital setting, these individuals improve, have a reduction of symptoms and frequently appear to be relatively well. These individuals often demand their release from hospital. There is a great deal of pressure from society to discharge these patients. You may ask, "How can society encourage the discharge of these patients?" There are two main reasons. The cost of psychiatric hospitalization is great and the medical insurance programs and governments develop policies to reduce the number of psychiatric beds. The second reason is based on society's concern with civil liberties. Because of the concern for civil liberties, legislation is passed to give the individual freedom if he is not dangerous to himself or others — even though they are unable to care for themselves adequately on an independent basis. These individuals who have chronic (long-standing) mental disorders are discharged into the community but frequently do not take their medications, do not attend follow-up appointments or accept the advice given to them in respect to their living circumstances. These individuals then end up "roaming the streets". Rather than receiving appropriate direction, proper meals, proper hygiene, medical treatment, and structured recreational and leisure activities that occur in a hospital setting, these individuals experience poor living conditions, terrible hygiene, inadequate meals and no health care. These individuals are sometimes referred to as going from "back wards to back streets". This group of severely mentally ill individuals represents a group of individuals who are, in fact, suffering more because of our "improved" treatments and humanitarian approach.

Reasons for Admission

Why is a person admitted to hospital? The most common reasons are:
1. Suicidal behavior
2. Homicidal behavior
3. Interpersonal conflict
4. Mental and physical changes related to alcohol and drug abuse
5. Acute crisis due to changes such as job or school
6. Grief reaction
7. Recurrence of long term mental illness
8. Abnormal reactions to major disasters
9. Reaction to abuse or violence

Involuntary Hospitalization

Hospitalization can be voluntary or involuntary.

"Voluntary hospitalization" occurs when an individual seeks medical care and accepts hospitalization voluntarily for diagnosis and treatment.

"Involuntary hospitalization" refers to individuals who are dangerous to themselves or others (suicidal or homicidal) and reject voluntary hospitalization. These individuals are "committed to hospital against their will. Every Canadian province and American state enacts legislation which is usually referred to as the "Mental Health Act". The Mental Health Act sets out firm rules as to which individuals could be hospitalized against their will. Each act lists procedures which must be rigidly followed before an individual could be hospitalized against his/her will. Every Act has clear rules as to who is allowed to hospitalize persons against their will and for what reasons. The rules include details as to the type of legal forms that must be completed. Individuals who are hospitalized against their will must be informed that they are being hospitalized against their will and that they have rights to appeal their hospitalization. Individuals may seek legal counsel and apply to a "board" to request their release from hospital. The board consists of several appointed persons. This board has the authority to recommend release or continued hospitalization.

Let me now describe what it means to be a voluntary patient in a psychiatric ward. This is part of a telephone conversation that I had with a physician me in reference to one of his patients.

Doctor A: "Good afternoon. I'd like to refer a patient to you. Laura is 52 years old and I have been treating her for six weeks. She is not doing well. Most of her day is spent crying. Two of her daughters recently came to my office to tell me that they are very worried about their mother who is talking about suicide. I treated her with antidepressants and tried to give her some direction but I think the problem is more than I can handle."

Doctor B: "Sure. What have you told Laura?

Doctor A: "Laura knows that she has a depression. We have tried her on two different antidepressants. She has never seen a psychiatrist before. None of the family have been treated by a psychiatrist. I spent a bit of time telling her about psychiatrists and psychiatric treatment. She seems quite agreeable."

Doctor B: "Why don't you send her to the emergency department tomorrow at 9:00 a.m. If she requires hospitalization, it's best that I see her early in the day when there is more staff on duty."

It is very important that the referring doctor have a positive attitude towards individuals who suffer emotional illness. It is also important that the physician views psychiatric care with a positive attitude. The referring physician must be kind, considerate, sympathetic and empathic. The referring physician must try and reduce fears and myths about psychiatric care. Unfortunately, referring physicians often are lacking knowledge and a positive attitude about psychiatric illness and psychiatric treatment. These physicians do not inform their patients adequately; do not educate them as to the need for proper medical and psychiatric care; and, may in fact, demonstrate negative attitudes towards mental illness and psychiatric treatment. Statements from the referring physician to the patient that represent negative attitudes may include "I don't know what else to do. There must be a problem in your head. I'm going to send you to a shrink". This type of attitude by professionals is still all too frequent.

This is an excerpt of the interview that took place with Laura in the emergency department:

Doctor B: "I am glad that Doctor A told you about depression and psychiatric care. From the information that you gave your doctor and me, I believe you have a severe depression. Because of the severity of the depression, I would like to hospitalize you today. You will be coming in as a voluntary patient. You will have the right to leave the hospital whenever you want to. We will not do any kind of investigation or treatment unless we inform you adequately. Our hospital consists of three different wards with a total of 70 beds. One of the wards is for the very severely ill individuals who need intensive care. The other two wards consist of 30 beds each. Most of the rooms are private rooms but some are semi-private. Each bedroom has its own bathroom. It is best that you wear your regular street clothes rather than hospital gowns."

Laura: "How long will I have to be in hospital?"

Doctor B: "The usual hospital stay is 30 days. There are some patients that remain in hospital for short periods of times such as one or two days but this would not be true for you."

Laura: "What kind of patients are on the ward?"

Doctor B: "There are many different types of patients on the ward. Some of the patients are quite young. Our youngest patient is 13 years of age. Some patients are quite old. My oldest patient on the ward today is 83 years of age. Some patients have been readmitted because their long-standing disorder has worsened. Many of the patients are like yourself. They are people who have functioned very well in their studies, work and family until they developed their emotional problems and required hospitalization."

Laura: "I'm so worried. This is so new to me."

Doctor B: "I would like to spend some time with you to discuss hospitalization. I know that there is very little good information written about psychiatric units. In fact, I can't think of one publication that is readily available in a bookstore for you to read. You are new to me. However, you have known your doctor for many years and I have had many referrals from him. I would like you to trust your doctor's judgement that he has made a proper referral in your case and that you will be very well cared for."

Laura: "Yes. He told me about other patients he has referred to you. I really do trust him."

The above discussion demonstrates a number of items. It is important that patients develop trust in their physicians and that physicians trust their patients. Trust is such a simple word but it means so much. It is only through the complex experience of trust that patients can gain confidence in the care offered them. Unfortunately, there seems to be a change in the pattern of medical care. Rather than patients developing a long term relationship with one physician or a clinic, patients are now obtaining medical care from a wide variety of physicians through emergencies and drop-in medical centers. There is a tendency to get medical care from many different sources. Long term and trusting relationships between patient and physician cannot develop in this setting.

The above discussion with Laura also focuses on the fact that the patient should be given information so that she can reach an independent decision about hospitalization. Laura has already received information from her family doctor. It takes time to give information. It is through adequate information, time and trust that appropriate attitudes towards emotional illness and treatment could occur. It is also obvious that Laura could not be given all the information in one sitting. She should be told that she will be gaining more information upon entrance into the hospital and that no diagnostic procedure or treatment will occur unless she agrees to it. It should be emphasized to patients that they are free to leave the hospital whenever they choose to do so. Patients fear losing control over their lives. They should be informed regularly that they do have control over decision-making within the hospital setting. Laura is introduced to her nurse.

Role of the Nurse

This is part of the conversation that was held between the patient and the nurse:

Carol (Nurse): "I will be your nurse on this shift Laura. For each of the three shifts, you will be assigned one nurse. Other nurses might be involved in your treatment. I will be your "primary nurse" and you can come to me at any time. I will help develop a program for you. I want you to feel protected and comfortable. I'm on your side."

Laura: "I don't know what I was expecting in the hospital. It is very different from what I expected."

Carol: "What do you mean?"

Laura: "I guess I'm foolish. I thought there were going to be bars on the windows. I had all sorts of dreams of how scary this place would be. It looks so normal. It looks like other hospital wards I've seen before. In fact, it looks a bit better than the usual hospital ward because there seem to be more sitting rooms and nobody is in a hospital gown. I feel a bit relieved."

Carol: "I have four sheets of paper with me. As you can see, there is a great deal written on these sheets. These are questions that I will be asking you. Some of the questions might be quite personal. You may choose not to answer some of the questions. However, the more we know about you, the more we will understand you and the better we will be able to treat you. I will be asking you such questions as "What brought you to hospital? When were you last well? What were you doing when you were well? Do you have any allergies? Do you have any history of taking street drugs or using alcohol?" This is called a "medical history"."

Laura: "Doctor A and Doctor B asked me a lot of those questions. I guess I might as well answer them for you also."

The following section is a sample of a "nursing medical history form".

NURSING MEDICAL HISTORY

I. DEMOGRAPHIC INFORMATION

Patient's name: _____

Name patient prefers to be called by _____

Date _____ Time of Admission to Unit _____

Mode of Admission   Ambulatory _____ Stretcher_____
                         Wheelchair _____ Other _____

                         Elective _____ Emergency _____

Accompanied by: _____

In case of Emergency, notify _____

Telephone #: _____ Relationship _____

II. PERSONAL HISTORY

General:

Male _____ Female _____ Eye _____ Color _____ Hair _____ Color _____

Skin Condition: _____

Rashes _____ Cuts _____ Bruises _____ Scars _____ Other _____

Turgor _____ Color _____ Hydration _____

Previous Illness:

Epilepsy _____ Diabetes _____ Cardiac _____ Psychiatric _____

Other _____

Current Medications:

Name of drug	Dosage	Hr. taken at home	Reason for taking

1. _____
2. _____
3. _____
4. _____
5. _____
6. Any non-prescriptive drugs/alcohol/tobacco _____

Frequency _____

III. GENERAL PHYSICAL APPEARANCE

_____
_____

IV. MENTAL STATUS

A. Self Awareness/Insight:

Why have you come to the hospital; were the reasons given to you; any recent changes in your life; in what way would you like to change your life; can we help you; how; what do you expect from us; what does your family expect; what has the doctor told you about your treatment?

B. Orientation
What day and date is it? What is the name of this place?

C. Mood/Affect:
Angry; friendly; cooperative, labile; depressed; euphoric

D. Actions/Behavior:
Eye contact; withdrawn; anxious; restless; tense; apprehensive; posturing; lethargic

---

E. Speech:
Content of speech; manner (slow; rapid; loud; circumstantial; mute; relevant)

F. Intellectual Functioning:
attention span; memory; decision-making ability; concentration

---

G. Preoccupation:
What are you concerned about most?

H. Stress:
Do you experience stress in your life?

I. Suicidal/Homicidal/Risks:
Have you felt life was not worth living; have you ever harmed yourself; do you feel like hurting someone?

J. Levels of Consciousness:
Alert; fully conscious; confused, delirious; lethargic; comatose

V. CONSENT FOR ADMISSION   (Signed by)
   Patient ——————————————— Next of Kin ———————————————

VI. ASSESSMENT PATTERNS OF DAILY LIVING
   A. Daily Activities:
   Describe a typical day; leisure time; people seen

   B. Ambulation:
   Degree of dependence/independence

   C. Vision/Hearing:
   Visual and hearing limitations

   D. Nutrition:
   Eating patterns; special diets; food fads; nutritional state

---

E. Reproduction:
Date of last menstrual cycle; pregnant; methods of birth control

F. Elimination:
Usual patterns; constipation; incontinence; use of laxatives; catheters

G. Sleep/Rest Patterns:
Usual hour of waking; retiring; night-time patterns; use of sedation

H. Personal Hygiene:
Bath/Shower/frequency

I. Physical Appearance:
Hygiene and grooming; general appearance; posture; weight

J. Recreation Activities/Interests:
Hobbies, sports; clubs, organizations; exercise routine; frequency of participation

VII. SOCIAL HISTORY
A. Language:
Primary language; other languages spoken/read; are questions understood

B. Education:
Years at school; other education or training; are you presently studying

C. Occupation:
Current occupation; length of time in current job; employment history

D. Living Arrangements:
Do you live alone; with someone else; who; relationship to person you are living with.

E. Family and/or Support Systems:
Number of brothers and sisters; position in family; help from family and/or support systems

Spouse/children; significant others; do you make friends easily; expected visitors

F. Religious Needs:
Do you wish to see the hospital chaplain; notify the clergyman; are there religious practices you would like honored

G. Finances:
Will your hospitalization cause any problems at home now or upon discharge (e.g. babysitting); debts; job or family problems

H. Involvement with other Agencies:
Clinics; other facilities; social services; clergy; contact employer

OTHER INFORMATION:

Completed by: _____ Date:_____

The nursing staff of a psychiatric unit are on duty 24 hours per day. They provide the minute to minute care for each patient. The nurse should appear concerned and protective. The nurse outlines the structure of the ward in terms of personnel, roles, programs, procedures, rules and expectations.

The nurses are usually organized in a specific manner. The staff nurse is responsible for a certain number of patients. This number varies depending on factors such as time of shift, severity of illness and other nursing duties such as leadership in therapeutic groups. The staff nurse communicates to other staff nurses during her shift and to staff nurses arriving for the next shift as to the patient's needs, problems and treatment program. The team leader (a nurse) supervises the staff nurses. The team leader is responsible to the unit manager. The unit manager is responsible to a nursing supervisor who may have one or more areas of the hospital under her jurisdiction. The nursing supervisor is then responsible to the acting supervisor of the hospital. The acting supervisor is responsible to the director of nursing.

Just in case you forgot, nurses are very, very human. Most are female but some are male. Some nurses are sooooo. . fat! Yes, the fat ones think of dieting. Sometimes doctors' eyes will suddenly shift quickly from their charts. Why? Because some nurses are so cute. I thought I should include this little paragraph. By the way, doctors are also very human. They may also be fat or cute.

The nurse is one member of a "multi-disciplinary team". Multi-disciplinary team refers to the fact that there are a variety of professionals working together to assist in the diagnosis and treatment of the patient. Other "disciplines" include psychology, social work, occupational therapy, psychiatrists, and medical consultants. The team usually meets at a formal meeting on a weekly basis to discuss the patients. Team members may meet more frequently or communicate through a series of notes written on the chart.

The Patient's Chart

Essentially all written communications about the patient are enclosed in the patient's "chart". The chart is usually subdivided into a number of sections including identification, legal, history, progress notes, nurses notes, doctor's orders, laboratory and other special tests, and consultations. The chart is an official document and is kept on the ward. When the patient is discharged from hospital, the chart goes to the Medical Records Department. The chart is a confidential document. Members of the team have access to the chart. However, anyone who is not on the team is not allowed to read the chart. The patient may sign a consent form which allows other specified individuals to have access to his chart. The chart is not generally given to the patient. However, some patients demand to read their chart. A patient has the right to access his own chart. The chart should be freely available to the patient. In fact, in some jurisdictions, the chart is considered to be "owned" by the patient. However, this may cause a number of problems. The chart frequently consists of medical terms that the patient may misunderstand or misconstrue. The chart can be considered a "working document" consisting of observations and interpretations of the patient at a given time. Each chart enclosure does not necessarily represent the final opinion of the staff. Patients might become upset with what is thought about them. If the chart is considered the patient's property, the staff will be less candid and will tend to write only generalized statements about the patient. This will interfere with the value of these written communications. Therefore, instead of a staff member writing in the chart "it appears that the husband is domineering and excessively controlling of his wife" (the patient), the staff member might write "there may be a relationship difficulty between husband and wife". As you can see, if the first phrase is written and the patient does not like the implications, then the patient may get angry at the staff or may threaten the staff with statements such as "you can't hear what I'm saying. You have your own mind made up. You don't know what you're doing. You are being unprofessional, etc." It is very difficult for the patient to become upset with a staff member if the second statement is written. However, it is clear that the first statement is much more communicative and may be helpful to the rest of the treatment team in understanding the total situation and eventually helping the patient and her husband.

Role of the Social Worker

This is part of the conversation that was held between the patient and the social worker:

Jean (Social Worker): "Doctor B. asked me to visit with you. I think he told you that I was going to talk to you about some of your difficulties."

Laura: "Yes. He told me that you were going to talk to me about my difficulties with isolation."

Jean: "I understand that you are spending most of your time at home alone. I understand you have your own house and that your finances are okay. I heard that you were very active when you were bringing up your children. You had a husband to take care of, the children needed a lot of attention, and you were involved in a business."

Laura: "Yes, but all that has gone. My youngest child is now 21 and left home three months ago. When my husband and I separated one year ago, everything was divided up and the business was sold. I feel like I'm not worth anything. It seems that there is nothing for me to do. It is as if life came to a stand still."

Jean: "You were a busy woman. I guess you must have had a lot to do with the school and other community activities that involved your children."

Laura: "I sure did. I was on the Parent-Teacher Association Board. In fact, a number of years ago I was president of the Parent-Teacher Association. Every minute of my time was taken up. My two boys were in hockey and I was always there to help out and encourage them."

Jean: "Doctor B told me that you were talking to him quite a lot about the fact that life came to a stand still. I want to talk to you about some of the organizations and activities that are in your area. I want to talk to you about taking care of yourself. About leisure and recreation. About having some fun. About starting your life in a different direction."

Laura: "You can talk. It's okay. I'm so low. I need any kind of help I could get."

Jean: "I would like to set some appointments with you. I would like to come and visit with you. I don't think it's proper for me just to come and say that I'm a social worker and that you should do this, that or the other thing. I think you and I should get to know each other really well. I think it's important that you and I talk about how hurt you feel at this time. I would like to help you plan some strategies that may be helpful when you return home."

Laura: "I'd like that."

Social workers are important members of the team within a hospital setting. No psychiatric program is complete without social workers. In the past, and unfortunately, in some situations at the present time, some physicians, other professionals, and members of our society think that social workers are simply involved in making sure that a person has a roof over their head and some food. Social workers offer more than financial assistance. Social workers are highly skilled members of the treatment team who have a good knowledge of human behavior. Aside from assisting patients in very specific manners such as housing, food and clothing, social workers are involved in evaluating and treating patients in individual and group settings.

Role of the Psychologist

The following is part of a conversation that occurred between the patient and the psychologist:

John (Psychologist): "Good morning, my name is John. I hope that you were told that I was to visit you."

Laura: "Yes, the nurse and Doctor B told me that you were going to talk to me about some tests and treatment."

John: "That's right. I was in a meeting yesterday with the rest of the staff. It seems that the whole staff believes that you are really quite intelligent and can contribute to society. I know something about your past work. I would like to do some tests and help you look at other choices of work for your future. Have you ever thought of retraining."

Laura: "Forget it. I'm too old. I'm worn out."

John: "I accept what you say. I know that you mean what you say. But, you are depressed and things have not gone well for you in your life. As a psychologist, I have helped people redirect their life and they are doing very well. I would like to do some intelligence testing with you. If we can show that you have a good ability to think, I think we can direct you into a government sponsored educational program. I know that you have some knowledge of typing and you have worked in a business before. There are so many jobs available for individuals who can handle a keyboard and a computer terminal. I would like to do some intellectual assessment and personality assessment. If the results show that you can handle a new educational program, we can get you a year of training and then get you placed with a company. We know that success in education and work, and, for that matter, other areas of life, leads to good feelings."

Laura: "I don't think there is anything good about me now."

John: "I know what you are saying. However, can you give me a chance? Will you agree to the testing?"

Laura: "Okay."

Psychologists are a necessary part of the treatment team in a psychiatric unit. Psychologists usually begin study for four years to receive a bachelor's degree in psychology. With further study, they may then be awarded a master's and/or doctoral degree in psychology. Psychologists specialize in areas such as testing, therapy or research. In Laura's case, the psychologist will be testing to evaluate the patient's intelligence and her personality qualities. Based on this information, the patient may then be referred to an educational program for upgrading. Some psychologists do not test patients. Instead, they are highly skilled in therapies such as relaxation, hypnosis, individual psychotherapy, family therapy or group therapy.

Recreational and Occupational Therapists

Most programs have recreational therapists and occupational therapists. Occupational therapists undergo a specified university training for their particular profession. Within a hospital setting, occupational therapists often become involved in developing recreation programs, leisure programs and specific occupational activities for hospitalized patients. The following is an example of a communication between the occupational therapist and Laura towards the end of Laura's hospitalization:

Ron (Occupational Therapist):   "Well Laura, you and I sure talked a lot and did a lot of things over the last four weeks. I'm really going to miss you now that you are leaving hospital."

Laura: "It was really a treat to meet with you Ron. When I came to the hospital I was fearful of everything. I thought that this was the last place in the world I ever wanted to be in. Actually, I feel a bit sad about leaving the hospital."

Ron: "I'm glad to hear that you feel good about the hospital."

Laura: "I sure do. You all made me feel so good. I almost feel like crying just thinking about how good you were to me."

Ron: "I hope things go well with you after you leave the hospital."

Laura: "When you first came to me and told me that I would be doing exercises each morning with you and other patients, I thought that you were being silly. I haven't done exercises for years. In fact, all I did was sit at home all last year."

Ron: "You did pretty good."

Laura: "It was nice to have music and the other patients during exercises. It was really a lot of fun. When you asked me to lead the group in exercises, I thought to myself "Gee, people like me. People are responding to me. This is like old times.""

Ron: "It just goes to prove that we all feel a lot better if we are doing something and if we are doing it with people. I hope that you get involved in some sort of a recreation program when you leave the hospital."

Laura: "I sure will. I sure could get these old flabby muscles going. I sure could enjoy the contact with others. I just hate being alone."

Ron: "Some of the ceramics you did were just excellent. Are you going to continue taking any kind of classes in ceramics when you leave."

Laura: "I really don't know. I do know that doing ceramics with others had a really good effect on me. I really do need people. If it's not ceramics, it's going to be something else. I'm really going to get involved."

Ron: "If I helped you as much as you say, it makes me feel good. I will always remember your laughter when we were at the movie with the other patients. When you laughed out, it seemed to catch on to everybody. Don't forget to keep laughing."

Laura: "It's been months since I laughed. You know, I haven't gone to a movie for three years. I haven't gone to any kind of entertainment for a long time. I guess you're telling me something. You're telling me to get my act together."

Ron: "Make sure you drop me a note and tell me how you are doing."

The Team Approach

Members of the "multi-disciplinary team" have an intense interest in people. It is not adequate for members of the team to have skills that they learned in university. They must have a certain sense of good will and humanism. The team member must be able to hear what the patients are saying. Team members must be careful not to impose their own set of values on the patients. For example, if a team member is highly religious, then that team member must be careful that he be able to accept the individual who is a professed atheist. If a team member believes strongly in marriage, then it is necessary that the team member not lecture a patient on how they must not live with their boyfriend or girlfriend before marriage. A team member must be secure in his/her role. Team members aim to cooperate and not compete with each other. For example, a psychologist should unconditionally accept the social worker and not think that psychology is more important or superior to social work. A goal of the team is to add their humility, humanitarianism and knowledge to the total understanding of each patient. The final goal is to help each patient achieve the highest level of functioning possible.

I hope that this chapter has given you some insight into the history of hospitalization of patients with emotional disorders. I hope that I have been able to remove a number of myths about psychiatric treatment. It is my hope that this chapter can be read and understood in the manner intended. I intended to show that psychiatric hospitalization can be a very positive experience occurring in a pleasant physical environment; that the members of the treatment team have a variety of skills to offer; and that beyond all else, an attitude of concern, interest, and hope is experienced by each and every patient. If I sounded too idealistic, I have no apology. Let's get rid of our fears of emotional illness and its treatment. Let's get on with diagnosis and treatment in a humanistic and scientific manner. Let's work together.

CHAPTER 14

Listener Contributions

LISTENER CONTRIBUTIONS

The exchange of letters was started by Carl Blashko, but now is carried on in particular by Drs. Janzen and Paterson. Listeners write in and their contributions are read over the air. Many of the contributions are written by listeners, others are taken from favorite books or the family album. For purposes of this chapter, listener contributions have been divided into sections. The philosophies expressed in most cases are self-explanatory. The authors would like to thank all participants for their help, whether or not your contributions are included or acknowledged.

Elderly

There have been many contributions about problems of the elderly to the hosts of "That's Living". This first excerpt was presented to John Paterson by Bill Matheson, one of "the Bills", who precedes our show. For about the first year of "That's Living", these comments with respect to "how you know you're growing older" were read over the air.

HOW TO KNOW WHEN YOU ARE GROWING OLDER

Everything hurts - and what doesn't hurt - doesn't work.
The gleam in your eyes is from the sun hitting your bifocals.
You feel like the night before and you haven't been anywhere.
Your little black book contains only names ending in M.D.
You get winded playing chess.

Your children begin to look middle aged.
You finally reach the top of the ladder - and find it's lean-
ing against the wrong wall.
You join a health club and you don't go.
Your mind makes contracts your body can't meet.
You begin to outlive enthusiasm.

You decide to procrastinate but then never get round to it.
A dripping faucet causes an uncontrollable bladder urge.
You know all the answers but nobody asks you the ques-
tions.
You look forward to a dull evening.
You walk with your head held high - trying to get used to
your bifocals.

Your favorite part of the newspaper is 25 years ago today.
You turn out the light for economic rather than romantic
reasons.
You sit in a rocking chair and can't make it go.
Your knees buckle and your belt won't.
You regret all those times you resisted temptation.

You're 17 around the neck - 42 around the waist - and 96
around the golf course.
You stop looking forward to your next birthday.
After painting the town red - you have to take a long rest
before applying a second coat.
Dialling long distance wears you out.
You're startled the first time you are addressed as "old
timer".

You remember today that yesterday was your wedding an-
niversary.
You just can't stand people who are intolerant.
The best part of your day is over when your alarm clock
goes off.
You burn the midnight oil after 9:00 p.m.
Your back goes out more than you do.
A fortune teller offers to read your face.
Your pacemaker makes the garage door go up when you
watch a beautiful girl go by.
You get exercise acting as a pallbearer for your friends who
exercise.

You have too much room in the house and not enough in the medicine cabinet.

You sink your teeth into a steak and they stay there.

It was in fact a discussion of those comments that resulted in another listener sending us *How To Stay Young*. This contribution follows:

HOW TO STAY YOUNG

Youth is not a time of life, it is a state of mind.
We grow old only by deserting our ideals. Years wrinkle the skin but to give up enthusiasm wrinkles the soul.

Worry, doubt, self-distrust, fear and despair - these are the long, long years that bow the head and turn the growing spirit back to dust.

There is in the hearts of all of us, whether seven or seventy, the love of wonder and the love of life.

We are as young as our faith and as old as our doubt - as young as our self-confidence and as old as our fear - as young as our hope and as old as our despair.

Author Unknown

One of the more poignant contributions is called *A Poem Found in a Hospital Locker*. Dr. Paterson read this poem after it was sent to us. The ideas from this contribution formed the basis of a number of topics on the radio show. A nurse sent in a reply, and we know that the author of the reply is Eleanor Hogben, but we have no details on where this was published. The reply too, makes good sense.

A POEM FOUND IN A HOSPITAL LOCKER

What do you see, nurses, what do you see? Are you thinking when you look at me?
A crabby old woman, not very wise
Uncertain of habit, with far-away eyes, Who dribbles her food and makes no reply When you say in a loud voice, "I do wish you'd try". Who seems not to notice the things that you do And forever is losing a stocking or shoe Who, unresisting or not, lets you do as you will. With bathing, and feeding, the long day to fill. Is that what your thinking? Is that what you see?

Then open your eyes nurse, you are not looking at me. I'll tell you who I am as I sit here so still. As I use at your bidding, as I eat at your will. I'm a small child often with a father and mother Brothers and sisters who love one another; A young girl of sixteen with wings on her feet Dreaming that soon now a lover she'll meet: A bride soon at twenty, my heart gives a leap, Remembering the vows that I've promised to keep. At twenty-five now I have young of my own Who need me to build a secure, happy home. A woman of thirty, my young now grown fast, Bound to each other with ties that should last. At forty my young sons, now grown will be found, But my man stays beside me to see I don't mourn. At fifty, once more babies play round me knee, Again we know children, my loved one and me.

Dark days are upon me, my husband is dead. I look to the future, I shudder with dread. For my young are all busy rearing young of their own, And I think of the years, and the love that I've known. I'm just an old woman now and nature is cruel, 'Tis her jest to make old age look like a fool. The body crumbles, grace and vigour depart,

There is now a stone where I once had a heart. But inside this old carcass a young girl still dwells, And now and again my battered heart swells, I remember the joy, I remember the pain, And I'm loving and living all over again. And I think of the years all too few - gone too fast And accept the stark facts that nothing will last.

So open your eyes, nurses, open and see Not a crabby old woman, look closer - see me.

A NURSE'S REPLY

"What do we see, you ask, what do we see? Yes, we are thinking when looking at thee! We may seem to be hard when we hurry and fuss. But there's many of you, and too few of us. We would like far more time to sit by you and talk, To bathe you and feed you and help you to walk. To hear of your lives and the things you have done; Your childhood, your husband, your daughter, your son, But time is against us, there's too much to do - Patients too many, and nurses too few.

We grieve when we see you so sad and alone. With nobody near you, no friends of your own, We all feel your pain, and know of your fear That nobody cares now your end is so near. But nurses are people with feelings as well, And when we're together you'll often hear tell Of the dearest old Gran in the very end bed, And the lovely old Dad, and the things that he said. We speak with compassion and love and feel sad, When we think of your lives and the joy that you've had. When time has arrived for you to depart, You leave us behind with an ache in our heart, When you sleep the long sleep, no more worry or care, There are other old people, and we must be there.

So please understand if we hurry and fuss - There are many of you, and too few of us."

Perhaps the other contribution having to do with the elderly that could be included was a contribution presented in a letter to Dr. Blashko. It is called *The Wall of Stone* and the message is obvious.

THE WALL OF STONE

Behind a wall of weathered stone There lived a lady - all alone. The wall was tall and strong and wide. So no one knew what it did hide. And neighbors whispered when they told About the wall so strange and old. Children passed with quickened feet Through the shadows on that street. And tales grew, to be told again, About the things those walls kept in.

But past the cheap and frightening talk, Through the wall and up the walk. A widow then, but once a wife, Was forced to live a lonely life. She'd sit and dream of joy that died And of a man, once by her side; A man whose laughter filled the hall; A man whose hands once built a wall.

The wall stood strong while he grew worse And soon his treasure was her curse. Then when he finally passed away, She found it best for her to stay Behind that wall he'd made of stone So lonely now but not alone. One glance at that weathered wall Would help that woman to recall When someone built with loving care A wall that still was standing there.

Then on a cold, cold winters day, A dying woman passed away. It wasn't long before the town, Sent men to knock the old wall down. As people stood, eyes opened wide, To see just what was found inside, Through the dust and by the stone They saw a house just like their own. The grass had turned a brownish-green And not one flower could be seen, A yard where only shadows play

Was bathed in sunlight on that day, And a wall that stood for years on end Was an enemy to its dearest friend.

A picket fence replaced the wall And flowers bloom now, bright and tall But somewhere, someone's still alone Behind a wall that's made of stone.

(written by a 19 year old boy)

Education

Two of the authors of this book are teachers, so one would expect that educational problems formed the basis for much of our discussion. Perhaps one of the nicest contributions to us was entitled *Teach Them Gently If You Can* and this is reproduced here.

TEACH THEM GENTLY IF YOU CAN

My young son starts school tomorrow. It's all going to be strange and new to him for awhile, and I wish you would sort of treat him gently.

You see, up to now, he's been our little boy.

He's been boss of the back yard. His mother has always been around to repair his wounds, and I've always been handy to soothe his feelings.

But now things are going to be different.

This morning he's going to walk down the front steps, wave his hand, and start out on the great adventure.

It's an adventure that will probably include wars and tragedy and sorrow.

To live his life in the world he will require faith, love, and courage.

So, world, I wish you would sort of take him by his young hand and teach him the things he will have to know.

Teach him also that for every scoundrel there is a hero; that for every selfish politician, there is a dedicated leader. Teach him that for every enemy there is a friend.

It will take time world, I know, but teach him, if you can, that a nickel earned is of far more value than a dollar found. Teach him to learn to lose and to enjoy winning.

Steer him away from envy, if you can, and teach him the secret of quiet laughter.

Let him learn early that the bullies are the easiest people to lick. Teach him it is far more honorable to fail than to cheat. Teach him to have faith in his own ideas, even if everyone tells him they are wrong. Teach him to be gentle with gentle people and tough with tough people.

Try to give my son the strength not to follow the crowd when everyone else is getting on the bandwagon. Teach him to listen to all men, but teach him also to filter all he hears on a screen of truth and take only the good that comes through.

Teach him, if you can, how to laugh when he is sad. Teach him there is no shame in tears. Teach him there can be glory in failure and despair in success.

Teach him to scoff at cynics and to beware of too much sweetness. Teach him to sell his brawn and brains to the highest bidders but never to put a price tag on his heart and soul.

Teach him gently, world, but don't coddle him, because only the test of fire makes fine steel. Let him have the courage to be impatient; let him have the patience to be brave.

Teach him always to have sublime faith in himself, because then he will always have sublime faith in mankind.

This is a big order, world, but see what you can do. He's such a fine little fellow, my son.

It should be noticed that Dr. Paterson has tried reading this on the air several times, but along with the next contribution, constitute two of the selections that he rarely gets through. Most parents will recognize "The Little Boy Who Didn't Pass".

THE LITTLE BOY WHO DIDN'T PASS

A sad faced little fellow, sits alone in deep disgrace; There's a lump rising in his throat and tears drop down his face. He wandered from his playmates; he doesn't want to hear. Their shouts of merry laughter, since the world has lost its cheer. He has sipped the cup of sorrow; he has dripped the bitter glass. And his heart is fairly breaking — the boy who didn't pass.

In the apple tree the robin sings a cheery little song. But he doesn't seem to hear it. Showing plainly something's wrong. Comes his faithful little Spaniel for a romp and a bit of play. And alone he sits in sorrow with his hair a tangled mass. And his eyes are red with weeping — the boy who didn't pass.

Oh, you who boast a laughing son, and speak of him as bright; And you, who love a little girl who comes to you at night. With shining eyes and dancing feet with honors from her school. Turn to that lonely lad that thinks he is a fool. And take him kindly by the hand, the dullest of his class. He is the one who most needs love — the boy who didn't pass!

Author unknown

Now our final words! It goes without saying that our team appreciates each and every reader who has shared our ideas. Trust us. Our next effort, *That's Living, Too* will be in the bookstores very soon.

BIBLIOGRAPHY

CHAPTER 2: SELF-CONCEPT

Andelin, H.B. (1974). *Fascinating Womanhood*. Bantam Books: New York.

Berry, J. (1978). *Can You Love Yourself?* Regal Books: California.
Branden, N. (1983). *Breaking Free*. Bantam Books: New York.
Branden, N. (1985). *Honoring The Self*. Bantam Books: New York.

Branden, N. (1986). *To See What I See and Know What I Know*. Bantam Books: New York.

Branden, N. (1987). *What Love Asks of Us*. Bantam Books: New York.

Branden, N. (1987). *How To Raise Your Self Esteem*. Bantam Books: Toronto.

Briggs, D.C. (1986). *Celebrate Yourself: Enhancing Your Own Self Esteem*. Doubleday: New York.

Jones, L.Y. (1980). *Great Expectations*. Ballantine Books: New York.

Rubin, T.I. (1986). *Compassion and Self-Hate: An Alternative to Despair*. Macmillan: Toronto.

Shostrom, E.L. (1968). *Man the Manipulator*. Bantam Books: New York.

CHAPTER 3:   FEARS AND PHOBIAS

Baured (1980). *Childhood Fears in Developmental Perspective.* N.L. Hersov, I. Berg (Eds)., *Out of School* (pp. 189-208). Wilkey and Sons: New York.

Blagg, N. (1987). *School Phobia and Its Treatment.* Lindan Croom Helm: New York.

Flatto, J.S. (1985). *Insomnia: Why Some People Can't Sleep.* Plymouth Press: New York.

Goldstein, A., Stainback, B. (1987). *Overcoming Agoraphobia.* Penguin Books: New York.

Jerrers, S. (1987). *Feel The Fear and Do It Anyway.* Fawcett Columbine: New York.

Kessler, Jane W. (1988). *Psychopathology of Childhood.* (2nd. Edit.) Prentice-Hall: Englewood Cliffs, New Jersey.

Lane, M.D., Milt, H. (1986). *Your Phobia: Understanding Your Fears Through Contextual Therapy.* Warner Books: New York.

Lowen, A. (1981). *Fear of Life.* Macmillan: New York.

Lucaire, E. (1988). *Phobophobia: The Fear of Fear Itself.* Putnam Pub. Group: New York.

Marks, I.M. (1969). *Fears and Phobias.* Heinemann: London.

Neuman, F. (1986). *Fighting Fear: Eight Week Program for Treating Your Own Phobias.* Bantam Books: New York.

Olshan, N., Wang, J. (1981). *Everthing You Wanted To Know About Phobias But Were Afraid To Ask.* Beaufort Books: New York.

Paolino, A. (1985). *Agoraphobia: Fear of Fear.* A. Paolino: New York.

Seidenburg, R., DeCrow, K. (1983). *Women Who Marry Houses.* Academic Press: New York.

Tec Leon (1978). *Fear of Success*. New American Library: New York.

Whitehead, T. (1983). *Fears and Phobias*. Arco: New York.

Woods, D.M. (1984). *Afraid of Everything: A Personal History of Agoraphobia*. R. and E. Pub: California.

CHAPTER 5:   HUMAN SEXUALITY

Bretcher, W. (1987). *Intimate Play*. Penguin Books: New York.

Calvin, W.H., Ojemann, G.A. (1980). *Inside The Brain*. New American Library: New York.

Carter, S., Sokol, J. (1987). *Men Who Can't Love*. Berkeley Books: New York.

Forward, S., Buck, C. (1978). *Betrayal of Innocence*. Penguin Books: New York.

Gazzaniga, M.S. (1988). *Mind Matters*. Houghton Mifflin Company: Boston.

Greenberg, J.S., Bruess, C.E., Sands, D.W. *Sexuality: Insights and Issues*. William C. Brown: Iowa.

Johanson, S. (1988). *Table Sex*. Penguin Books: New York.

Masters, W.H., Johnson, V.E. (1966). *Human Sexual Response*. Little Brown and Co.: Boston.

Nicarthy, G. (1986). *Getting Free*. Seal Press: Seattle, Washington.

O'Conner, D. (1986). *How to Make Love To The Same Person For the Rest of Your Life and Still Love It*. Bantam Books: New York.

Pearsall, P. (1988). *Super Marital Sex-Loving for Life*. Oxford Press: New York.

Shacuitz, M.H. (1987). *Sexual Static*. Little Brown and Co. New York.

CHAPTER 6:   PSYCHOSOMATIC MEDICINE

Crisp, A. H. (1980). *Anorexia Nervosa -Let Me Be*. Academic Press: London.

CHAPTER 9:   ALZHEIMER'S DISEASE

Heston, L.L., White, J.A. (1983) *Dementia: A Practical Guide To Alzheimer's Disease and Related Illnesses*. W.H. Freeman: Toronto.

Shamoian, C.A. (1984). *Biology and Treatment of Dementia in the Elderly*. American Psychiatric Association: Washington D.C.

CHAPTER 10:   HABIT CONTROL

Azrin, N.H., Besalel, V.A. (1979). *A Parent's Guide To Bedwetting Control*. Simon and Schuster: New York.

Bobrow, M. (1987). *Habit Breakthrough*. Loiry Pub. House: London
Davis, D.S. (1987). *Habit of Fear*. Scribner Press: New York.

Dunlap, K. (1949). *Habits: Making and Unmaking*. Liveright: London.

Floyd, K. (1986). Sandman's Land. *Alberta Psychology*. Vol. 15 (5).

Morrison, E. (1988). *Counseling Through the Media: An Approach to Smoking Cessation*. Unpublished M.Ed. Thesis, University of Alberta: Edmonton.

Pomerleau, O.F., Pomerleau, C.S. (1984). *Break the Smoking Habit*. Behavioral Med. Press: New York.

Peck, M. Scott (1983). *People of the Lie: The Hope for Healing Human Evil*. Simon and Schuster: New York.

Sheehy, G. (1976). *Passages*. E.P. Hutton: New York.

Thorkelson, L. (1984). *Emotional Dependency*. New American Library: New York.

CHAPTER 11:   ADDICTIONS

Burton, S., Kiley, L. (1986). *Beyond Addictions Beyond Boundaries*. Brookridge: New York.

Carmi, A., Schneider, S. (1985). *Drugs and Alcohol*. Springer-Verlag: New York.

Peterson, R., Jaffe, J. (1980). *Addictions: Issues and Answers*. Harper and Row: New York.

Steiner, C. (1971). *Games Alcoholics Play*. Ballantine Books: New York.

Taylor, N. (1970). *Narcotics-Natures Dangerous Gifts*. Dell Books: New York.

CHAPTER 12:   EDUCATION IS EVERYONE'S BUSINESS

Allport, G.W. (1955). *Becoming: Basic Consideration for a Psychology of Personality*. Yale University Press: New Haven, Connecticut.

Boegehold, B.D. (1984). *Getting Ready to Read*. Ballantine Books: New York.

Bloom, B.S. (1985). *Developing Talent in Young People*. Ballantine Books: New York.

Catterall, C.D. (1979). Psychological Rights Campaign. *International School Psychology WGR*. Vol 6 (4).

Declaration of the Rights of the Child. (1973). United Nations Office of Public Relations: New York.

Elkind, D. (1987). *Miseducation-Preschoolers at Risk*. Alfred A. Knopf: New York.

Glasser, W. (1975). *Schools Without Failure*. Harper and Row: New York.

Larrick, N. (1982). *A Parent's Guide to Childrens Reading*. Bantam Books: Toronto.

Mitchell, W. (1985). *The Power of Positive Students*. Bantam Books: Toronto.

Moore, R., Moore, D. (1984). *Home Style Teaching*. Word Books: Waco, Texas.

Oppenheim, J., Brenner, B., Boegehold, B.D. (1986). *Choosing Books for Kids*. Ballantine Books: New York.

Ostrander, S., Schroeder, L. (1986). *Super Learning*. Dell Books: New York.

Sattler, J.M. (1988). *Assessment of Children* (3rd. Ed.). Jerome M. Sattler Publisher: San Diego, California.

Sternberg, R.J. (1985). *Beyond I.Q.*. Cambridge University Press: London.

Woolfolk, A.E., McCune-Nicolich, L. (1984). *Educational Psychology for Teachers*. Prentice-Hall: Englewood Cliffs, New Jersey.

CHAPTER 13:   PSYCHIATRIC HOSPITALIZATION

McElroy, E. (1987). *Children & Adolescence with Mental Illness: A Parent's Guide*. Woodbine House: Toronto.